IARIA

eLmL 2017

The Ninth International Conference on Mobile, Hybrid, and On-line Learning

March 19 – 23, 2017

Nice, France

eLmL 2017 Editors

Luca Andrea Ludovico, Università degli Studi di Milano, Italy

Ahmed Mohamed Fahmy Yousef, Fayoum University, Egypt

Printed from e-media with permission by:

Curran Associates, Inc.
57 Morehouse Lane
Red Hook, NY 12571

CURRAN ASSOCIATES INC.
proceedings.com

Some format issues inherent in the e-media version may also appear in this print version.

Printed by Curran Associates, Inc. (2017)

International Academy, Research, and Industry Association (IARIA)
412 Derby Way
Wilmington, DE 19810

Phone: (408) 893-6407
Fax: (408) 527-6351

petre@iaria.org

Additional copies of this publication are available from:

Curran Associates, Inc.
57 Morehouse Lane
Red Hook, NY 12571 USA
Phone: 845-758-0400
Fax: 845-758-2633
Email: curran@proceedings.com
Web: www.proceedings.com

Table of Contents

Estimation and Adaptation Method for Students' Learning Styles on Web-based Learning Environment 1
Ashery Mbilinyi, Shinobu Hasegawa, and Akihiro Kashihara

Survey on e-Learning Implementation in Eastern-Europe - Spotlight on Romania 5
Ioana Goldbach and Felix Hamza-Lup

Development of a Support System for Japanese Extensive Reading: Supporting learners' autonomous learning outside the classroom 13
Teiko Nakano

Content Management and Support in 3.0 E-learning Model 17
Raadila Bibi Mahmud Hajee Ahmud-Boodoo, Tomayess Issa, Vanessa Chang, and Pedro Isaias

The Methods to Measure the Achievement of Learning Using Lecture Contents 25
Ryosuke Takata, Naka Gotoda, Toshihiro Hayashi, Hiroshi Murai, Ken'ichi Fujimoto, and Rihito Yaegashi

ICT Operational Model and ICT Operational Pattern which Express Teacher's Operation in a Lecture 29
Naoya Okada, Naka Gotoda, Toshihiro Hayashi, Norifumi Suehiro, Keizo Saisho, Hiroshi Oota, and Rihito Yaegashi

Saudi Arabian Students' Attitudes to and Perceptions of Social Networking for Educational Purposes 33
Sulaiman Alqahtani, Tomayess Issa, Theodora Issa, and Pedro Isaias

Developing Students' Vocabulary Knowledge in Content Subjects: A Computational Linguistic Approach 41
Kirk L. B. Dowswell

Smartphones as a Support for the Language of Images in Continuing Professional Development 47
Laura Rayon Rumayor, Ana Maria de las Heras Cuenca, Yolanda Munoz Martinez, and Antonio Bautista Garcia-Vera

Speech Shadowing Support System in Language Learning 51
Carson Lee and Shinobu Hasegawa

ADPT++ Technology-Based Combined Strategy for Problem Solving 55
Claudia Martinez-Araneda, Matilde Basso-Aranguiz, Claudio Oyarzo-Vera, and Marcia Munoz Venegas

EFL in Openness: A Project Based Language Learning with MOOCs and Online International Exchange 61
Yayoi Anzai

Towards Automatic Coding of Collaborative Learning Data with Deep Learning Technology 65
Chihiro Shibata, Kimihiko Ando, and Taketoshi Inaba

The Web MIDI API in On-Line Applications for Music Education 72
Luca Andrea Ludovico

A Web-based Petri Nets Application To Teach Music Analysis and Composition 78
Adriano Barate

Collaborative Music Composition Using Cloud Tools 84
Marco Morandi

Method for Quick Identification of Computer Operations Performed by a Student 90
Kenta Morita, Haruhiko Takase, and Naoki Morita

CoWaBoo: A Descriptive Protocol of Learning Driven Applications 94
Athanasios Priftis and Jean-Philippe Trabichet

Learner Satisfaction in eTexbook Co-reading: A Comparative Study of Internal and External Forums 101
Sinini Paul Ncube and Hussein Suleman

Proposed Model for Using Open Educational Resources in Massive Open Online Courses (MOOCs) 109
Ahmed Hosny Saleh Metwally and Yining Wang

Personalized Links Recommendation Based on Learning Analytics in MOOCs 115
Ahmed Mohamed Fahmy Yousef

eLmL 2017

Forward

The ninth edition of the International Conference on Mobile, Hybrid, and On-line Learning (eLmL 2017), held in Nice, France, March 19 - 23, 2017, focused on the latest trends in e-learning and also on the latest IT technology alternatives that are poised to become mainstream strategies in the near future and will influence the e-learning environment.

eLearning refers to on-line learning delivered over the World Wide Web via the public Internet or the private, corporate intranet. The goal of the eLmL 2017 conference was to provide an overview of technologies, approaches, and trends that are happening right now. The constraints of e-learning are diminishing and options are increasing as the Web becomes increasingly easy to use and the technology becomes better and less expensive.

eLmL 2017 provided a forum where researchers were able to present recent research results and new research problems and directions related to them. The topics covered aspects related to tools and platforms, on-line learning, mobile learning, and hybrid learning.

We take this opportunity to thank all the members of the eLmL 2017 Technical Program Committee as well as the numerous reviewers. The creation of such a broad and high-quality conference program would not have been possible without their involvement. We also kindly thank all the authors who dedicated much of their time and efforts to contribute to the eLmL 2017. We truly believe that, thanks to all these efforts, the final conference program consists of top quality contributions.

This event could also not have been a reality without the support of many individuals, organizations, and sponsors. We are grateful to the members of the eLmL 2017 organizing committee for their help in handling the logistics and for their work to make this professional meeting a success.

We hope that eLmL 2017 was a successful international forum for the exchange of ideas and results between academia and industry and for the promotion of progress in eLearning research.

We also hope that Nice provided a pleasant environment during the conference and everyone saved some time for exploring this beautiful city.

eLmL 2017 Chairs

eLmL Steering Committee
Herwig Mannaert, University of Antwerp, Belgium
Stephen White, The University of Huddersfield - Queensgate, UK
Maiga Chang, Athabasca University, Canada
Hironori Washizaki, Waseda University, Japan
Krzysztof Szklanny, Polish-Japanese Academy of Information Technology, Poland
Christian M. Stracke, Open University of the Netherlands, The Netherlands
Ivan Ganchev, University of Limerick, Ireland / Plovdiv University "Paisii Hilendarski", Bulgaria
Tomayess Issa, Curtin University, Australia
Yifat Ben-David Kolikant, Hebrew University of Jerusalem, Israel
Mudasser Wyne, National University - San Diego, USA

eLmL Industry/Research Advisory Committee
Michael Verhaart, Eastern Institute of Technology Hawke's Bay, New Zealand
Guglielmo Trentin, Institute of Educational Technology of the Italian National Research Council (ITD-CNR), Italy
Nick Louloudakis, Institute of Computer Science, Foundation of Research and Technology Hellas (ICS-FORTH), Greece

eLmL 2017

COMMITTEE

eLmL Steering Committee

Herwig Mannaert, University of Antwerp, Belgium
Stephen White, The University of Huddersfield - Queensgate, UK
Maiga Chang, Athabasca University, Canada
Hironori Washizaki, Waseda University, Japan
Krzysztof Szklanny, Polish-Japanese Academy of Information Technology, Poland
Christian M. Stracke, Open University of the Netherlands, The Netherlands
Ivan Ganchev, University of Limerick, Ireland / Plovdiv University "Paisii Hilendarski", Bulgaria
Tomayess Issa, Curtin University, Australia
Yifat Ben-David Kolikant, Hebrew University of Jerusalem, Israel
Mudasser Wyne, National University - San Diego, USA

eLmL Industry/Research Advisory Committee

Michael Verhaart, Eastern Institute of Technology Hawke's Bay, New Zealand
Guglielmo Trentin, Institute of Educational Technology of the Italian National Research Council (ITD-CNR), Italy
Nick Louloudakis, Institute of Computer Science, Foundation of Research and Technology Hellas (ICS-FORTH), Greece

eLmL 2017 Technical Program Committee

Ali Ahmad Alawneh, Philadelphia University, Jordan
Cristina Azevedo Gomes, Polytechnic Institute of Viseu, Portugal
Juarez Bento da Silva, Universidade Federal de Santa Catarina, Brazil
Werner Beuschel, Technical University Brandenburg, Germany
Mohsin Bilal, Umm Al Qura University, Saudi Arabia
Julien Broisin, University of Toulouse, France
Eglė Butkevičienė, Kaunas University of Technology, Lithuania
José Carlos Metrolho, IPCB, Portugal
Maiga Chang, Athabasca University, Canada
Steven Chen, United Daily News, Taiwan
Lorraine Cleeton, Northcentral University / Walden University, USA
David Comiskey, Ulster University, Northern Ireland
Andre Constantino da Silva, Federal Institute of São Paulo – IFSP, Brazil
Ana de las Heras, Udima Universidad a Distancia de Madrid, Spain
Giuliana Dettori, Istituto per le Tecnologie Didattiche, Genova, Italy
Ramon Fabregat Gesa, University of Girona, Spain
Joseph Finkelstein, Center for Bioinformatics and Health Analytics - Columbia University, USA
Sue Folley, University of Huddersfield, UK
Ivan Ganchev, University of Limerick, Ireland / Plovdiv University "Paisii Hilendarski", Bulgaria
Leonardo Garrido, Tecnológico de Monterrey, Mexico
Henrique Gil, Escola Superior de Educação do Instituto Politécnico de Castelo Branco, Portugal
Giuliana Guazzaroni, Università Politecnica delle Marche, Italy

David Guralnick, Kaleidoscope Learning & Columbia University, New York, USA
Felix Hamza-Lup, Armstrong State University, USA
Oriel Herrera, Universidad Católica de Temuco, Chile
Taketoshi Inaba, Tokyo University of Technology, Japan
Tsunenori Ishioka, The National Center for University Entrance Examinations, Japan
Tomayess Issa, Curtin University, Australia
Adel Jebali, Concordia University, Canada
Mike Joy, University of Warwick, UK
Katerina Kabassi, TEI of Ionian Islands, Greece
Konstantinos Kalemis, Kapodistrian University of Athens, Greece
Keiichi Kaneko, Tokyo University of Agriculture and Technology, Japan
Charalampos Karagiannidis, University of Thessaly, Greece
Ilias Karasavvidis, University of Thessaly, Greece
Yifat Ben-David Kolikant, Hebrew University of Jerusalem, Israel
Bernd Krämer, FernUniversität in Hagen, Germany
Miroslav Kulich, Czech Technical University in Prague | Czech Institute of Informatics, Robotics, and Cybernetics, Czech Republic
Joseph C. Kush, Duquesne University, USA
Ivan Kuzio, Technical Trainers College, Riyadh, Saudi Arabia
Cynthia Y. Lester, Georgia State University, USA
Ken W. Li, Hong Kong Institute of Vocational Education (Tsing Yi), Hong Kong
Andreas Lingnau, Humboldt-Universität zu Berlin, Germany
Giorgos Liodakis, TEI of Crete, Greece
Martin Llamas Nistal, Universidade de Vigo, Spain
Nick Louloudakis, Institute of Computer Science, Foundation of Research and Technology Hellas (ICS-FORTH), Greece
Hwangji Sherrie Lu, Ashford University, USA
Luca Andrea Ludovico, Università degli Studi di Milano, Italy
Stefania Manca, Institute of Educational Technology - National Research Council of Italy, Italy
Giuseppina Rita Mangione, INDIRE (National Institute for Documentation, Innovation and Educational Research), Italy
Herwig Mannaert, University of Antwerp, Belgium
José Manuel Machado, University of Minho, Portugal
Alke Martens, University of Rostock, Germany
Paulo Martins, University of Trás-os-Montes e Alto Douro (UTAD), Portugal
Bruce R. Maxim, University of Michigan-Dearborn, USA
Natarajan Meghanathan, Jackson State University, USA
Santiago Mengual Andrés, University of Valencia, Spain
Begoña Montero-Fleta, Universitat Politecnica de Valencia, Spain
Rafael Morales Gamboa, Universidad de Guadalajara, Mexico
Umberto Nanni, Universita' di Roma "La Sapienza", Italy
Jari Palomaki, Tampere University of Technology - Pori, Finland
Andreas Papasalouros, University of the Aegean, Greece
Hugo Paredes, INESC TEC / University of Trás-os-Montes e Alto Douro, Portugal
Arna Peretz, Ben-Gurion University of the Negev, Israel
Maria Potes Barbas, Escola Superior de Educação de Santarém, Portugal
Tamara Powell, Kennesaw State University, USA
Francesca Pozzi, Istituto Tecnologie Didattiche - CNR, Genoa, Italy

Copyright Information

Estimation and Adaptation Method for Students' Learning Styles on Web-based Learning Environment

Ashery Mbilinyi[1], Shinobu Hasegawa[2]
[1]School of Information Science,
[2]Research Center for Advanced Computing Infrastructure
Japan Advanced Institute of Science and Technology
Nomi, Japan
e-mail:[1]ashery.mbilinyi, [2]hasegawa@jaist.ac.jp

Akihiro Kashihara
Dept. of Information and Communication Engineering
The University of Electro-Communications
Tokyo, Japan
e-mail:akihiro.kashihara@inf.uec.ac.jp

***Abstract*—Learning Style is an important factor that determines how students acquire knowledge. In this paper, we present our approach for recognition of students learning styles on the web-based learning environment and adaptation features that will help to personalize their learning experience leading to improved learning outcomes.**

Keywords-text; Adaptation; Learning Style; Web-based Learning.

I. INTRODUCTION

With the development of sophisticated e-learning environments, which characterize the huge information, the strong interactivity, the great coverage and no space-time restrictions [1], personalization is becoming an important feature in e-learning systems. The large numbers of students, the main users of such systems have differences in background, goals, capabilities and learning styles [2]. Adapting these differences especially on web-based systems will personalize their learning experience and therefore increase their motivation and learning outcomes especially when they are completely self-directed learners. Learning Styles as one of these individual differences every student possesses can be defined as everything that is characteristic to that particular individual when he/she is learning, i.e., a specific manner of approaching a learning task, the learning strategies activated in order to fulfill the task [3]. Various researches have tried to provide adaptation on the web, based on this important trait, but the main challenges still remain on how to effectively detect and adapt learning styles without destructing student-learning experience. So in this paper, we are outlining different methods especially implicit methods used by related works and then explain our approach and why we think it is effective.

The paper has been arranged as follows: In Section 2, an overview of learning styles estimation methods is given while Section 3 points out the details of implicit methods. Section 4 explains our approach and the last section gives a conclusion and future work to be done.

II. LEARNING STYLES ESTIMATION METHODS

Most of the approaches proposed can be categories into either an explicit or implicit approach. Explicit approaches estimate learning styles by directly gather information using one or more users` query methods while implicit approaches rely on actions and behavior of users observed during their interaction with the system. The latter means the user models are updated by using information that is collected automatically [4].

III. IMPLICIT METHODS

The implicit approaches fall into 2 types, which are literature based approaches and data-driven approaches. In literature-based approaches, behavior and actions of users are monitored and used as hints about their preferences by applying the simple rule method [5] to estimate the match with predefined learning style classes. The advantage of this approach is its ability to deduct learning style without the need of training data since it depends entirely on learning style models [4]. Data-driven approaches depend on real users' data and therefore have a high chance of being accurate but the main challenge is a representative dataset is needed to be available to build an accurate classifier [6][10]. The following are classification methods used by most of the existing data-driven systems.

A. Artificial Neural Networks

Neural Networks are a computational approaches with a model that base on the biological neural structure of the brain. They comprise of input layer, which has neurons that receive signals from the environment, hidden layer transmits signals to other neurons after getting the input from other neurons and output layer that sends output signals to the environment. Feed Forward Neural Network, which is one type of neural network was used by Villaverde et. al [7] to model learning styles from students' actions by identifying ten patterns of behavior to be a network input. The output of this model represents three dimensions of Felder-Silverman learning styles model. The good thing about this method is, it can be updated quickly since it relies on history profiles and therefore, it can distinguish changes in users' behavior.

B. Bayesian Networks

Since a Bayesian Network (BN) is a directed, acyclic graph whose nodes are labeled by random variables [8], it can be used to model the relationship between the learning styles and the factors determining them. Garcia et al [9] used this approach to implicitly detect students learning styles by observing their behavior in SAVER system. The random variables were the different dimensions of Felder-Silverman Learning styles and the factors that determine each of these aspects and these factors were extracted from the students' interaction data with the system. The reported reasons to use BN are its natural representation of probabilistic information, its efficiency, and its support to encode uncertain expert knowledge. Fig.1 shows an example of the structure of BN, where leaf nodes represent student's observable behavior and root nodes represent the learning style to infer [9][10].

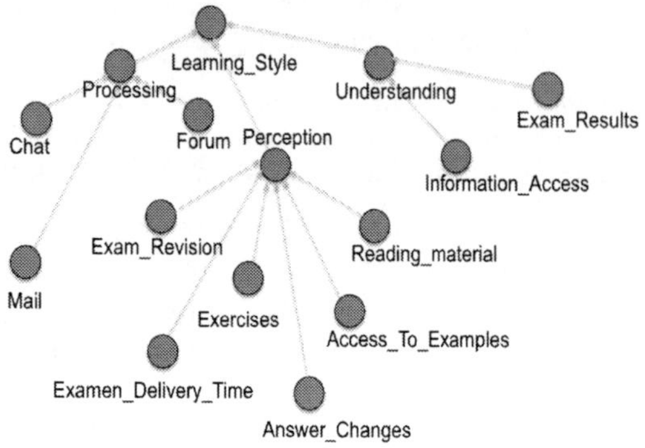

Figure 1. Bayesian Network Modelling Students' Learning Styles.

C. Decision Trees and Hidden Markov Model

Decision trees (DT) are an AI classification algorithm frequently used in estimating learning styles because of its simplicity, the rules of classification are visible and easy to understand, and it is appropriate when many attributes are relevant [10] .Cha et al [11] used this approach with 58 patterns of behavior to automatically deduce the 4 dimensions of Felder-Silverman model [12] of 70 students in a web-based learning course. He used together with Hidden Markov Model (HMM). His DT structure consisted of leaves that represent the learning styles to be inferred, and the nodes that represent the features tracked that lead to those learning styles [10].

IV. OUR APPROACH

A. Learning Style Estimation

Since most of the implicit approaches rely on available data, we think at the initial stage when the system does not have enough data about a new log in user, a direct feedback from a user should be used to estimate their preference. This approach helps to solve "cold start" problem. "Cold start" is the problem whereby a new user of the system starts with nothing in his/her profile, and therefore a training period is required to train the profile before it accurately reflects user's preferences [13]. To solve this problem, most systems use collaborative filtering approach in which a prediction is made about a new user based on the similarity between the interest profile of that user and those of other users [14][15][16]. This may be suitable in other domains like e-commerce, but in learning environment may not be effective because no matter how similar users might be, they still have their own unique way of learning. Then, during their learning period, their interaction data should be the one to be used. This means we are using both explicit and implicit approaches with initial and learning process stages respectively.

Initial Stage:

When a new user logs into the system, the Kolb's Learning Style Inventory questionnaire (LSI) will be given. LSI was "designed to measure the degree to which individuals display different learning styles" in accordance with Kolb's learning style model [4][17]. Kolb's model as one of the many learning style models found in the literature is probably the most famous one. This model articulates that people learn from experience so the learning is a continual process, which follows the cycle. Therefore, it is very unlikely that people will always have the same learning style, but changes during the knowledge construction process, which involves the person and the environment they find themselves [18]. It categorizes students into 4 classes of learning styles, which are Accommodators, Assimilators, Convergers, and Divergers. So the system will place a student within one of these four categories based on the response to the questionnaire. We have decided to use this model over others because it base on the idea that people learn through experience so it can accommodate the dynamism of their learning styles with respect to change in time [19]. This means in the next stage where dynamic data about user will be captured, Kolb's model will still act as a better framework that guide the inference of students' categories.

During Learning Process:

Since the learning types of Kolb's are associated with experience and therefore the types of materials users would like to access to accomplish a learning task. We want to estimate their ranking preference of these materials based on the frequency of clicks on a particular material page link at this stage. The idea is based on assumption that frequency and duration of access are two major indicators of a user interest in a page [20][21]. But, we haven't used the duration because in learning environment duration might not necessary give the clear indication of user interest on a page. For example, a slow learner might spend much time on page which he/she don't like but difficult for him/her to comprehend, while a faster learner can still spend much time on the same page because he/she likes the content materials. Also, the size of the page might also affect the duration of access. On the other hand, we think clicking frequency gives a clear indication of learning material preference. This can be seen clearly especially during assessments because users will always go back to revisit the pages of the kind of materials that better give them the understanding to respond to the assessments.

So, the material types and their urls are as follows: Problems solving tasks (url_p), Examples (url_e), Theory (url_t) and Exercises (url_x). Given a session a user initiates we want to determine the preference of Exercises material types with respect to other materials. To do that we take the number of clicks in exercises page (url_x) over the total clicks made in different pages material within a session as shown in (1):

$$Frequency_{urlx} = \frac{\sum Clicks_{urlx}}{\sum Session\ clicks} \quad (1)$$

We are taking the assumption that the higher the frequency of clicks of a given url with respect to other urls within the session, the higher the preference of that kind of material.

B. Adaptation Features

Fragment Sorting:

Fragment Sorting is the technique in which educational resources are presented in a different order considered suitable for each student [19] [22]. This is one of our system's adaptation features. At the "initial stage", different orders of materials to each learning style the Kolb's questionnaire categorizes a user will be given. The orders have the most suitable material at the top to the least one at the bottom. The font size and color of each link to the material is also different with top one larger and bottom one smaller in descending order. This will help users reduce the cognitive effort of deciding which material to access first and therefore help their navigation process. Fig. 3 shows the orders of materials for each student type at the initial stage.

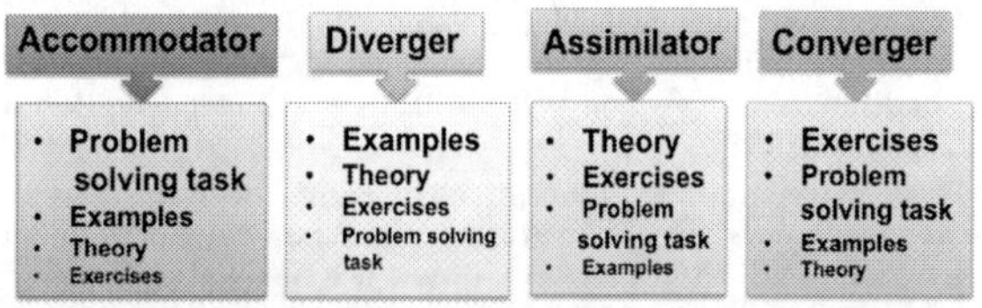

Figure 2. Fragment Sorting for each learning style type.

This order manually ranked based on Kolb's Experiential Learning cycle shown in Fig. 3:

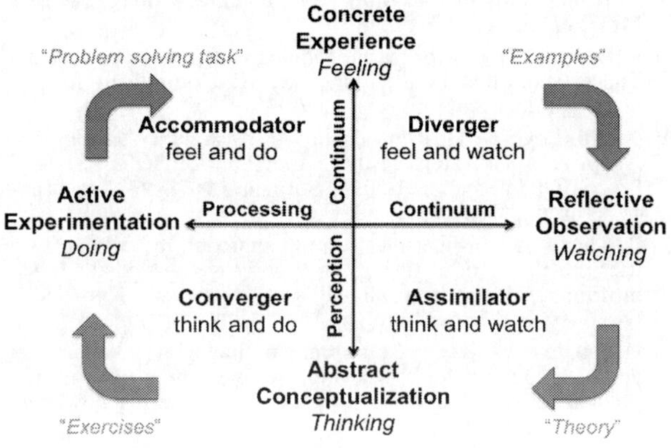

Figure 3. Kolb's Experiental Learning Cycle.

Based on the ranking order in Fig. 2,we want to estimate the value of importance of each material type to a student using reciprocal rank measure [23]. We are calling this importance value as Kolb's Value (KV) and will be calculated using (2) below:

$$KV = \frac{1}{rank_i} \quad (2)$$

where KV refers to the Kolb's value of a particular material type and $rank_i$ refers to its ranking position from the top.

Since our main idea of using Kolb's model at the start, based on our mutual belief with Kolb that users learning style changes with experience and knowledge. We want to provide different fragment sorting each time a user session starts, as we believe his/her preference of learning might change as his/her knowledge of particular topic advances. To do that, we have to estimate and combine the value of importance of each learning material type at the "initial stage" which is Kolb's value and the "learning process" stage, which is the previous active session of the student. The Equation (3) shown below is the combination of (1) and (2), to get the total importance of particular material type based on its url.

$$I_{url} = KV + Frequency_{url} \quad (3)$$

The order now will be changing dynamically in each new session, following the higher the importance value of the material type. For example, If $I_{urlp} > I_{urle} > I_{urlt} > I_{urlx}$ then the order will be Problem Solving Task⇒Examples⇒Theory⇒Exercises.

Adaptive Link Generation

We want to provide navigation support to a user especially during assessments as we believe at this moment is when he/she will revisit materials so as to help him/her to perform assessment tasks. The idea that users always jumps back during assessment is derived from the study conducted on 140,546 students participated in 4 Massive Open Online Courses (MOOCs) by Guo et al [24]. This study found that, despite the linear structure imposed on students-chronological ordering of weeks and learning sequences-learners predominantly navigate through MOOCs in a nonlinear way, on average students skip 22% of learning sequences entirely and perform back jumps, most often from assessments back to early lectures. But because for our case, the situation is different due to the fact that different material types are given for a particular topic. We want a user to be able to easily navigate to the particular material type of his preference when attempting the test.

So after a user opens the test page and attempt all questions, the system then evaluates the results and generates a link based on the previous importance values of urls of different material types for a user. If the score is below 60%, a link to most important material type will be shown. Next links will continue being generated based on the decreasing importance value every time a user re-attempt the exam and get below 60%, otherwise, a user will be allowed to continue to the next learning topic.

V. CONCLUSION AND FUTURE WORK

In this paper, we have presented a method to estimate and adapt student's' learning style, which combines both explicit and implicit approaches. The key idea is that our method can leverage the "cold start" problem faced by most data-driven methods, as they don't have enough data at the beginning of student interaction with the system. And also we think in learning environment it is individual actions that are most important, so we have used frequency of clicks information with the expectation that it will give more accurate inference about a user rather than relying on collaborative-filtering approaches used by different existing systems where a user learning style is estimated using data about similar users.

In the future, we would like the system to be updated with more data-driven approaches. This approach will be more suitable as a system continues to build a "rich profile" of the user as he/she continue to learn while interacting with the system. We want to incorporate time spent on materials information in more efficient way by considering the size of pages (materials), and also consider the comparison on duration spent on the same size of material with respect to different learners' performances. We also want to include more users' data about preference of on certain types of system tools like chats, forum, etc. This will help to perform cluster analysis of different type of users and can lead to better recommendation of what types of users should work together in tasks that need collaborative work.

ACKNOWLEDGMENT

This work is supported in part by Grant-in-Aid for Scientific Research (B)(No. 26282047), from Ministry of Education, Science and Culture of Japan and Japan International Cooperation Agency (JICA) under ABE Initiative Program.

REFERENCES

[1] R. Anane, S. Crowther, J. Beadle and G. Theodoropoulos, "eLearning content provision" In Proceedings of the 15th international workshop on database and expert systems applications (DEXA'04) , pp. 420-425, 2004

[2] A. Klasnja-Milicevic,M.Ivanovic and A. Nanopoulos, "Recommender systems in e-learning environment:a survey of the state-of-the-art and possible extensions, " Artificial Intelligence Review, vol. 44, pp. 571-604, Sept. 2015, doi:10.1007/s10462-015-9440-z.

[3] E. Popescu, P. Trigano, and C. Badica, "Toward a unified learning style model in adaptive educational systems," In 7th Proc. IEEE International Conference on Advanced Learning Technology, pp. 804-808, 2007.

[4] A. Al-Azawei and A. Badii, "State of the art of learning styles-based adaptive educational hypermedia systems," International Journal of Computer Science & Information Technology(IJCSIT), vol. 6,No 3, pp. 1-19, June 2014,doi:10.5121/ijcsit.2014.6301.

[5] S. Graf and P. Kinshuk, "An Approach for Detecting Learning Styles in Learning Management Systems," Sixth IEEE Int. Conf. Adv. Learn. Technol., pp. 161–163, 2006.

[6] S. Graf ,"Adaptivity in learning management systems focusing on learning styles," Ph.D. thesis,Vienna University of Technology,9801086 Neulinggasse 22/12A 1030,Vienna, 2007.

[7] J. Villaverde, S. Godoy, and A. Amandi, "Learning styles' recognition in e-learning environments with feed-forward neural networks," J. Comput. Assist. Learn.,vol . 22 no. 3, pp. 197-206,May 2006.

[8] F. Jensen. "An introduction to Bayesian Networks," Springer Verlag,1996.

[9] P. Garcia and A. Amandi, "Using Bayesian networks to detect students' learning styles in a Web-based education system," Proc ASAI, Rosario,no.11,pp. 29-30,2005.

[10] J. Feldman, A. Monteserin, and A.Amandi, "Automatic detection of learning styles:state of the art ," Artificial Intelligence Review, vol. 44, pp. 157-186, May 2014, doi:10.1007/s10462-014-9422-6.

[11] H. Cha, Y. Kim, S. Park, and T.Yoon, "Learning Styles Diagnosis Based on User Interface Behaviors for Customization of Learning Interfaces in an Intelligent G. Eason, B. Noble, and I. N. Sneddon, "On certain integrals of Lipschitz-Hankel type involving products of Bessel functions," Phil. Trans. Roy. Soc. London, vol. A247, pp. 529–551, April 1955.

[12] F.R. Silverman, "Learning and Teaching Styles in Engineering Education," Engineering Education, vol 78(7), pp. 674-681, 1988.

[13] P. Resnick and H. Varian, "Recommender Systems,," Communications of the ACM,40(3):pp. 56-58 ,1997.

[14] D. Billsus and M. J. Pazzani. "Learning collaborative information filters". Papers from The AAAI Workshop on Recommender Systems WS-98-08, AAAI Press, Menlo Park, California, 1998.

[15] D. R. Greening. Collaborative filtering for web marketing efforts. Papers from The AAAI Workshop on Recommender Systems WS-98-08, AAAI Press, Menlo Park, California, 1998.

[16] P. Resnick, N. Iacovou, M. Suchak, P. Bergstrom, and J. Riedl. Grouplens: An open architecture for collaborative filtering of netnews. In Proceedings of the ACM Conference on Computer Supported Cooperative Work, pages 175–186, 1994.

[17] D. Kolb, "Individual learning styles and the learning process," MIT 1971.

[18] E. Brown, "The use of learning style in adaptive hypermedia," Thesis submitted to the university of Nottingham for the degree of doctor of philosophy, 2007.

[19] A. Mbilinyi, S. Hasegawa, and A. Kashihara, "Design for Adaptive User Interface for Modelling Students' Styles," Proc. HCI International 2016, Springer,LNCS 9735,pp. 168-177,Toronto,Canada,July 2016 .

[20] P. Chan, "A non-invasive learning approach to building web user profiles," In Workshop on Web usage analysis and user profiling , Fifth International Conference on Knowledge Discovery and Data Mining,pp. 7–12,1999.

[21] H. Liu, and V. Keselj,. "Combined mining of web server logs and web contents for classifying user navigation patterns and predicting users' future requests". Data and Knowledge Engineering 61(2):pp. 304–330, 2007 .

[22] P. Brusilovsky, "Adaptive Hypermedia," User Model. User-Adap. Interact .11,pp. 87-110, 2001.

[23] Mean reciprocal rank.Available from: https://en.wikipedia.org/wiki/Mean_reciprocal_rank .

[24] P. J. Guo and K. Reinecke, "Demographic differences in how students navigate through MOOCs," In Proceedings of the First ACM Conference on Learning' Scale Conference,pp. 21-30,2014.

Survey on e-Learning Implementation in Eastern-Europe Spotlight on Romania

Ioana R. Goldbach
Center for Research and Studies in Management and Marketing
University of Targoviste
Targoviste, Romania
e-mail: Ioana.Goldbach@icstm.ro

Felix G. Hamza-Lup
Computer Science and Information Technology
Armstrong State University
Savannah, Georgia USA
e-mail: Felix.Hamza-Lup@armstrong.edu

Abstract — **Rapid proliferation of mobile technology and the Internet in Eastern-Europe for the past decade has had a significant impact on information distribution and has facilitated the introduction of novel e-Learning systems and technologies. The rapid growth and use of technology, as well as the ongoing transition towards a knowledge-based society of the workforce, has triggered in Romania the need and pressure to learn continuously. The paper provides an overview on e-Learning developments in Eastern-Europe taking as case-study Romania. As part of the European Union (EU), Romanian's education system is developed and evolves in the context of EU's regulations. However, recent developments in the area of online learning in Eastern Europe, specifically the fast pace of development of these systems in Russia could have a strong impact on regional markets. A comparison with US developments in e-Learning is provided to emphasize common issues in the development and adoption of e-Learning systems.**

Keywords – e-Learning; Romania; Eastern Europe; Online Learning; Learning Management Systems.

I. Background

E-Learning systems have been deployed in the US for several decades and currently more than one in four students take an online course according to a 2015 survey of online learning [1]. While in Eastern-Europe (EE), online programs are in their infancy, with the advent of high-speed Internet and mobile technology even in remote areas, the potential for rapid growth is tremendous.

An important factor for the implementation of online programs in EE is the reduced cost associated with attending these programs, as well as the time flexibility provided to students and instructors. One can attend these courses from home without additional costs associated with travel, on a flexible schedule that allows keeping a full time job.

Smarter/wider use of technology in teaching is generally seen as a promising way of controlling costs [2]. Higher education is being affected by the "cost disease" [3] since universities have high costs for infrastructure and labor, with reliance on expensive face-to-face provision. The urgent need to boost university productivity in US has been noted by many [4]-[6]. Likewise, productivity is a growing factor for e-Learning adoption in EE as well.

This survey is structured as follows: in Section 2 an overview of e-Learning initiatives in Europe is provided, particularly highlighting some of the European Commission (EC) initiatives and some initiatives that fall outside EC jurisdiction. Since Russia is a major player in this field in EE, we provide a brief overview of systems employed there. In Section 3 the current state of e-Learning initiatives in Romania are presented, focusing on the seeds of online learning in different areas – from K-12 to industry. Section 4 illustrates the driving force behind e-Learning systems and investigates future trends. A parallel is drawn between e-Learning implementation in EE and US since most "*Dos and Don'ts*" are invariable across continents and cultures. The Conclusion section summarizes the trends and requirements for a successful adoption of e-Learning in Romania.

II. E-Learning in Europe – West and East

The EC funds online collaborative platforms that bring education and training professionals together. These platforms allow education and training professionals to share ideas and experiences, learn new approaches or techniques from their peers and discuss important challenges faced by their colleagues around Europe. The digital single market - digital economy and society [7] focuses on experimentation with such online platforms.

The Electronic Platform for Adult Learning in Europe [8] is an example of the EC initiative for e-Learning. The platform is a multilingual open membership community for teachers, trainers, researchers, academics, policy makers and anyone else with a professional role in adult learning across Europe. It was launched in 2015 and is Europe's largest adult learning community.

While EC has the funding to bring novel ideas to fruition, a large set of initiatives outside the EC domain have been taking shape in recent years. eTwinning [9] for example, is a platform for staff (teachers, head teachers and librarians), working in a school environment to communicate, collaborate, develop projects and share knowledge using online tools. eTwinning is now part of the Erasmus+ program [10] and, as of September 2016, there were approx. 40,000 teachers, 50,000+ projects and 160,000+ schools participating in this e-Learning community. eTwinning impact on schools as measured through a survey in 2016 has proven (by an 84% teachers vote) that the platform significantly facilitates and improves the relationship among teachers and students. Moreover, 77% of the teachers surveyed agree that eTwinning has had a moderate to high impact on fostering EU citizenship values in schools.

The conclusions emerging from the eTwinning studies show that innovative schools promoting international collaboration and self-study among the teachers benefit the most from such an online system. eTwinning is now focusing on developing a full cycle of schools and on recruiting teachers for each school level [11].

Another initiative that brings together the main players in the education system in EU: teachers, experts, policy makers, non-governmental associations, etc., is the School Education Gateway [12]. Sponsored through the Erasmus+ Program, it went live on February 2015 and is available in 23 languages.

Shifting the analysis from Western to Eastern Europe, one notices Russia's early efforts into upgrading the education system to cover the growing gap between rural and urban education. Russians have a long history of distance education; since 1920s the government Committee for the Advancement on Self-Education organized a nationwide correspondence education system to cope with the population spread over vast distances (e.g., since 1924 courses were taught in the area of agriculture, engineering, social sciences - through radio broadcasts for remote regions) [13]. Western e-Learning systems needed translation and some required software licensing posing a barrier in their adoption in Russia, hence, the need to develop in-house solutions. Russia is considered a leader in e-Learning systems development in EE with a yearly growth rate of approximatively 16% as illustrated in Fig. 1.

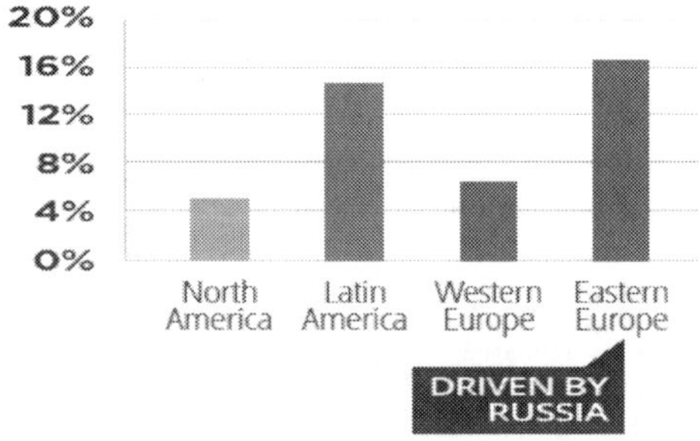

Figure 1. E-Learning growth by region [14]

The avant-garde of e-Learning systems in EE is led by the Russians through the use of software systems like Moodle, Khan Academy and Coursera. Moreover a partnership between Intel and the Volnoe Delo charitable foundation spawn in 2007 the program "Computers for Students". The partnership aims at donating over 1 million laptops at the national level as well as setting up the "11e-learning" program for the K-4 schools in Russia. Of particular interest are the Massive Open On-line Courses promoted by the Moscow-based Digital October Technology Center [15] geared towards self-taught, self-paced learners.

In addition to Russia, a number of EE countries are devoting significant efforts to grow and adopt e-Learning systems specifically in the mobile learning area. Countries like Azerbaijan, Kazakhstan, Moldavia and Ukraine lead these efforts as illustrated in Fig. 2.

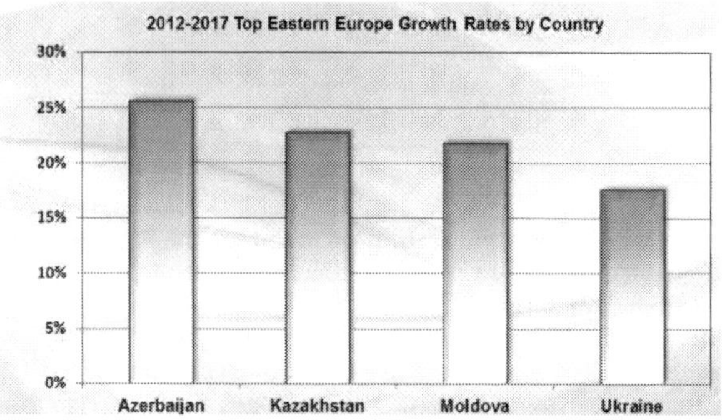

Figure 2. Mobile learning growth in the past 5 years [16]

Russia, like the other EE countries faces many problems in course management systems deployment, including the need to localize content by translating it from English into the local language, a difficult adjustment of online courses to the country's rigid universities' curricula, as well as social acceptance of online learning as an alternative to traditional classrooms.

III. E-LEARNING IN ROMANIA

As a member of the European Union (EU), albeit part of the EE block, Romania is guided by decisions made at the EU level. In this context, in Romania, within the general strategy of the EU's Information and Communication Technologies, the Ministry of Education and Research, has been trying to implement the online assessment, as well as the e-Lessons for various subjects. EU defines e-Learning as "*the use of new multimedia technologies and the Internet to improve the quality of learning by facilitating access to resources and services, as well as remote exchanges and collaboration*" [17].

The e-Learning concept was introduced in Romania approximatively two decades ago through the Virtual University paradigm, however, the first in-house Java based e-Learning software systems were surfacing in 1999 around major university centers [18].

Since then, the e-Learning concept has been more frequently used in Romania. Currently, all Romanian universities, as well as some governmental and non-governmental organizations use e-Learning platforms with a slow but increasing frequency. The main goal of these platforms is to provide distance education for a growing workforce in the service sector, as well as to re-train Romanian workforce.

The growth of the Romanian IT sector for the past decade has triggered the need for rapid education in a variety of technological areas. The great advantage of the sector is the presence of a highly skilled workforce that has determined the development of software and services, with an amazing growth rate of approximately 40% since 2000 [19]. Using online courses for training eliminates the need to provide a full classroom setting for employees, greatly reducing the costs for establishing and maintaining an educational space for the Romanian workforce. Moreover, when the learner has control over when the material is being presented, they are better prepared to retain the information instead of feeling rushed or stressed.

In Romania the older segment of the population has been experiencing the Digital Divide [20] and the rural segment the Urban-Rural Divide [21] due to the slow penetration of technology in the first years of the post-revolution era (i.e., 1989). E-Learning technology can alleviate these gaps by allowing people of all ages and trades to learn new skills without the restrictions of a traditional classroom. Young and old alike can use online courses to learn a new skill, help improve their career or just to narrow the Digital Divide gap.

While e-Learning implementation is still lagging behind in Romania, we identified a series of efforts in this direction. The e-Learning trend has not been uniformly adopted in the Romanian university system however, islands of initiatives can be found in other areas. The following sections present these initiatives classified based on their area of application.

A. E-Learning in K-12

There are roughly 80 virtual high schools [22] in 18 different countries in Europe right now, with about 50% being private. Most K-12 initiatives have around 500 students and are targeted towards social inclusion for students outside the bounds of traditional schools. They represent a complete pedagogical spectrum from 100% online through to significant face-to-face interaction [23]. The schools tend to serve: the long-term sick, disabled students, young parents or pregnant young women, travelers, bullied or school-phobic, students with behavior problems, drop-outs, imprisoned youth or the geographically isolated. Other schools serve students with special language needs, expatriates or elite performers.

One of the first e-Learning initiative in Romania [24] is targeted at secondary high school education and it is designed to prepare Romanian children who intend to continue their studies at an American University.

A novel initiative in Romania along the trend set by the EU projects is the Romanian Teachers Online portal iTeach [25]. iTeach is a virtual online environment based on Web 2.0 paradigms, facilitating the collaboration on didactic projects, socio-professional collaborations, learning and experience exchange, as well as familiarization with novel technology for e-Learning. Currently iTeach hosts seven online courses: two DigitalEdu courses – targeted towards teaching educators project based learning use in K-12 schools, as well as online tools for class interaction, an introduction to eTwinning and a module for international collaborations in which theoretical solution and their practical implementation is pursued. Other courses are targeted at collaboration quality assessment, teaching quality assessment, as well as a course on using digital systems and software tools in education.

A research survey of new technologies in the teaching and learning process at both rural and urban schools conducted by the Center for Development and Innovation [26] shows that the frequency of using the e-Laboratories in the urban area (24.8%) is increased due to the large number of students, comparative to rural areas (19.5%), illustrated in Fig. 3.

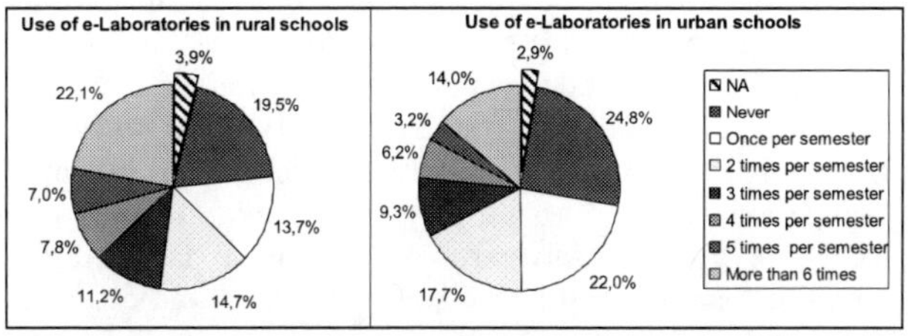

Figure 3. Frequency of using the e-Laboratories

The survey concludes with the need to expand development of e-Learning management systems in Romania at both rural and urban levels.

B. E-Learning in Higher Education

The slow deployment of e-Learning in Romanian universities is mainly due to the rigidity of the curriculum backed by the reluctance of the instructors, professors and academic leaders to support such systems for reasons similar to other countries (e.g., US), summarized as follows.

Resistance to change – Change entails the development of new skills and requires leaders to become learners, generating for some uncomfortable situations. Studies show that in higher education institutes, only 10% to 15% of faculty is open to adopt e-learning tools and techniques. Approximately 70% – 80% constitutes the reluctant majority who has to be convinced that e-Learning rewards would benefit them also [27].

Short-sighted policies – Quality versus Costs – a simplistic view of e-Learning as a medium to increase enrollment and revenue is flawed. A successful implementation entails the right technology, reliability, security of student data, and ease of use for both faculty and students.

Budgetary limitations – Money is a limited resource while technology is a field of moving targets, with many new products and services. Many pathways exist for the successful delivery of e-Learning, with selection and provision depending on factors, such as organization size, mission and priorities. Technology is as good as one's ability to manage and exploit it.

Unqualified decision makers – Administrators in charge often do not really have the background or knowledge of instructional design, compliance, intellectual property and experience to implement online courses. Such issues can be alleviated by selecting a qualified team of professionals with relevant experience and by being prepared to understand and identify the e-Learning finest practice tools and services that would best differentiate the institution in the marketplace.

An example of such an initiative is the Virtual University of Bucharest [28]. University of Bucharest, the second ranked University in Romania, has introduced e-Learning at the Economic Studies Academy and the National School of Administrative and Political Studies. The first online master program was attempted by the Faculty of Communication and Public Relations in 2004 [29]. A related effort is the Economic Studies Academy that deployed the first online Master program based on case studies form Harvard Business School. Subsets of online learning (e.g., blended learning) are also explored.

The Polytechnic University of Bucharest has several ongoing e-Learning projects, some of them targeted at instructional design, others at developing new methodologies for teaching and most importantly projects devoted to experiential learning.

With the rapid proliferation of networking technology in Romania, another initiative, the Center for Resources, Development, Information and Services, offers an online course dedicated to CISCO network specialization.

There is a new trend for major Romanian Universities to provide online courses. Timisoara Polytechnic for example, provides an online platform, UniCampus, offering a Mobile e-Commerce course and aiming at the development of the first Romanian Massive Open Online course. Such open and free systems resemble international initiatives like Coursera, EdX, FutureLean [30].

A premiere for Eastern Europe, the Online Admission System recently deployed in Romania proposes online management of admission for Universities in Romania. So far five universities have joined the system: Romanian-American University, Technical University for Building Management, Ovidius University of Constanta, Polytechnic University of Timisoara and Technical University "Gheorghe Asachi" from Iasi. Similar platforms were implemented some time ago in Western countries, for example UCAS from 1996 in Britain, Studielink in Holland and CommonApp in US.

C. E-Learning in Industry

Preferably, every company should have a strategy to set out career development paths and the required training curricula that will enable the personnel to develop the necessary knowledge and skills. These training initiatives should be monitored and managed through a consistent and reliable tracking system that can be stored, consulted and analyzed as required. The system's data will be useful for management reports on productivity and for assessing individuals' career advancement. This system of training management, referred to as a learning management system (LMS), is a key element of an effective professional development plan.

The workforce training/re-training is a major issue in Romania and e-Learning platforms for these tasks are in their infancy. A survey of the Northern European countries shows that workers in North Europe are four times more willing to be taught by their employers than the workers in the South [31]. A recent survey in Romania [32] answered by a total of 405 students, 904 graduates and 825 employers illustrates a positive view on e-Learning initiatives with the main priority on the increase in quality, the emphasis on practical aspects, and links with the realities of the economy and the labor market.

An example of such an initiative is the Virtual Business University [33]. Its main goal is the advancement of online/distance learning aimed at filling in the workforce market needs. It offers online courses and advice for young entrepreneurs and it is providing theoretical and practical experience to its users. Students are required to attend these courses through comprehensive online interaction tools like discussion forums and chat channels. Upon completion they receive a certificate and the course credits can be used towards a graduate degree if the students decide to pursue a Master program in the area. The Virtual University has built partnerships with various marketing, communication and investment organizations (e.g., Finantate.ro, Markmedia.ro, Comunicare.ro and Comunicareonline.ro).

A similar effort, Timsoft [34] has been focusing on e-Learning for about four years and has offered over twenty online courses in IT, Counselling, Management, Marketing, and e-Training. Other Romanian software houses like Siveco [35] and Softwin have developed the AeL e-Learning system in an effort to facilitate the understanding of educational subjects and increase the efficiency of the learning process. AeL has a user friendly interface and can be easily translated in any language.

Online Academy [36] is an e-Learning portal developed by InsideMedia with the help of experts from the Science and Education Institute and the Association for Excellence in Career. It offers a set of basic courses targeted to lifelong learning. The portal and courses' modular structure facilitates active participation and collaboration among participants.

D. E-Learning in GO and NGOs

Governmental Organizations (GO) in Romania have shown significant interest in e-Learning technologies especially in the context of the e-Government initiatives (e.g., the use of information and communication technologies to improve the activities of the organizations in the public sector). Non-Governmental Organizations (NGOs) in Romania have received in the past decade a significant amount of financial support through EU grants.

The Foundation for the Development of the Civic Society [37] with the financial support of the Trust for Civil Society in Central and Eastern Europe deployed a few years ago an e-Learning platform to: provide technical assistance, information, advertisement and research, to improve the impact of the NGOs in the community; present a comprehensive view of the NGO interests and involvement in other sectors of the society; improve the visibility and transparency of the NGOs. The goal of the foundation is to enable through the use of e-Learning technologies a strong and influential civil society with responsible citizens that promote the community interests and values.

The results of an assessment survey on the performance of the e-Government is illustrated in Fig. 4.

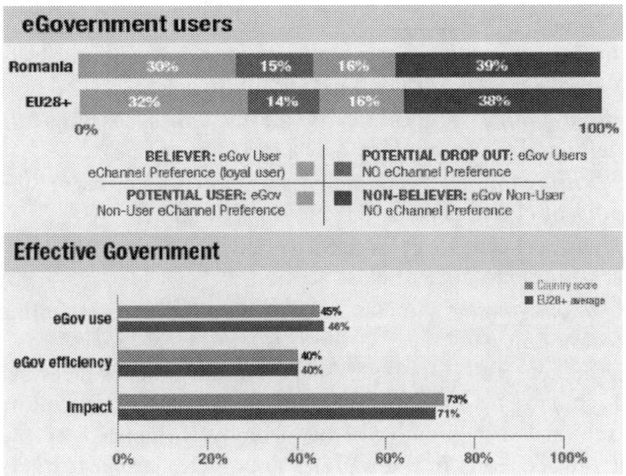

Figure 4. e-Government performance in Romania [38]

The e-Government implementation in Romania is beginning to show positive developments with 30% of the citizens using these services at present.

IV. Aligning to Current and Future Trends

There are many advantages in using an e-Learning system but the efficiency of such a system depends on many factors. Current and future trends are driven by several major aspects as highlighted in the following paragraphs.

A. Continuous Education and Professional Development

When people continue their education, they are growing, becoming more involved and curious, they develop skills that the modern job market requires, and they are cognizant and engaged in the world around them. Continuing education is essential in most areas and disciplines particularly in the technological sector. However, since technology is permeating in all areas and disciplines it triggers automatically the need for continuous learning. From job performance to promotion and advancement, continuous education is acknowledged as of upmost importance, as illustrated in Fig. 5.

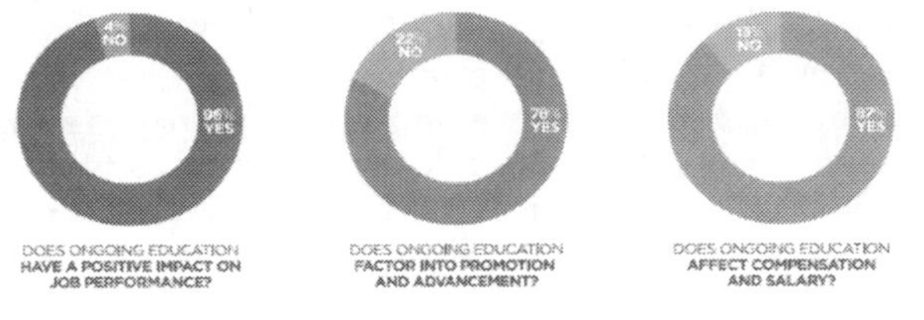

Figure 5. Importance of continuing education [14]

B. Adoption of Mobile Technology

Mobile learning is a revolution in e-Learning. It is defined as "*learning across multiple contexts, through social and content interactions, using personal electronic devices*" [39]. From the perspective of learning technology, mobile delivery is the second most important priority for development in EU, as illustrated in Fig. 6.

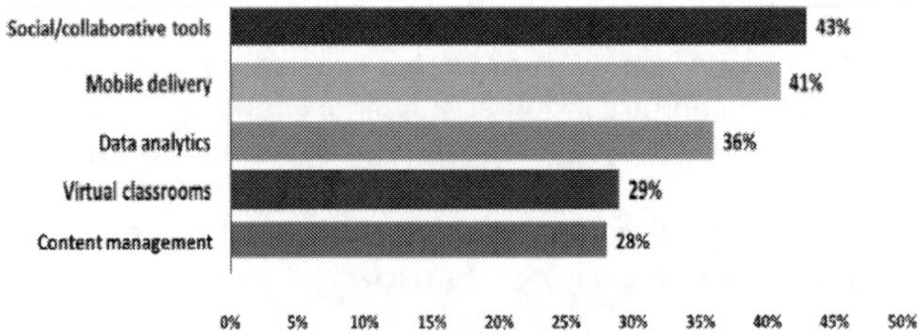

Figure 6. Top 5 learning technology priorities [14]

With the rapid and wide spread of handheld technology, currently there are more than 7 million smartphone users in Romania (i.e., one out of three Romanians is using a smartphone). It is estimated that by 2020 one out of two Romanians will use a smartphone [40]. Hence, the hardware required to deploy mobile learning applications is already available.

C. The Cloud Effect

Cloud-based learning management systems are hosted on the Internet and can be accessed by logging into a service provider's site. Rather than having to install course design and management software, instructional designers can simply use their Internet browsers to upload course content, create new courses, and communicate with learners directly. This is all done through a secure LMS, giving designers the ability to store information on the cloud, which can be remotely accessed by other, approved users.

Major benefits of deploying an e-Learning platform on the Cloud include [41]:

- *Lower startup costs* - there is no software to purchase, no need to devote the time or human resources to installing programs and working out glitches;
- *Enhanced data security* – data is hosted on platforms that are better encrypted and safer to use;
- *Improved accessibility* – better accessibility for both learners and course designers. Learners are able to learn on-the-go, anywhere and anytime, instructional designers can utilize their tablets and any other internet-ready device to upload content and communicate;
- *Faster deployment* – cloud-based eLearning is faster to set up and requires less time to actually deploy. There's no hardware of software involved, so one can have immediate access to the LMS;
- *Cost predictability* – cloud-based LMS offers administrators the ability to choose between plans based on registered users or plans based on activity;

- *Easier to maintain* – cloud-based LMS service providers have IT staff on hand. One does not have to worry about dealing with glitches and other LMS operation issues;
- *More storage space* – all of the data will be uploaded directly to the LMS, releasing space on user devices. Other users, such as collaborators and content creators, will be able to share information with ease, given that it's being stored on a remote (and secure) server;
- *Fully customizable and scalable* - regardless of whether it is a smaller organization or a large corporation, cloud-based LMS offers the best of both worlds in the form of customizability and low cost. Owners can modify and scale their learning cloud-based LMS, providing the best learning experience for their users.

V. COMPARISON WITH US, BLENDED LEARNING

The Gartner Group Research Institute in the United States anticipated that the world's e-Learning sales would grow 14.5% annually from 2006 to 2011 [1]. Campuses will still be active, however, technology will transform the way education is delivered and accessed, and the way value is created by higher education providers. A 4% growth for US is forecasted as related with 16% for Eastern Europe (Fig. 1).

While in US more than 1 in 4 students take an online course, in EE we estimate the current ratio at about 1 in 30. However, when compared to Europe, similar issues plague the e-Learning system deployment. As mentioned in Section III.B, resistance to change, short-sighted policies, budgetary limitations and unqualified decision makers are universal problems in this area. However, another important factor is the maturity of the learner. Fully online programs are meant for those who live far from campus or may have jobs that prevent them from attending campus classes, but at the same time such programs require a mature learner that is self-paced, responsible and motivated. To be successful in a fully online learning environment requires a strong sense of self-directed learning. Of course many strategies exist to promote student engagement (e.g., enable students to monitor their own progress, help students set achievable goals in the course); however, often these strategies fail and sometimes are not correctly implemented due to the lack of expertise in instructional design.

An alternative solution, especially useful for transitioning from a traditional course to an online course is Blended Learning [42]. The term Blended Learning is being used with increasing frequency in academic writing but there is no consensus on its meaning [43]. An alternative term, Hybrid, is defined as being of "mixed character; composed of different elements" [44], and Blended is defined as "an unobtrusive or harmonious part of a greater whole" [45]. Blended Learning has been described as a hybrid instructional approach combining aspects of e-Learning and a traditional classroom environment [46] and defined as courses that deliver material both face-to-face and online and where students interact with instructors both online and face-to-face. Many colleges in US offer hybrid courses, which combine traditional face-to-face with online instruction. Previous research proves that this combination may promote learner-centered and active learning [47]. A similar trend is foreseen in Europe as well, specifically in Eastern Europe and particularly in Romania where e-Learning systems are still in their infancy.

As an example of this strategy the public University System of Georgia [48] defines the following:

- *Fully online*: All or nearly all the class sessions are delivered via technology (96% to 100% online);
- *Partially online*: Technology is used to deliver more than 50% of class sessions (51% to 95% online);
- *Hybrid*: Technology is used to deliver at least one class session up to 50% of class sessions;
- *Campus/on-site*: No class sessions are replaced by online technology.

Whether fully or partially online, the successful deployment of e-Learning systems in Romania will follow the regional trends and will be strongly influenced by the political decisions in the region. Young Romanian learners seem to be very flexible and motivated specifically in the technology sector. They know that e-Learning enables global learning, breaking the boundaries of local knowledge and they are eager to explore the possibilities.

VI. CONCLUSION

The paper provides an insight into e-Learning technologies and their evolution in Europe. The focus is set on Eastern Europe, particularly on the developments in Romania along several dimensions: e-Learning in high schools, higher education, government, as well as the private sector. Several important factors that influence the adoption and success of e-Learning systems are presented and should be considered by policymakers and educators.

Spawning from the need for continuous education, e-Learning generates advantages for both the young and the mature learner in Romania. Mobile and Cloud technology are fundamental factors for e-Learning growth and provide major benefits not only in terms of content storage and management but also in terms of content presentation and availability.

U.S and East European e-Learning trends show common expectations from faculty, administrators and students, highlighting the need for a gradual and better managed introduction to online teaching. As a first step of this transition, a careful analysis along the main strengths, weaknesses, opportunities and threats of online teaching must be accomplished, and the subset of courses to be taught online must be identified. Online teaching pedagogy courses must be subsequently offered to faculty and students, as well as training describing the features and the use of the LMS of choice. Ultimately a successful implementation of the e-Learning paradigms depends on all the actors involved: administrators, faculty, students and policy makers.

REFERENCES

[1] I. E. Allen, J. Seaman, R. Poulin, and T. T. Straut, “Online Report Card Tracking Online Education in the United States,” 2016. [Online]. Available from: http://onlinelearningconsortium.org/read/online-report-card-tracking-online-education-united-states-2015, 2016.10.27

[2] W. G. Bowen, M. M. Chingos, K. A. Lack, and T. I. Nygren, “Online learning in higher education,” Education Next, vol. 13(2), pp. 58-64, 2013.

[3] W. J. Baumol, “Macroeconomics of unbalanced growth: The anatomy of urban crisis,” The American Economic Review, vol. 57(3), pp. 415-442, 1967.

[4] B. Massy, “Initiatives for containing the cost of higher education,” Washington: American Enterprise Institute, 2013.

[5] T. A. Sullivan, C. Mackie, W. F. Massy, and E. Sinha, “Improving measurement of productivity in higher education,” Washington: National Academics Press, 2012.

[6] B. G. Auguste, A. Cota, K. Jayaram, and M. C. A. Laboissiere, Winning by degrees: The strategies of highly productive higher-education institutions, Washington, DC: McKinsey and Company, 2010.

[7] Commission Staff Working Document Online Platforms Accompanying the document Communication on Online Platforms and the Digital Single Market, {COM (2016) 288}. [Online]. Available from: https://ec.europa.eu/digital-single-market/en/online-platforms-digital-single-market, 2016.09.25

[8] EPALE - Electronic Platform for Adult Learning in Europe. [Online]. Available from: https://ec.europa.eu/epale, 2016.10.28

[9] D. Cassells, A. Gilleran, C. Morvan, and S. Scimeca, Growing Digital Citizens. Developing active citizenship through eTwinningm, Central Support Service for eTwinning, Brussels, Oct. 2016, ISBN 978-9-49241-445-8

[10] Erasmus+, EU programme for education, training, youth and sport. [Online]. Available from: http://ec.europa.eu/programmes/erasmus-plus/node_en, 2016.10.19

[11] eTwinning’s impact on schools. [Online]. Available from: https://www.etwinning.net/ro/pub/highlights/etwinnings-impact-on-schools.htm, 2016.10.18

[12] School Education Gateway. [Online]. Available from: http://www.schooleducationgateway.eu/en/pub/index.htm, 2016.10.16

[13] O. Zawacki-Richter, and A. Kourotchkina, “The Development of Distance Education in the Russian Federation and the Former Soviet Union,” The International Review of Research in Open and Distributed Learning, Vol. 13, no. 3, pp.165-184, 2012.

[14] El. Market, E-Learning Market Trends and Forecast 2014 - 2016 Report A report by Docebo | March 2014, [Online]. Available from: https://www.docebo.com/landing/contactform/elearning-market-trends-and-forecast-2014-2016-docebo-report.pdf 2016.11.17

[15] Digital October. Creation of technology ventures aimed at global markets and global resources. [Online]. Available from: http://www.digitaloctober.ru/en/about, 2016.09.26

[16] S. S. Adkins, “Ambient Insight Premium Report. The 2012-2017 Worldwide Mobile Learning Market. Quantitative Market Analysis,” 2013. [Online]. Available from: http://www.ambientinsight.com/resources/documents/Ambient-insight-2012-2017-worldwide-mobile-learning-market-executive-overview.pdf, 2016.09.26

[17] Commission of the European Communities, 2005. [Online]. Available from: http://ec.europa.eu/information_society/doc/factsheets/005-e-Learning.pdf, 2016.09.25

[18] I. Salomie, F. G. Hamza-Lup, and R. Bot “Design Decisions for a Virtual University in the Framework of CONED Tempus Project,” in Web-Based Educational Technology, Casa Cartii de Stiinta, Cluj Napoca, pp. 223-234, 2000, ISBN 973-686-066-3

[19] PC TEL NET, “Futurallia Bucharest 2015”. [Online]. Available from: http://www.futuralliabucharest2015.com/en/ccib-ro-fr-association/ccib-s-mission/growth-sectors-of-the-romanian-economy.html, 2016.09.30

[20] S. D. Şandor, “Romania`s Digital Divide and the Failures of E-Government,” Transylvanian Review of Administrative Sciences, 16: 154-162, 2006. E-government in Romania. In Klumpp (ed.), One-stop-Europe: Citizen centered government, Alcatel-Lucent Stiftung, Germany, pp. 5-10, 2007.

[21] V. Stoica, A. Ilas, “Rural-Urban Digital Divide in Romania,” in the Digital Public Administration and E-Government in Developing Nations: Policy and Practice, IGI Global, pp. 317-333, March, 2013.

[22] Researching Virtual Initiatives in Education. [Online]. Available from: http://www.virtualschoolsandcolleges.eu/index.php/Category:Virtual_schools_in_Europe, 2016.09.23

[23] P. Glader, “Blended Learning, International, K12, Personalized Learning, Private, Public, Required, Technology.” Online EDUCA: A Closer Look at 8 Virtual K-12 Schools in Europe, 2012. [Online]. Available from: http://www.wiredacademic.com/2012/12/online-educa-a-closer-look-at-8-virtual-k-12-schoolsineurope/?share=email, 2016.09.26

[24] L.O.T.B. American High Schools in Bucharest Romania, A United States High School. [Online]. Available from: http://americanonlinehighschools.com/american-highschools-in-Bucharest-Romania.html, 2016.09.22

[25] iTeach online platform. [Online]. Available from: http://iteach.ro, 2016.09.21

[26] Centre for Innovation in Education. [Online]. Available from: http://www.tehne.ro, 2016.09.25

[27] M. Gaebel, V. Kupriyanova, R. Morais, and E. Colucci, “E-Learning in European Higher Education Institutions, Results of a Mapping Survey Conducted in October-December 2013,” in the European University Association, Brussels, 2014.

[28] M. Logofatu, C. Logofatu, and B. Logofatu, “A Virtual University Platform for University of Bucharest, Romania,” International Conference the Future of Education, Florence, June, 2013.

[29] National School of Political and Administrative Studies. [Online]. Available from: http://www.snspa.ro, 2016.09.29

[30] Curs m-commerce pe UniCampus, 2016. [Online]. Available from: http://elearning.upt.ro/cursul-m-commerce-pe-unicampus/n-32-70-199/d, 2016.09.25

[31] Nosco Learning [Online]. Available from: http://www.nosco-learning.ro, 2016.09.30

[32] R. L. Andronica, et al, A. O. Andronica, E. Dovalb, I. Lepdatua, O. Negulescub, C. Rulea, "Opinions about distance learning in Romania – a comparative," International Conference on Education and Educational Psychology, ICEEPSY, 2012.

[33] The Virtual University - a Center of Continuous Training and Learning. [Online]. Available from: http://www.uva.ro, 2016.09.30

[34] Timsoft e-Learning. [Online]. Available from: http://www.timsoft.ro/indexen.php, 2016.09.23

[35] Business-to-Business Solutions and Business-to-Public Solutions. [Online]. Available from: http://www.siveco.ro, 2016.09.23

[36] Online Academy, e-Learning site. [Online]. Available from: http://www.academiaonline.ro, 2016.10.03

[37] Civil Society Development Foundation. [Online]. Available from: http://www.fdsc.ro/eng, 2016.10.03

[38] E-Government in Romania, January 2015. [Online]. Available from: https://joinup.ec.europa.eu/sites/default/ files/ egov_in_romania_-_january_2015_-_v.12.0_final.pdf, 2016.10.04

[39] H. Crompton, "A historical overview of mobile learning: Toward learner - centred education," in Z. L. Berge and L. Y. Muilenburg (Eds.), Handbook of mobile learning, Florence, KY: Routledge, pp. 3-14, 2013.

[40] The Statistics Portal Statistics and Studies. [Online]. Available from: https://www.statista.com/statistics/566182/ predicted-number-of-smartphone-users-in-romania, 2016.10.06

[41] e-Learning Industry, Learning Management Systems. [Online]. Available from: https://elearningindustry.com/8-top-benefits-of-using-a-cloud-based-lms, 2016.10.07

[42] F. G. Hamza-Lup, and S. White, "Design and Assessment for Hybrid Courses: Insights and Overviews," International Journal of Advances in Life Sciences, Vol. 7(3), pp. 122-131, 2015.

[43] R. T. Osguthorpe, and C. R. Graham, "Blended learning environments," Quarterly review of distance education, vol. 4, 2003, pp. 227-233, 2015.

[44] Oxford dictionaries. "Hybrid." [Online]. Available from: www.oxforddictionaries.com/definition/english/hybrid, 2015.11.16

[45] Oxford dictionaries. "Blend." [Online]. Available from: www.oxforddictionaries.com/definition/english/blend, 2015.11.16

[46] K. L. Smart, and J. J. Cappel, "Students' perceptions of online learning: A comparative study," Journal of Information Technology Education, vol. 5, pp. 201-219, 2006.

[47] Y. J. Dori, and J. Belcher, "How does technology-enabled active learning affect undergraduate students' understanding of electromagnetism concepts?" Journal of the Learning Sciences, vol. 14, pp. 243-279, 2005.

[48] "Armstrong State University Course Program Definitions". [Online]. Available from: http://archive.armstrong.edu/images/office_online_learning/ ArmstrongCourseProgramDefinitions.pdf, 2015.11.16

Development of a Support System for Japanese Extensive Reading:

Supporting learners' autonomous learning outside the classroom

Teiko Nakano
Shobi University
Saitama, Japan
email: t-nakano@b.shobi-u.ac.jp

***Abstract*—This paper reports on the investigation of a support system for Japanese extensive reading. This system was developed for Japanese learners outside the classroom to learn Japanese through e-learning by reading digital books with autonomy. From the results of the questionnaire and the amount of reading by participants, it was found that video clips and a comment board are useful functions for self-study. Additionally, the findings suggest that, unless there are no discussions among learners, reading communities are useful in that learners are made aware of other learners' presence.**

Keywords-online library; Japanese graded readers; reading community.

I. INTRODUCTION

Extensive reading (ER) is part of an approach for teaching English to speakers of other languages to build vocabulary and develop reading comprehension [1] [2] [3]. The development of graded readers (GRs) has a long history, and a large number of GRs have been published. Extensive reading has not been a common approach in education programs because it is time consuming and qualitatively different compared with existing reading courses that are typically offered; however, through the development of a module that can hold students accountable for their reading [4], ER outside the classroom has been made possible.

There has been a gradual increase in the number of Japanese GRs, and digital books of Japanese GRs have been prepared. Considering that most learners of foreign languages are studying outside the countries where the target language is used, an online library of GRs is useful for providing learning materials. Online systems have the most benefit for learners who learn autonomously outside the classroom. Currently, there is no system of Japanese ER which is available to independent learners outside the classroom. This study designs and develops a support system for Japanese ER on the basis that an online GR library is appropriate for autonomous learning [5], where learners select their reason or way of learning.

It is recognized that, despite limitations, Video-Based Learning represents an effective learning method that replace teacher-led learning approaches [6]. In this study, video clips and a comment board were used in the self-ER support system as a preliminary study. Based on the results of a post-questionnaire and the amount of reading, the usefulness of the self-ER support system is discussed. Moreover, this study

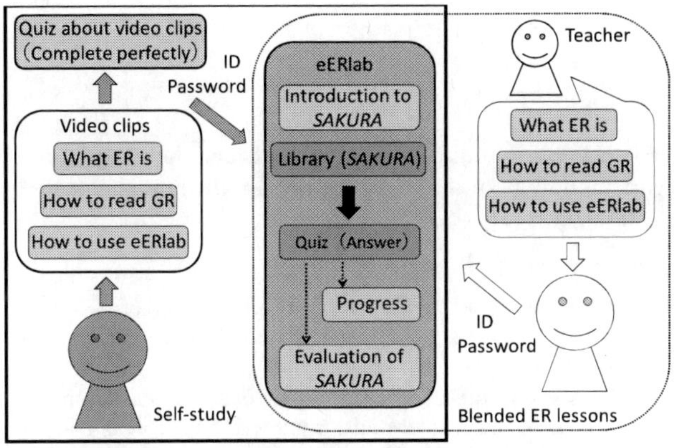

Figure 1. Schematic of a Support System for ER

discusses the potential of post-reading activities for learners who study independently through a reading community on Facebook (FB), where learners discuss books with each other.

This paper aimed to address the following questions:

(1) Can the video clips replace teachers?

(2) As an indicator of the presence of other learners, is a comment board useful for encouraging reading?

(3) Is an ER FB group that discusses books useful for encouraging reading?

In section II, we will discuss the design of this system. Then, in section III, we will look at the methodology of this study. In section IV, we will examine how useful this system was based on the results of a post questionnaire and amount of reading. In section V, we will conclude this study.

II. A SUPPORT SYSTEM FOR AUTONOMOUS LEARNING

Fig. 1 shows a schematic of the support system for ER, which has two purposes and functions. First, the system supports blended ER lessons (blended-ER support system), which are designed for teachers who provide such lessons. Second, it is a support system for learners who study by themselves (self-ER support system). This system was designed to facilitate learning outside the classroom, and provides an online library of Japanese GRs such that learners can select their method and reason for learning. The common functions between the two systems are libraries and quizzes.

In the blended-ER support system, the teacher explains ER, how to read GRs, and how to use the eERlab. The teacher can also provide post-reading activities, such as initiating discussions about the readings. A blended ER lesson using the blended-ER support system was implemented, and the availability of the system was confirmed [7][8][9].

In contrast, the self-ER support system was designed for learners who learn independently through the system, without teachers. In this system, video clips are used in place of the teacher's explanation so that learners can learn the same lessons as those in the blended-ER support system. Additionally, a comment board, on which learners write their impressions about books, was added to the eERlab to ensure that learners were aware of the presence of other learners. It is expected that knowing other learners' progress would promote reading among learners visiting the comment board [10].

III. METHODS

First, I will introduce the participants and then, explain the methodology of the study. Lastly, I will show the post questionnaire.

A. Participants

Ten international students (5 Chinese, 5 Korean) at a Japanese language school participated in this study. To understand participants' needs and abilities, the Simple Performance-Oriented Test (SPOT), a vocabulary assessment, and pre-questionnaire were administered. SPOT was used to assess grammar [11]. A Japanese language proficiency test was used to assess vocabulary.

The pre-questionnaire asked about the length of time spent learning Japanese, whether the respondent has devices for reading digital books, whether he or she uses social networking services (SNS), and whether he or she would join the ER FB group. The participants' average period of learning Japanese was 1 year and 8 months, with the shortest being 4 months, and the longest 3 years and 3 months. The results of the pre-questionnaire indicate that all the participants had devices for reading digital books and used SNS. Five (4 Chinese, 1 Korean) of 10 participants reported that they would join the ER FB group. Those 5 participants were asked about the kind of SNS used, device used, frequency of use per week, with whom they communicated and the language used. Four of the 5 participants used FB. Four of the 5 participants used smartphones to access SNS. Four participants used SNS every day and the other participant used SNS 2–3 days per week. Participants used SNS mostly with "friends in their country", followed by "family" and "friends in Japan". That is, participants mainly used SNS to communicate with others living in their home countries and used their first language. Four participants used both their first language and Japanese, and 1 participant used only their first language.

B. e-Extensive Reading Lab

Fig. 2 shows a schematic of the self-ER support system. "Video clips" are used to teach "what ER is," "how to read GR" and "how to use eERlab". The time required to watch each video clip is 3, 2, and 5 min, respectively. "The quiz about the video clips" was prepared for participants to check their understandings of the video clips.

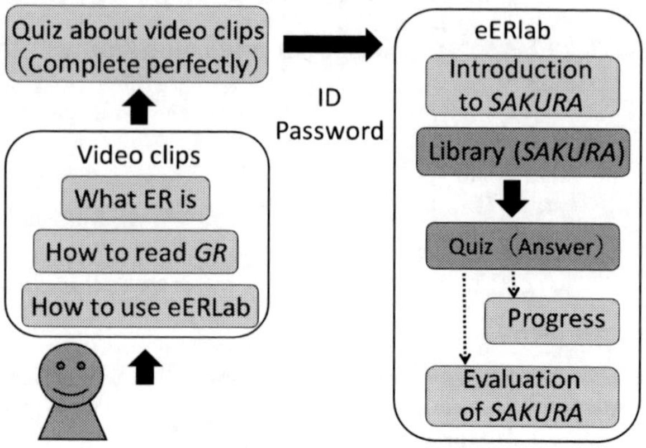

Figure 2. Schematic of a Self-ER Support System

The "Library" contains *SAKURA* which is a small collection of Japanese GRs divided into eight levels from A, beginner to H, higher middle level [12]. "Introduction to *SAKURA*" provides information on each title, such as a brief introduction, number of letters, and vocabulary level.

On the "Quiz" page, participants were required to answer some questions about the book that they had read. Participants were asked five questions with four choices each to gauge their reading comprehension. Additionally, participants were required to complete a questionnaire. Therein, they evaluated the length, difficulty, and contents of the reading, and were asked to report the hours spent reading and the frequency of dictionary usage using a five-point Likert scale. The final part of the "Quiz" page featured a comment board, on which participants could write their impressions about a given story. The data on the amount of reading were displayed in the "Progress" page, and the answers to the questionnaire and the participants' comments were displayed on the "Evaluation of *SAKURA*" page, along with the participants' IDs.

The procedures were as follows:

(1) The participants watch the video clips. After they complete the quiz section about the video clips perfectly, they log into eERlab using their user IDs and passwords. Nicknames are used as IDs.

(2) Participants read books from the library on their devices. Participants are required to read from the lower level of *SAKURA*. eERlab was used for 3 weeks.

(3) Participants answer questions about the story that they read, and complete a questionnaire to evaluate the book. They are then asked to enter their comment about the story.

C. ER Discussion Group on Facebook

The experimenter created a private group on FB and invited participants who opted to join the ER FB group on the pre-questionnaire. The members of the ER FB group were not classmates. Participants used their real names on FB.

(1) The experimenter writes questions about each title on FB.

(2) After completing the relevant reading, participants in the ER FB group are required to post their answers to the questions on the FB group wall.

(3) Participants of ER FB group are also required to comment on other participants' answers and comments.

D. Post-Questionnaire

In the post-questionnaire, participants were asked:

(1) How much did you understand the explanations of the video clips? What are the strengths of the video clips and what needs to be improved? How many times did you take the quiz about the video clips until you achieved a perfect score?

(2) How do you rate eERlab and the difficulty of the quizzes?

(3) Please give your reason if you did not write a comment on the comment board.

(4) Please state why you did or did not find the "Progress" and "evaluation on eERlab" sites useful.

(5) Please evaluate the ER FB group. What are the strengths of the ER FB group and what points need to be improved? Please state the reason if you did not write a comment on the ER FB group page.

(6) Please give your reason if you did not comment on other participants' posts on FB.

Questions (5) and (6) were intended only for members of the ER FB group.

IV. Results and Discussion

First, we discuss the functions of the self-ER support system. Then, we examine the effect of the ER FB group. Lastly, we discuss the usability and effect of this system on users' Japanese proficiency.

A. Availability of the Video Clips

To the question, how much did you understand the explanations of the video clips, 80% of participants answered "understood very well". Among the strengths of the video clips, participants reported that the activities were: "easy because [they] just imitated the video clip;" "explained plainly;" and that "the speed of speaking was appropriate." The points needing improvement were: "the speaking volume was low" and "the explanation was long." The average number of times needed to complete the quiz about the video clips to achieve a perfect score was 1.2 times. This result shows that the video clips could replace teachers' explanations.

B. Availability of a Comment Board

Four of the 10 participants in this study posted their impressions of the readings to the comment board. Participants who did not post their comments gave the following reasons: "I am not good at writing," "I did not have anything to post," "I did not have time to write comment," "I did not notice the space for posting comments on the site," and "it was troublesome." However, regarding the function of displaying their comments on the comment board, 80% of participants reported that they found this useful. For the reason, six participants answered, "I thought it would be interesting to read other participants' comments," and two participants answered, "I thought that I should do the reading when I saw that other participants had already done so." Participants who answered that "it [the comment board] was not useful" gave the following reasons: "I was not affected by other participants' opinions" and "it was stressful."

It is predicted that participants who had not yet completed the reading were motivated to read by observing other participants' progress. A reading community outside the classroom in which learners can know that other learners are also reading may be effective in motivating learners who have not yet read the book to begin reading.

C. Effect of ER Facebook Group

Three participants (2 Chinese, 1 Korean) in the ER FB group posted their responses to the discussion questions, which the experimenter had posted on FB. However, there was no discussion because the participants did not comment on one another's posts. Although all FB comments were marked "seen by everyone," no participants used FB's "Like" function on their peers' comments.

In the post-questionnaire, participants who posted comments on FB answered that the comment function "allows participants to exchange ideas" as a positive point of having an ER FB group. For points needing improvement, they answered, "Using FB for discussion was good, but it was not useful in this experiment. The rules for commenting should be less rigid."; and "The more members, the better the discussion." In addition, participants stated that "the effect of [having a] FB group depends on whether each member is active or not."

A participant who did not write a comment on FB, but wrote comments on the comment board stated the following in an interview, "I could write on the comment board, but I could not write on FB. I could not [express] my real feelings in Japanese." Another participant who did not write on the comment board or on FB selected "interesting" in post-questionnaire question about the ER FB group, giving the reason, "I was able to learn the other participants' opinions."

Although there was no discussion, participants' impressions about the ER FB group were positive.

D. Effect of Other Learners' Presence on ER

Table I shows the effect of the ER FB group on the posted comments. "Vocabulary" and "grammar" show average scores. "Amount of reading" shows the average number of titles that participants had read. "Quiz" shows the average rate of correct answers to the questions about each story. "Comment" and "FB" show the number of participants who posted their comments on the comment board and on FB, respectively. There was no significant difference in Japanese proficiency between the participants who joined the group and those who did not. In addition, the difference in quiz scores was not large. However, "Amount of reading" among those who joined the group was almost double that of those who did not. Furthermore, the rate of participants who posted their comments on the comment board among those who joined the group was higher than that of those who did not. Three of the four participants who posted their comments on the comment board had joined the group.

Table II shows the relationship between the amount of reading and comment posting. Participants are divided into upper or lower groups depending on the amount read. The five

TABLE I. EFFECT OF ER FB GROUP PARTICIPATION ON POSTED COMMENTS

ER FB group	Vocab	gram mar	Quiz	Amount of reading	Comment board	FB
Joined	77	83	90	7.8	3	3
Did not	83	80	85	4.0	1	

TABLE II. COMMENT POSTING AND AMOUNT OF READING

	Amount of reading	Comment board	ER FB group
Upper	10.4	4 / 4	3 / 3
Lower	1.4	0 / 4	0 / 3

TABLE III. JAPANESE PROFICIENCY AND ER

		Vocab	Grammar	Amount of reading	Quiz
Vocab	Upper	89	85	5.2	96
	Lower	71	77	6.6	79
Grammar	Upper	84	90	5.6	85
	Lower	76	73	6.2	90

participants in the upper group read 10.4 books on average, and the five participants in the lower group read 1.4 books on average. All the participants who posted their comments on the comment board and the ER FB group wall belonged to the upper group. This result suggests that the presence of a reading community encourages participants to read books.

The amount of reading among members of the ER FB group was higher than that among those nonmembers. Although there was no discussion, participants were made aware of the other learners' presence. However, it was suggested that membership in the ER FB group is an important indicator of participation in FB discussions. The effect of ER FB group membership on FB commenting and the effect of the comment board of the self-ER support system were almost the same in that they encouraged learners to read by making them aware of the other learners' presence. These results indicate that an ER FB group is not necessary, but that a comment board is useful in the self-ER support system.

E. Japanese Proficiency and ER

Table III shows the relationship between participants' Japanese proficiency and ER. As for the amount of reading, the lower groups in both vocabulary and grammar read more on average than upper groups. According to the logs of the self-ER support system, the time required to read in the upper group was shorter than that in the lower group. However, the results show that participants in the upper group who could read faster than those in the lower group did not always read more than those in lower group. Two of the three participants who read more than 13 books belonged to the lower groups of both vocabulary and grammar. However, three participants who read only one book belonged to the upper groups of vocabulary or grammar. In the post-questionnaire, these participants stated, "if I was given something that was appropriate to my level, I would have read;" "I did not know my level when I started;" "it was boring because there were same words appeared too many times in the texts." According to these results, implementing a vocabulary level test that judges the appropriate level of *SAKURA* for learners to start reading is necessary.

V. CONCLUSION

To develop an environment where independent learners outside the classroom can learn autonomously, we confirmed the usefulness of video clips and a comment board as functions of the self-ER support system. We also found that a comment board and FB group were effective in making independent learners aware of the presence of other learners.

Further work is needed to improve the current system and to develop an environment where learners can learn through Japanese GRs independently.

ACKNOWLEDGMENT

This work was supported by JSPS KAKENHI Grant Number 15k02650.

REFERENCES

[1] S. D. Krashen, "Some new evidence for an old hypothesis," Paper presented at the Georgetown Round Table for Lanuguage and Linguistics. April, 1992.

[2] P. Nation, "The language learning benefits of extensive reading," The Language Teacher. 21, 5, pp. 13-16, 1997.

[3] R. R. Day and J. Bamford, "Extensive reading in the second language classroom," Cambridge: Cambridge University Press, 1998.

[4] T. Robb and M. Kano, "Effective extensive reading outside the classroom: A large-scale experiment," Reading in a Foreign Language, vol. 25, No. 2, pp. 234–247, Octover 2013.

[5] N. Aoki, "Examining Definitions of Learner Autonomy," Handai Nihongo Kenkyu 10, pp.129-148, Mar. 1998. [Online]. Available from: http://hdl.handle.net/11094/8114. [retrieved: January 2017]

[6] M. A. Chatti, M. Marinov, O. Sabov, R. Laksono, Z. Sofyan, A. M. F. Yousef, and U. Schroeder, "Video annotation and analytics in CourseMapper", *Smart Learning Environments* 3(1), 10, 2016.

[7] T. Nakano, Introduction of extensive reading using electronic teaching materials, *Shobi University Sogoseisaku Ronshu* 17, pp.137–144, 2013.

[8] T. Nakano, "Implementing Extensive Reading in Japanese as L2 Environment: A Case Using Facebook to Build a Reading Community", Proceedings of The Third World Conference on Extensive Reading, Chap. 8, pp. 69-78. [Online]. Sept. 2015, Available from: http://erfoundation.org/wordpress/ [retrieved: January 2017]

[9] T. Nakano, "Extensive Reading for Second Language Learners of Japanese in Higher Education: Graded Readers and Beyond", *The Reading Matrix*, Vol.16, No. 1, pp. 119-132. [Online]. Available from: http://readingmatrix.com/ [retrieved: January 2017]

[10] N. Kuga, T. Nakano, Y. Cong, J. Jung, and S. Mayekawa, "A Study of Social Facilitation Effect on e-Learning", *Proceedings of e-Learn* 2006, 1659-1664, 2006.

[11] N. Kobayashi, "SPOT: Measuring Japanese language ability," *The 31th annual meeting of the Behaviormetric Society of Japan*, 110–113, 2003.

[12] B. Reynolds, T. Harada, M. Yamagata, and T. Miyazaki, "Towards a framework for Japanese graded readers: Initial research findings," *Papers of the Japanese Language Teaching Association in honor of Professor Fumiko KOIDE*, Vol.11, pp.23–40, 2003.

Content Management and Support in 3.0 E-learning Model

Raadila Hajee Ahmud-Boodoo*, Tomayess Issa**, Vanessa Chang***
Department of Information Systems, CBS
Curtin University of Technology
Perth, Western Australia
e-mail: *r.hajeeahmud@postgrad.curtin.edu.au,
**Tomayess.Issa@cbs.curtin.edu.au,
***Vanessa.Chang@cbs.curtin.edu.au

Pedro Isaias
Institute for Teaching and Learning Innovation (ITaLI)
The University of Queensland
Queensland
e-mail: pedroisaias@gmail.com

***Abstract*—A number of E-learning models have been proposed in the literature capturing critical success factors of E-learning in an attempt to denote how E-learning can be made effective to achieve the best learning outcomes. In fact, E-learning has redefined the way education is dispensed across the world. It is viewed as a modern, effective and efficient alternative to education for a number of reasons including an alternate means to cater for the increasing demand for higher education and to cater for the increasing expectations to make the learning process more customised to learners' needs to achieved the best learning outcomes. The concept of Web 3.0 is often associated with the Semantic Web, which is a recent effort to make the Web more meaningful to machines. In fact, the Semantic Web is seen as a promising technology to meet E-learning requirement. Consequently, this study represents an attempt to provide a holistic representation of E-learning critical success factors as well as Semantic Web characteristics. The study proposes a combined E-learning and Semantic Web model, E-learning 3.0, derived from the literature review outlining four main characteristics namely Content Management, Teaching and Learning, Support and Technology. It focuses on two of these characteristics namely Content Management and Support, which are further analysed via surveys conducted within the Mauritian higher educational sector from students and lecturers. Results following an exploratory factor analysis on the 2 dimensions surveyed provided a regrouping of their sub characteristics allowing for a more integrated representation of these characteristics within the combined model.**

Keywords-E-learning; Semantic Web; Critical Success Factors; Content Management; Support

I. INTRODUCTION

In the research and development world, there is great stress upon the need to develop educational models that will meet the expectations of the higher-education community where effective learning occurs with the best outcomes. In fact, over recent years, more emphasis is given to the development of education systems that involve intelligent technologies and the World Wide Web [11]. With the need to make the learning process faster with well organised learning materials specific to learners' needs as well as customised online services initiated by user profiles, efforts are now being directed in building 3.0 E-learning systems in line with the Semantic Web [15].

As the name suggests, the Semantic Web aims to add a level of meaning to the Web so that it can be more easily manipulated by computer programs, and thereby used more effectively by humans [23]. In fact, the semantic web is about adapting content to specific users where instead of having to search a long list of web sites for the required information, users have access to a customised file where the content is translated, personalised and adapted to meet specific needs [1]. It encompasses efforts to build a new WWW architecture that enhances content with formal semantics, which enables better possibilities for navigating through the web and accessing its contents [22].

As a matter of fact, the static approach to learning content limits the willingness of many people to use information and communication technologies to learn [29]. Expectations with regards to E-learning lie in having a learning process which is timely and efficient capturing the needs for suitable learning content, as well as a mechanism to organise learning materials based on learner's needs and pace [22]. The concept of Web 3.0 is often associated with the Semantic Web and is seen as having the potential to improve the semantics interoperability for e-learning components and as such provide the best capabilities for learning content composition and access [35]. Central to this is the use of ontologies which is the backbone of the Semantic Web. Ontologies allow for learning domains to be described from different perspectives allowing for a richer description and retrieval of contents [7].

In an effort to remain competitive and maintain their market share, many traditional higher education institutions are offering web-based or web supplemented learning to compete with the growing number of virtual higher education institutions[25]. As such, E-learning is carving its way as an alternate medium of course delivery in many countries including Mauritius which aims to be the centre of excellence in education, attracting international universities and students from all over the region. In fact, in the wake of being a digital island, Mauritius regroups all the necessary ingredients in fostering E-learning as an alternative mode to traditional method of teaching [34]. However, one of the biggest drawbacks of the current educational system in the country is the under utilisation of technologies to enhance learning. E-learning platforms in Mauritius are usually used as means of delivery information on the Internet in static ways [34]. With internal university politics, omnipresent technological transformations in education and Government policies to democratise tertiary education, tertiary institutions, particularly public ones, are forced to reconsider the traditional class room delivery model and the roles that educators and learners play in the learning environment [33]. Undeniably, Mauritius is no exception to the growing need for post secondary education. With limited capacity of existing classrooms at academic institutions and the prohibitive cost of building new facilities, E-Learning is an attractive alternative [27]. In line with the aim to become a knowledge based economy, E-learning is seen as part of the solution in converting the island into a knowledge hub, complementing educational infrastructure needs, widening access and eliminating distance barriers and promoting a student centered learning environment [34].

With the numerous benefits that E-learning could bring to countries like Mauritius coupled with Semantic Web technology, which is seen as a promising technology to meet E-learning requirements, this paper aims to look at current literature and provide an overview of E-Learning critical success factors (CSFs) and Semantic Web characteristics in a combined 3.0 E-learning model. The paper will then empirically validate two characteristics outlined from the proposed 3.0 E-learning model namely Content Management and Support through surveys conducted within tertiary institutions in Mauritius. Section II of the paper describes the initial proposed model based on existing literature, Section III outlines the research methodology followed by the survey analysis of the characteristics Content Management and Support in Section IV. The paper ends with the conclusion and directions for future explorations in Section V.

II. INITIAL PROPOSED 3.0 E-LEARNING MODEL

A comprehensive literature search and review clearly revealed that E-learning CSFs which are relevant to the Semantic Web are often omitted or seldom integrated into existing 3.0 E-learning models. In an attempt to provide a holistic representation of a 3.0 E-learning model based on the combined characteristics of the Semantic Web and E-learning CSFs, an initial 3.0 E-learning model is proposed in Fig. 1 as an effort to synthesize existing literature review on E-Learning CSFs and Semantic Web characteristics. It seeks to capture the most prominent set of E-learning CSFs and Semantic Web characteristics derived from the literature review. However, for any E-learning system to be effective, users' perceptions and needs must be taken into consideration. As a result, this review cannot be claimed to be exhaustive. In order to ensure that the new model meets the needs and expectations of higher education E-learning users, namely students and lecturers, the model needs to be evaluated. For this purpose, the proposed 3.0 E-learning model is evaluated within the higher education sector in Mauritius. It consists of four main characteristics which are further broken down into a number of sub characteristics as follows.

A. Content Management consisting of: Content Creation, Content Retrieval, Content Reuse and Knowledge Representation

A systematic approach to managing knowledge is considered to be an essential pre-requisite for knowledge seekers to access relevant learning materials as and when required [16]. In fact, the prevalence of materials and resources to support the learning settings is deemed as critical to the success of online delivery strategies within higher education institutions [32]. As such, content management, which refers to the access, manipulation and maintenance of learning content, is seen as a key characteristic for 3.0 E-learning [31]. Central to this is the creation and retrieval of learning materials based on their degree of difficulty and knowledge levels of students. Furthermore, the Semantic Web is seen as an opportunity to enhance learning content descriptions via the use of ontologies, which provide a formal representation of learning content allowing for better conditions for composing and reusing learning materials [12][30].

B. Teaching and Learning consisting of: Curriculum, Pedagogy, Personalised Learning and Collaboration

According to [17], well-designed courses, curriculums and learning materials are key factors that influence learning performance. He further stated that that the structure and coherence of the curriculum components and of the learning material are major factors for facilitating meaningful learning. Additionally, personalised learning where students are provided with learning content which meet their specific needs and motivations as well as knowledge and skills level based on their particular learning and cognitive styles, is considered key to the success of E-learning environments [11]. Reference [4] further stated that productive learning outcomes are most likely to occur when learners perceive that their actual learning environment matches their preferred learning environment. In fact, according to [10], E-learning is concerned with ensuring learners' learning goals are met, synchronous and asynchronous communications occur, as well as collaboration between learners and instructors. The Semantic web is seen to further support teaching and learning, allowing students to determine their learning agenda and be in control of their learning [8].

C. Support consisting of: Instructional Support, Systems Support, Organisational Support and Government Support

According to [27], the success of E-learning in higher education is a shared responsibility between e-learning stakeholders. Students, lecturers, educational institutions and the Government have key roles to play in the success of E-learning. In fact, organisational support is identified as a critical success factor for E-learning success in the literature review [14][36][38]. Reference [28] stated that successful implementation of e-learning requires the same management commitment as other mission-critical, university-wide initiatives. This includes the right teaching and learning support to lecturers and students to faciliate online learning acceptance and the necessary technical infrastructure and technical to support the E-learning environment. Students should be provided with the resources to develop and enhance their skills and knowledge of online learning management systems in terms of timely feedback on learning progress, appropriate online learning tools such as FAQs, discussion forums, emails and collaboration among peers [2] [20]. Similarly, lecturers should be provided with the support needed to allow for the shift in mindset and skillset necessary to perform effectively in an online learning environment [32]. It is even argued that the perception of how one is supported within an E-learning environment contributes significantly to its success [20]. In addition, especially in developing countries, such as Mauritius where public tertiary institutions rely a lot on Government's funding, political backing and support from policy makers are essential [3].

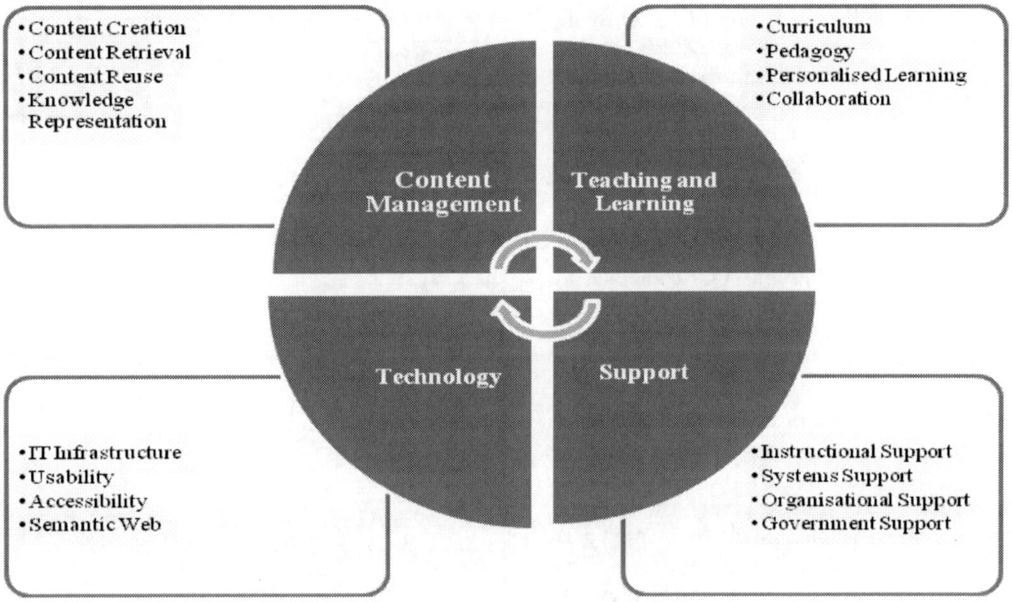

Figure 1. Initial proposed 3.0 E-learning model.

D. Technology consisting of: IT Infrastructure, Usability and Accessibility and Semantic Web

The acceptance of E-learning depends a lot on the efficient and effective use of Information Technology [5]. A reliable IT infrastructure capable of supporting online delivery is considered as a critical success factor for E-learning [14]. Systems usability and accessibility are key as systems users, especially students, will not care about didactics as long as as they can find the information they are looking for and their needs are satisfied [16]. The interface design as well as the ease of navigation and consistency in the manner that the online learning environment is presented and organised play vital roles in fostering a friendly and less intimidating learning environment [5]. In addition, the E-learning environment can be further enhanced by Semantic Web technologies where personal profile of students including previous knowledge and experience, preferred learning styles and educational goals can facilitate semantic web retrieval of content to allow for best individuals learning experiences. Semantic Web technologies through the use of ontologies can provide well structured databases to allow better knowledge handling by machines opening the gate to a learner centered learning environment which promotes collaboration, reuse and where learners can manage their own learning content [2].

III. METHODOLOGY

Two web-based surveys were conducted to gather the perceptions of students and lecturers on the initial proposed 3.0 E-learning model. One survey was directed towards students from the Mauritian higher education sector and one was directed towards lecturers of the Mauritian higher education sector. Web-based surveys have several advantages including short response time, lower cost to the researcher(s), instant access to the audience irrespective of their geographical location, better design options, speed and accuracy of data collection and immediate access to results in different formats [6] [18] [39]. However, there have been concerns about the reponse rate of web-based surveys which is highly dependent on Internet and email technology as well as participants characteristics [37]. Bearing these in mind and looking at the target participants for this study, namely students and lecturers from Mauritian higher education institutions, web-based surveys were considered as appropriate.

The development of the survey required a thorough understanding and accurate interpretation of E-Learning CSFs and the Semantic Web characteristics from the literature review. The surveys' questions were then based on the characteristics identified in the initial proposed model as per Fig. 1 in order to gather the perceptions of Mauritian students and lecturers on these characteristics.

In order to collect a sample that represents the point of view of Mauritian higher education students and lecturers, a research agency in Mauritius was contacted to distribute the survey. The respective links of the surveys were distributed to students and lecturers from both public and private tertiary institutions via emails. With the response rate of web-based surveys also dependent on the number of contacts made to participants, participation rate was monitored and follow ups emails were sent to participants to ensure as many responses as possible [24][21].The data collection process was anonymous. Participants provided consent before moving to the next part of the survey by reading the Informed Consent form. The fom clearly stated that by completing the survey, they are consenting to participate.

Both surveys were structured in a simple manner and consisted of different types of questions including multiple choice questions, five-point Likert scale questions and free text boxes. Participants were provided with a brief explanation of each section at the beginning of each section.

Section one of both surveys captured general information about participants' demographics. Each of the characteristics in the proposed model had a dedicated section to it with a number of statements using a five point likert scale to determine how strongly participants agree or disagree with the statements. The scale ranged from one to five and consisted of the following values: Strongly Agree, Agree, Neutral, Disagree, and Strongly Disagree with a '5' representing the participant strongly agree with the statement and a '1' representing the participant strongly disagree with the statement. At the end of each section, participants were given the option to write any comments regarding each section should they wish to do so via a free text box.

IV. SURVEY ANALYSIS

300 students and 105 lecturers from the public and private tertiary institutions participated in the surveys. Table I provides some statistics on the students' and lecturers' surveys participation.

TABLE I. ONLINE SURVEY STATISTICS

	Lecturers' Survey	Students' Survey
Number of participants	105	300
Gender		
Male participants	50%	43%
Female participants	50%	57%
Types of Institutions		
Public	51%	48%
Private	49%	52%
Age (Students)		
16-25		97%
26-35		3%
36-45		-
46-50		-
51 and above		-
Age (Lecturers)		
22-35	18%	
36-45	27%	
46-50	41%	
51-55	12%	
56-60	2%	
61 and Above	-	
Fields of Study/Faculty		
Agriculture	-	-
Art & Design	10%	7%
Business, Accounting & Finance	16%	6%
Engineering	1%	6%
Health	1%	3%
Information Technology and Systems	9%	10%
Law and Management	27%	12%
Science	-	6%
Social Studies & Humanities	14%	12%
Tourism	18%	23%
Others	4%	15%
Qualifications		
Foundation	-	3%
Undergraduate Certificate	-	7%
Undergraduate Diploma	-	22%
Undergraduate Degree/Bachelor Degree	5%	62%
Postgraduate Diploma	13%	4%
Postgraduate Degree/Masters	67%	2%
PhD/Research	15%	-
Others	-	-

SPSS software version 22.0 was used to analyse the surveys' results. Exploratory factor analysis was used to "explore the underlying dimensions of a construct" in order to ensure a more consistent interpretation of data from the original groupings in the proposed model [9]. To ensure the appropriateness of factor analysis for this study, the Kaiser-Meyer-Olkin measure of sampling adequacy (KMO) and the Bartlett's test of sphericity which examines if variables are related were used [13] [26]. KMO recommends a minimum of 0.5 while the Bartlett's test of sphericity is significant when $p = .05$ or smaller [19]. The KMO for statements related to Content Management and Support characteristics are outlined in Table II. The KMO results met the minimum standards required for both groups although Content Management seemed to be a concept more familiar to lecturers as compared to students. The Bartlett's tests were significant for both characterisics and groups. Factor analysis was therefore deemed appropriate for this study.

TABLE II. KMO AND BARTLETT'S TEST

		Content Management		Support	
		Lecturers' Survey	Students' Survey	Lecturers' Survey	Students' Survey
KMO Measure of Sampling Adequacy		.797	0.54	0.699	0.824
Bartlett's Test of Sphericity	Sig.	.000	.000	0.000	.000

With these initial tests and findings, factor extraction was then performed on both characteristics to determine the smallest number of factors that can be used to best represent the interrelationships among the set of variables [19]. Kaiser's criterion where only factors with an eigen value greater than 1.0 was then used to determined the number of factors to be retained [19].

For Content Management for both the lecturer's and the student's survey, there were 2 components with eigenvalues greater than 1; these 2 components accounted for 57 % (lecturer's survey) and 62% (student's survey) of the total variance of the data set. Similarly, for Support, 2 components accounted for 54 % (lecturer's survey) and 57% (student's survey) of the total variance of the data set. To assist further in the analysis of these 2 characterisitcs, Varimax rotation method, a widely used orthogonal method which attempts to minimise the number of variables by keeping the high loadings variables for each factor, was then used to determine which factors loaded on each of the dimensions [9][19].

With respect to Content Management, for the lecturers' survey, the items that cluster on the same components suggest that component 1 represented Content Relevance and Responsibility while component 2 represented Content Representation. As for the students' survey, component 1 was very much related to that of the lecturers' survey and was termed as Content Relevance and Accessibility while component 2 was termed Content Responsibility . Based on these results, Content Management was reviewed to include Content Relevance, Content Accessibility, Content Responsibility and Content Representation as per Table III and Table IV.

TABLE III. CONTENT MANAGEMENT FACTOR LABELS - LECTURERS

Statements from Lecturers' Survey	Component 1	Component 2	Factor Labels
Learning content should match the unit's aims	.764		**Content Relevance and Responsibility**
Learning content should match students' needs	.659		
Students can contribute to learning content creation (e.g. Students' portfolios, presentations etc)	.645		
Only lecturers can create learning materials	.640		
Learning content should be reusable		.908	**Content Representation**

TABLE IV. CONTENT MANAGEMENT FACTOR LABELS - STUDENTS

Statements from Students' Survey	Component 1	Component 2	Factor Labels
Learning content should be quick to search	.795		**Content Relevance and Accessibility**
Learning content should match students' needs	.778		
Only lecturers can create learning materials		.867	**Content Responsibility**
Students can contribute to learning content creation (e.g. Students' portfolios, presentations etc)		-.544	

TABLE V. SUPPORT FACTOR LABELS - LECTURERS

Statements from Lecturers' Survey	Component 1	Component 2	Factor Labels
Training to use the system is important	.875		**Types of Support**
Effective and appropriate technology infrastructure is important	.833		
Ongoing IT Support is important (e.g. help, FAQs, Help desk)	.556	.402	
Students should assist their peers			
Ongoing feedback to students about their learning performances is important		.734	**Stakeholder's Support**
Ongoing feedback from students about their learning experience is important		.724	
Lecturers should support students (e.g. students'; encouragements, provision of study materials, assessment and exams hints, use of different teaching styles)		.681	

TABLE VI. SUPPORT FACTOR LABELS - STUDENTS

Statements from Students' Survey	Component 1	Component 2	Factor Labels
Ongoing IT Support is important (e.g. help, FAQs, Help desk)	.818		Types of Support
Effective and appropriate technology infrastructure is important	.804		
Training to use the system is important	.600		
I should be able to provide feedback about my learning experience	.535	.445	
Lecturers' support is important (e.g. through students' encouragements, provision of study materials, assessment and exams hints, use of different teaching styles)		.713	Stakeholders' Support
Peer assistance is important to me		.712	
Ongoing feedback from lecturers about my learning performance is important		.668	

TABLE VII. SUMMARY OF FACTORS FOR CONTENT MANAGEMENT AND SUPPORT

		Results derived after Students' Survey Analysis	Results derived after Lecturers' Survey Analysis	Results derived after Students' and Lecturers' Surveys Analysis
Content Management	Content Relevance			√
	Content Accessibility	√		
	Content Responsibility			√
	Content Representation		√	
Support	Types of Support			√
	Stakeholders' Support			√

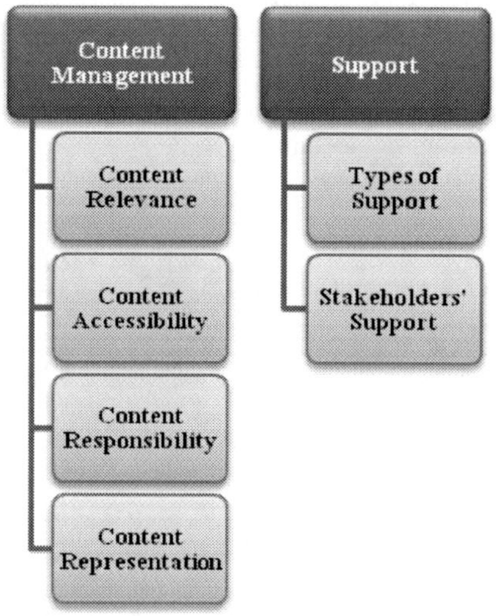

Figure 2. Revised Content Management and Support characteristics.

As for Support, for both surveys, factor loadings after rotation showed clustering on component 1 to represent the types of support expected and therefore renamed as Type of Support. Component 2 for both surveys converged towards the idea of who should be providing the support and was renamed as Stakeholders' Support. Table V and Table VI outline the factors for Support chactacterisitcs.

The revised Content Management and Support Characteristics are shown in Fig 2. For Content Management, the resulting factors Content Relevance and Content Responsibility were derived from both the students' and lecturers' surveys while Content Accessibility and Content Representation were factors derived from the students' and lecturers' surveys respectively. The Support characteristic consists of Types of Support and stakeholders' Support resulting from analysis of both students' and lecturers' survey. Table VII provides a summary of the factors derived , clearly outlining factors common to both surveys' analysis.

To examine the internal reliability of each dimension, Cronbach alpha was calculated on the 2 dimensions resulting in alpha coefficients of 0.737 and 0.778 respectively indicating sufficient level of reliability. Based on these results, it can be concluded that these two dimensions namely Content Management and Support represents different aspects of the 3.0 E-learning model.

V. CONCLUSION AND FUTURE WORK

Higher educational institutions are required to understand the critical success factors affecting E-learning to be able to make the best use of the Internet. With Semantic web technologies viewed as a promising technology to meet E-learning requirements, the need for a combined model capturing the CSFs of E-learning as well as the main characteristics of the Semantic Web is deemed necessary.

This study is significant because it proposed a combined model representing the CSFs of E-learning with the Semantic web, namely a 3.0 E-learning model. The study identified four main characteristics within the proposed 3.0 E-learning model and provided empirical evidence and indicative support of the importance of two of these characteristics namely Content Management and Support. This study additionally provided a deeper analysis of Content Management and Support characteristics via exploratory factor analysis further regrouping the sub characteristics of these two dimensions to provide a more holistic view of what they represent within the model.

In terms of future directions, since the results of this study are based on survey outcomes from Mauritian Higher educational sector, they can be further assessed by interviewing experts in E-learning within the Mauritian higher educational sector. Future research should also aim to generalise these results to consider other environments and countries. Additionally, more characteristics and sub characteristics can be added to the E-Learning and Semantic Web Combined Model, as well as new groupings can be made following further analysis.

ACKNOWLEDGMENT

The authors wish to thank all participants for their useful insights on the issue at hand and for taking the time to participate in the surveys.

REFERENCES

[1] A. Chisega-Negrilă, "Web 3.0 in Education" The Eight International Conference on eLearning and Software for Education (eLSE) Bucharest, Apr. 2012, pp. 455-160, doi:10.5682/2066-026X-12-073.

[2] A. Karunasena, H. Deng, and X. Zhang, "A Web 2.0 Based E-Learning Success Model in Higher Education," Lecture Notes in Information Technology, vol. 23, pp. 177, 2012, available from: http://search.proquest.com/openview/96f7e80b7208282c2da97ab71ada177d/1?pq-origsite=gscholar&cbl=1956339

[3] A. S. Andersson and Å. Gronlund, "A Conceptual Framework for E-Learning in Developing Countries: A Critical Review of Research Challenges," The Electronic Journal of Information Systems in Developing Countries, pp.38, 2009, Available from: http://144.214.55.140/ojs2/index.php/ejisdc/article/view/564/291

[4] A. Yarrow, J. Millwater and B. J. Fraser, "Improving University and Primary School Classroom Environments through Preservice Teachers' Action Research," International Journal of Practical Experiences in Professional Education, vol. 1 no. 1, pp. 68-93, 1997.

[5] B. Cheawjindakarn, P. Suwannatthachote, and A. Theeraroungchaisri, "Critical Success Factors for Online Distance Learning in Higher Education: A Review of the Literature," Creative Education, vol.3, no. 08, pp. 61, Dec. 2012, doi:10.4236/ce.2012.38b014.

[6] C. M. Fleming and M. Bowden, "Web-Based Surveys as an Alternative to Traditional Mail Methods," Journal of Environmental Management, vol. 90, no. 1, pp. 284-292, Jan. 2009, doi:10.1016/j.jenvman.2007.09.011.

[7] D. Castellanos-Nieves, J. T. Fernández-Breis, R. Valencia-García, R. Martínez-Béjar, and M. Iniesta-Moreno, "Semantic Web Technologies for Supporting Learning Assessment," Information Sciences, vol. 181, no. 9, pp. 1517-1537, May. 2011, doi:10.1016/j.ins.2011.01.010.

[8] E. Moreale and M. Vargas-Vera, "Semantic Services in E-Learning: An Argumentation Case Study," Educational Technology & Society, vol. 7, no. 4, pp. 112-128, Oct. 2004, Available from: http://www.jstor.org/stable/jeductechsoci.7.4.112

[9] F. Alhija, "Factor Analysis: An Overview and Some Contemporary Advances," International Encyclopedia of Education, pp. 162-170, 2010, doi:10.1016/b978-0-08-044894-7.01328-2.

[10] F. Ghaleb, S. Daoud, A. Hasna, J. M. ALJa'am, S. A. El-Seoud, and H. El-Sofany, "E-Learning Model Based on Semantic Web Technology," International Journal of Computing & Information Sciences, vol. 4, no. 2, pp. 63-71, Aug. 2006, Available from: http://www.ijcis.info/Vol4N2/pp63-71.pdf

[11] F. P. Rokou, E. Rokou and Y. Rokos, "Modeling Web-Based Educational Systems: Process Design Teaching Model," Educational Technology & Society, vol. 7, no. 1, pp. 42-50, Jan. 2004, Available from: http://www.jstor.org/stable/jeductechsoci.7.1.42

[12] G. Šimić, D. Gašević and V. Devedžić, "Semantic Web and Intelligent Learning Management Systems" Workshop on Applications of Semantic Web Technologies for e-Learning, Aug. 2004, Available from: http://s3.amazonaws.com/academia.edu.documents/30656784/SWEL04-ITS04-proceedings.pdf?AWSAccessKeyId=AKIAIWOWYYGZ2Y53UL3A&Expires=1485048663&Signature=P49tQrRgfCD5b2He5VXerMkhk6c%3D&response-content-disposition=inline%3B%20filename%3DSemantic_web_and_intelligent_learning_ma.pdf

[13] H. F. Kaiser, "An Index of Factorial Simplicity," Psychometrika, vol. 39, no. 1, pp. 31-36, Mar. 1974, doi: 10.1007/BF02291575.

[14] H. M. Selim, "E-Learning Critical Success Factors: An Exploratory Investigation of Student Perceptions," International Journal of Technology Marketing, Vol. 2, No. 2, pp. 157-182, 2007, doi:10.1504/IJTMKT.2007.014791

[15] H. Tao, et. al. "Semantic Web-Based Educational Knowledge Service System (Ekss) for E-Learning," Proc. 2006 First International Conference on Communications and Networking in China, IEEE, Oct 2006, doi: 10.1109/CHINACOM.2006.344834.

[16] I. Pah, I. Maniu, G. Maniu and S. Damian, "A Conceptual Framework Based on Ontologies for Knowledge Management in E-Learning Systems," Proc. 6th WSEAS International Conference on Education and Educational Technology, Italy, Nov. 2007, pp. 283-286, Available from:

http://www.wseas.us/e-library/conferences/2007venice/papers/570-623.pdf

[17] J. Brophy, Jere, "Teaching. Educational Practices Series—1," international Bureau of Education, pp. 37, 2000, Available from: http://www.ibe.unesco.org.

[18] J. Ilieva, S. Baron and N. Healey, "Online Surveys in Marketing Research: Pros and Cons," International Journal of Market Research, vol. 44, no.3, pp. 361-376, Jan. 2002, Available from: https://www.researchgate.net/publication/27398278_On-line_surveys_in_international_marketing_research_pros_and_cons

[19] J. Pallant, SPSS survival manual. McGraw-Hill Education (UK), 2013.

[20] J. W. Lee and S. Mendlinger, "Perceived Self-Efficacy and Its Effect on Online Learning Acceptance and Student Satisfaction," Journal of Service Science and Management, vol. 4, no. 3, pp. 243, Sep. 2011, doi: 10.4236/jssm.2011.43029.

[21] K. B. Sheehan and M. G. Hoy, "Using E-Mail to Survey Internet Users in the United States: Methodology and Assessment," Journal of Computer-Mediated Communication, vol. 4, no. 3, pp. 0-0, Mar. 1999, doi: 10.1111/j.1083-6101.1999.tb00101.x.

[22] L. Stojanovic, S. Staab and R. Studer, "Elearning Based on the Semantic Web" WebNet2001-World Conference on the WWW and Internet, 2001 pp. 23-27, Available from: http://citeseerx.ist.psu.edu/viewdoc/download?doi=10.1.1.16.295&rep=rep1&type=pdf

[23] M. Bucos, B. Dragulescu and M. Veltan, "Designing a semantic web ontology for E-learning in higher education," 9th International Symposium on Electronics and Telecommunications, Timisoara, pp. 415-418, Nov. 2010, doi: 10.1109/ISETC.2010.5679298.

[24] M. J. Kittleson, "Determining Effective Follow-up of E-Mail Surveys," American Journal of Health Behavior, vol. 21, no. 3, pp. 193-196, May. 1997, Available from: http://web.b.ebscohost.com.dbgw.lis.curtin.edu.au/ehost/detail/detail?sid=63d78955-000f-44ab-b03b-c5b1773529f2%40sessionmgr102&vid=0&hid=125&bdata=JnNpdGU9ZWhvc3QtbGl2ZQ%3d%3d#db=rzh&AN=107263899&anchor=AN0006258503-4

[25] M. Q. Huynh, U. N. Umesh and J. S. Valacich, "E-Learning as an Emerging Entrepreneurial Enterprise in Universities and Firms," Communications of the Association for Information Systems, vol. 12, no. 1, pp. 3, 2003, Available from: http://aisel.aisnet.org/cais/vol12/iss1/3

[26] M. S. Bartlett, "A Note on the Multiplying Factors for Various X 2 Approximations," Journal of the Royal Statistical Society. Series B (Methodological), vol. 16, no. 2, pp. 296-298, Jan. 1954, Available from: http://www.jstor.org/stable/2984057

[27] N. L. Wagner, K. Hassanein and M. M. Head, "Who Is Responsible for E-Learning Success in Higher Education? A Stakeholders' Analysis," Educational Technology & Society, vol. 11, no. 3, pp. 26-36, 2008, Available from: http://profs.degroote.mcmaster.ca/ads/headm/Articles/Who%20is%20responsible%20for%20eLearning%20Success%20in%20Higher%20Education.pdf

[28] P. Henry, "E-Learning Technology, Content and Services," Education+ Training, vol. 43, no. 4, pp. 249-255, 2001, Available from: http://elibrary.mediu.edu.my/books/2015/MEDIU01271.pdf

[29] P. Kanaksabee, M. P. Odit and A. Ramdoyal, "A Standard-Based Model for Adaptive E-Learning Platform for Mauritian Academic Institutions," Journal of International Education Research, vol. 7, no. 1, 2011, doi: http://dx.doi.org/10.19030/jier.v7i1.3541.

[30] P. Monachesi, K. Simov, E. Mossel, P. Osenova and L. Lemnitzer, "What Ontologies Can Do for Elearning," Proc. IMCL 2008, Apr. 2008, Available from: http://www.lt4el.eu/content/files/IMCL08Final.pdf

[31] R. B. M. Hajee Ahmud-Boodoo, "E-Learning and the Semantic Web: A Descriptive Literature Review," In Artificial Intelligence Technologies and the Evolution of Web 3.0, T. Issa and P. Isaias, USA: IGA Global, pp. 66-100, 2015.

[32] R. Oliver, "Assuring the Quality of Online Learning in Australian Higher Education," Proc. 2000 Moving Online II Conference Lismore, 2001, pp. 222-231, Available from: http://ro.ecu.edu.au/cgi/viewcontent.cgi?article=5791&context=ecuworks

[33] S. Gunness, Learner-Centred Teaching through Oer. Open educational resources and social networks: Co-learning and professional development. London, Scholio: Educational Research & Publishing, 2011.

[34] S. Pudaruth, Sameerchand, R. K. Moloo, A. Mantaye and J. N. Bibi, "A Survey of E-Learning Platforms in Mauritius" Proc. World Congress on Engineering, Vol. 1, Jun 2010, Available from: https://www.researchgate.net/profile/Sameerchand_Pudaruth2/publication/45534420_A_Survey_of_E-Learning_Platforms_in_Mauritius/links/573858ab08ae9f741b2bba62.pdf

[35] S. Rashid, R. Khan and F. Ahmed, "A Proposed Model of E-Learning Management System Using Semantic Web Technology," Daffodil International University Journal of Science and Technology, vol. 8, no. 1, Jan. 2013.

[36] T. Govindasamy, Thavamalar, "Successful Implementation of E-Learning: Pedagogical Considerations," The internet and higher education, vol. 4, no. 3, pp. 287-299, 2001, Available from: http://elibrary.mediu.edu.my/books/2015/MEDIU01323.pdf

[37] T. H. Shih and X. Fan, "Comparing Response Rates in E-Mail and Paper Surveys: A Meta-Analysis," Educational Research Review, vol. 4, no. 1, pp. 26-40, 2009, doi: http://dx.doi.org/10.1016/j.edurev.2008.01.003.

[38] V. Benigno and T. Guglielmo, "The Evaluation of Online Courses," Journal of computer assisted learning, vol.16, no. 3, pp. 259-270, Sep. 2000, doi: 10.1046/j.1365-2729.2000.00137.x.

[39] W. Fan and Z. Yan, "Factors Affecting Response Rates of the Web Survey: A Systematic Review," Computers in Human Behavior, vol. 26, no. (2), pp. 132-139, Nov. 2009, doi: http://dx.doi.org/10.1016/j.chb.2009.10.015.

Methods to Measure the Achievement of Learning Using Lecture Contents

Ryosuke Takata *, Naka Gotoda †, Toshihiro Hayashi †, Hiroshi Murai ‡,
Ken'ichi Fujimoto ‡ and Rihito Yaegashi §,
*Graduate School of Engineering, Kagawa University,
Hayashi-cho 2217-20, Takamatsu, Kagawa 761-0396, Japan
Email: s15g471@stu.kagawa-u.ac.jp
†Information Technology Center, Kagawa University,
Saiwai-cho 1-1, Takamatsu, Kagawa 760-8521, Japan
Email: {hayashi, gotoda}@eng.kagawa-u.ac.jp
‡University Consortium for E-Learning, Shikoku Center, Kagawa University,
Saiwai-cho 1-1, Takamatsu, Kagawa 760-8521, Japan
Email: {murai, kfujim}@cc.kagawa-u.ac.jp
§Faculty of Engineering, Kagawa University,
Hayashi-cho 2217-20, Takamatsu, Kagawa 761-0396, Japan
Email: rihito@eng.kagawa-u.ac.jp

Abstract—**In recent years, learning analytics has been attracting attention. Learning analytics is the measurement, collection, analysis and reporting of data about learners and their contexts for purposes of understanding and optimizing learning and the environments. Generally, its information are stored in Learning Management System (LMS) and Course Management System (CMS). However, LMS and CMS did not have the method to measure the achievement of learning using lecture contents. This paper proposes the methods to measure the achievement of learning using lecture contents.**

Keywords–Lecture Contents; Learning Analytics; Measurement of Learning Achievement.

I. Introduction

Recently, many educational institutions offer various mechanism for the educational advance using information communication technology (ICT). A massive open online course (MOOC) [1][2][3] is a model for delivering learning content online to any person who wants to take a course, without any limitation on attendance. MOOC delivers not only text media (syllabus, handout, etc.), but also sound contents and movie contents. Coursera [4] is also the service provider to deliver a lecture of a university as MOOC. Coursera is delivering courses of more than 1000 by 120 universities and has more than 13,000,000 participants. It's learned using lecture contents by open online course. Hori [5] shows the user is viewing only one or two lecture contents by open online course. Hori also shows 80 percent of user view and stopped half of lecture contents and the average viewing hour is 30 minutes. Generally, lecture contents is 90 minutes in Japan. Because lecture contents are generated by recording real lecture. This result shows it is difficult to secure time to view all of lecture contents.

We developed the lecture contents viewing system using lecture contents metadata [6][7]. The system which we developed has three functions, index function, unit/content viewing function and playlist function. The index function can view lecture contents from utterance time of indexing term by using index metadata. The unit/content viewing function can be played back selected unit and learning content of lecture content by using syllabus metadata generated from the syllabus. The playlist function can view plural units and learning contents continuously. This system provides various mechanism of viewing lecture contents on learning. This system provides the mechanism which the learner views the lecture contents little by little and complete viewing with several days. In recent years, learning analytics [8] has been attracting attention. Learning analytics is the measurement, collection, analysis and reporting of data about learners and their contexts for purposes of understanding and optimizing learning and the environments. Its information stored Learning Management System (LMS) [9] and Course Management System (CMS) [10]. However, LMS and CMS did not have the method to measure the achievement of learning using lecture contents. And the system which we developed has the mechanism to acquire viewing history of learners [11]. However, this system can not measure the achievement of learning using lecture contents. This research proposes the methods to measure the achievement of learning using lecture contents.

This paper is organized as follows. Section II describes lecture contents viewing system using lecture contents metadata. Section III describes method to measure the achievement of learning using lecture contents. Section IV describes conclusion.

II. Lecture Contents Viewing System Using Lecture Contents Metadata

This section describes lecture contents metadata and lecture contents viewing system using lecture contents metadata.

A. *Lecture Contents Metadata*

The lecture contents and lecture contents metadata are stored in the database. Its database is called lecture contents archives. Lecture contents metadata consist of general information, index metadata and syllabus metadata. General information are name of lecture contents, creation date of lecture contents, etc. The index metadata is generated from text data which is converted by teacher's utterance in lecture

```
<contents name="JAD02">
  <index>
    <term name="Encoding">
      <time>00:04:39</time>
    </term>
    <term name="Symbol">
      <time>00:07:32</time>
      <time>00:14:12</time>
      <time>00:46:08</time>
      <time>01:07:29</time>
      <time>01:07:54</time>
    </term>
    <term name="Codeword">
      <time>00:08:03</time>
      <time>00:12:11</time>
      <time>00:46:08</time>
    </term>
    <term name="Length of code">
      <time>00:10:23</time>
    </term>
    <term name="Average code length">
      <time>00:10:37</time>
      <time>00:25:46</time>
    </term>
    ...
  </index>
</contents>
```

Figure 1. The Index Metadata

```
<lecture title="Fundamentals of Telecommunication Engineering">
  <unit id="1">
    <unitstart">00:00:00</unitstart>
    <unitend">00:31:45</unitend>
    <unittitle">Encoding of Information</unittitle>
    <content id ="1">
      <contentstart>00:00:00</contentstart>
      <contentend>00:06:41</contentend>
      <contenttitle>Information Transimission</contenttitle>
    </content>
    <content id ="2">
      <contentstart>00:06:41</contentstart>
      <contentend>00:09:57</contentend>
      <contenttitle>Symbol and Code</contenttitle>
    </content>
    ...
  </unit>
  <unit id="2">
    <unitstart">00:31:45</unitstart>
    <unitend">00:50:08</unitend>
    <unittitle">Information Content</unittitle>
    ...
  </unit>
  ...
</lecture>
```

Figure 2. The Syllabus Metadata

contents using a voice recognition technology. Figure. 1 shows index metadata. In index metadata, the information of lecture contents describes contents tags, indexing term describes term tags and utterance time of indexing term describes time tags. According to Figure. 1, indexing term "Codeword" is uttered 00:08:03, 00:12:11 and 00:46:08 in the lecture content (JAD02).Using index metadata, the contents created by this system don't need the play back from the beginning but from the midstream.The syllabus metadata is generated from the syllabus. Figure. 2 shows the syllabus metadata. Figure. 2 shows the lecture contents (JAD02) consists of various units and learning contents. This unit consists of "Encoding of Information" and "Information Content". This learning content (Encoding of Information) consists of "Information Transmission" and "Symbol and Code". The lecture contents

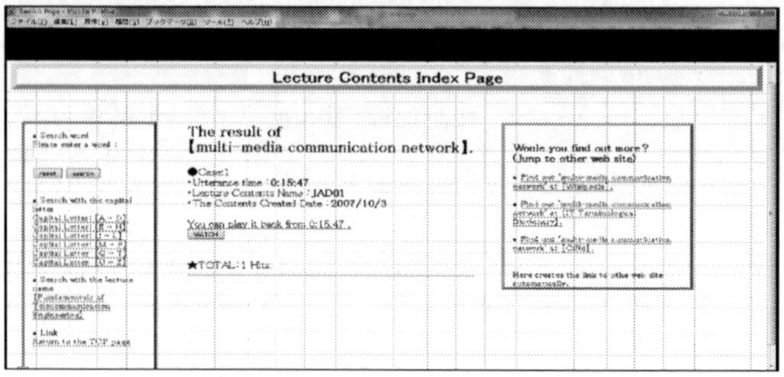

Figure 3. Result Window of index function

```
<smil>
  <head>
    <layout>
      <region id="1" width="480" height="320"fit="fill"/>
    </layout>
  </head>
  <body>
    <par>
      <video src="JAD01.rm" region="movie1"clip-begin= " 3008s" />
      <textstream src="JAD01.rt" region="text1" clip-begin= " 3008s">
    </par>   </body>
</smil>
```

Figure 4. SMIL generated by indexing function

can be played back selected units and learning contents by using syllabus metadata.

B. Lecture Contents Viewing System Using Lecture Contents Metadata

The lecture contents viewing system has three functions, indexing function, unit/content viewing function and playlist function.

1) Indexing Function: The indexing function has three retrieval methods, (a) Input indexing term to input form, (b) Select indexing term from initial letter of indexing term, (c) Select indexing term from indexing list for each lecture. Figure. 3 shows the result window. In indexing function, the lecture contents can be played back the midstream uttered indexing term. This function uses Synchronized Multimedia Integration Language (SMIL) [12]. Using SMIL, the lecture contents created by this system can play back from the scene of indexing term. Figure. 4 shows SMIL file generated by indexing function. The lecture contents (JAD01) uttered indexing term "Entropy" is played back from 3008 seconds.

2) Unit/Learning Content Viewing Function: The unit/learning content viewing function can be played back selected unit and learning content of lecture content by using syllabus metadata. This function also uses SMIL. Figure. 5 shows SMIL file generated by this function. Its shows the lecture contents (JAD02) is played back unit of information content from 1905 seconds to 3008 seconds. These information are based on syllabus metadata, which the authors defined in this research. Figure. 6 shows lecture content using SMIL file.

3) Playlist Function: The playlist function can view plural units and learning contents continuously. Using SMIL, the

TABLE I. Obtained Viewing History of Lecture Contents

No.	Starting Time	Ending Time	Playback Start Position	Playback Ending Position	Playback Time
1	1/16/2015 10:28:00	1/16/2015 10:31:16	0:06:41	0:09:57	196 seconds
2	1/16/2015 10:31:16	1/16/2015 10:39:31	0:31:45	0:40:00	495 seconds
3	1/16/2015 10:39:31	1/16/2015 10:46:12	0:00:00	0:06:41	401 seconds
4	1/16/2015 10:46:12	1/16/2015 10:49:28	0:06:41	0:09:57	196 seconds
5	1/16/2015 10:49:28	1/16/2015 10:59:38	0:40:00	0:50:08	608 seconds

```
<smil>
  <head>
    <layout>
      <region id="1" width="480" height="320"fit="fill"/>
    </layout>
  </head>
  <body>
    <video clip-begin="1905s"clip-end="3008s" src="JAD02.rm"
      title="Information Content"region="1"/>
  </body>
</smil>
```

Figure 5. SMIL generated by unit/learning content function

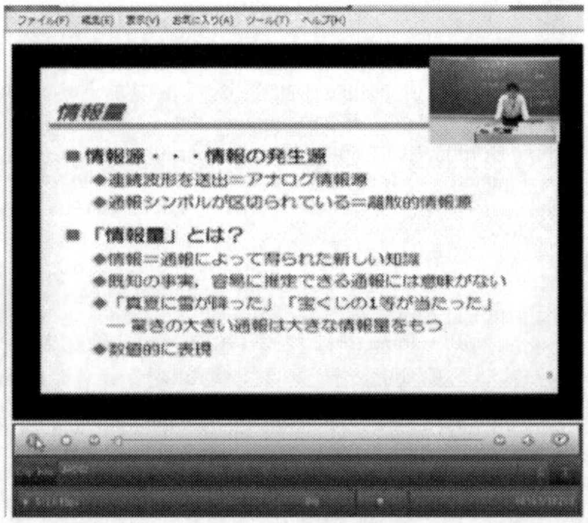

Figure 6. Played Lecture Contents

lecture contents created by this system can play back plural units and learning contents continuously. Figure. 7 shows SMIL file generated by playlist function. According to Figure. 7, the lecture contents (JAD02) is played back from 3008 seconds (00:50:08) to 4267 seconds (01:11:07) and from 401 seconds (00:06:41) to 597 seconds (00:09:57) continuously. The playlist function can play not only the same lecture contents but also different lecture contents continuously.

III. The Methods to Measure the Achievement of Learning Using Lecture Contents

We developed the function to acquire viewing history of learners [11]. This sectoin proposes the two kinds of method to measure the achievement of learning using lecture contents. It's the method to measure the achievement of each student and the

```
<smil>
  <head>
    <layout>
      <region id="1" width="480" height="320"fit="fill"/>
    </layout>
  </head>
  <body>
    <seq>
      <video clip-begin=" 3008s " clip-end=" 4267s "
        src=" JAD02.rm " title=" Entropy " region=" 1"/>
      <video clip-begin=" 401s " clip-end=" 597s "
        src=" JAD02.rm " title=" Length of code " region=" 1"/>
  </body>
</smil>
```

Figure 7. SMIL generated by playlist function

method to measure the achievement of all students. These are measured based on data which the function to acquire viewing history of learners creates.

A. The Method to Measure the Achievement of each Student

A function which acquires viewing history consists of indexing history acquisition function and viewing time acquisition function. The indexing history acquisition function acquires a total number of views using indexing function. TABLE.I shows viewing history obtained by the viewing time acquisition function. This is a viewing history of lecture content (JAD02) by a certain learner. No.1 of Table.1 means that the learner views lecture content (JAD02) from January 16, 2015 10:28:00 to January 16, 2015 10:31:16. Also, it means that lecture content (JAD02) is playback from 00:06:41 to 00:09:57. Therefore, the learner views lecture content (JAD02) for 196 minutes from 00:06:41 to 00:09:57. As shown in the syllabus metadata of Figure. 2, lecture content (JAD02) is played back about " Symbol and Code " from 00:06:41 to 00:09:57. Therefore, it means the learner views " Symbol and Code " of lecture content (JAD02). Figure. 8 presents the measurement obtained by this method. This is measured based on data which the function to acquire viewing history of learners creates. Figure. 8 shows that Student X is viewing all contents of No.1, 80% of contents of No.2. However, student X is viewing only 30% of contents of No.5.

B. The Method to Measure the Achievement of all Students

Section III.A describes the method to measure the achievement of each student. It is important that a teacher sees the measurement on each all students, and a teacher correspond appropriately to it. And it is also important to grasp the

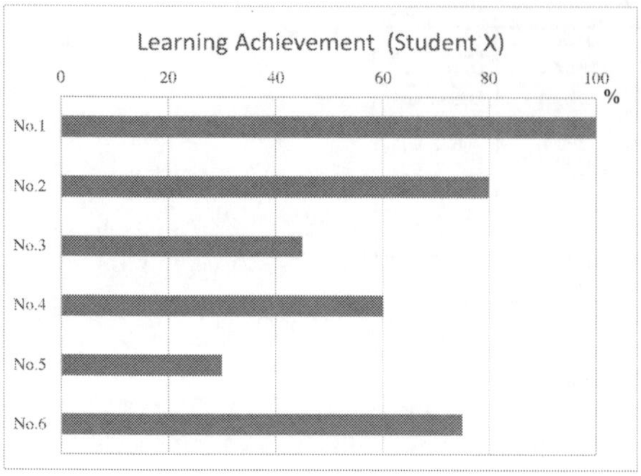

Figure 8. Learning Achievement (Student X) of each Lecture Content

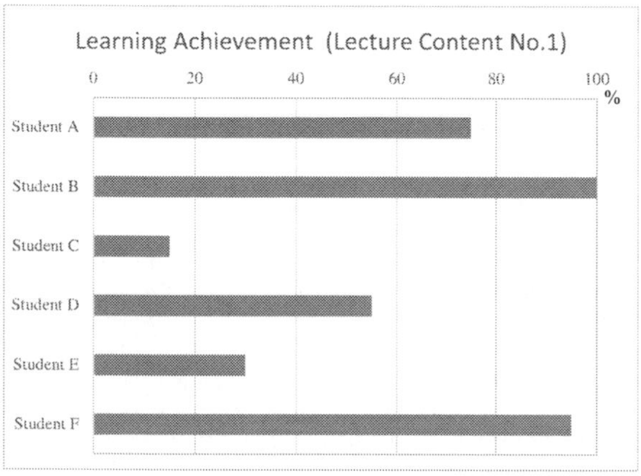

Figure 9. Learning Achievement (Lecture Content No.1) of each User

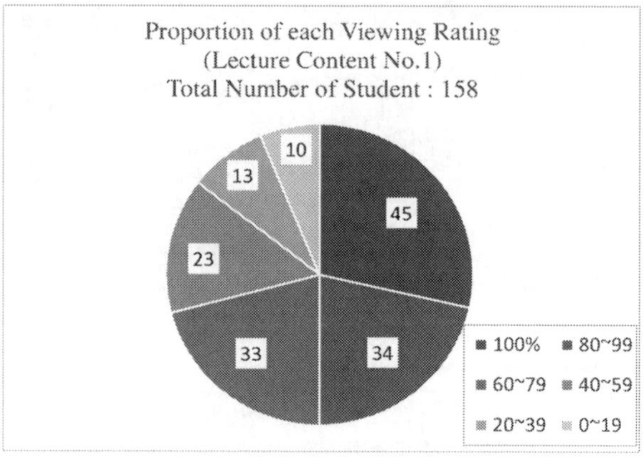

Figure 10. Proportion of each Viewing Rating

achievement of all students. This is also measured based on data which the function to acquire viewing history of learners creates. Figure. 9 is indicated the measurement obtained by this method. Figure. 9 shows student A is viewing 75% of contents of No1, student B is viewing all contents of No.1. And student C is viewing only 15% of contents of No.1. Figure. 10 shows proportion of each viewing rating. Figure. 10 shows the students who view 100% of contents of No.1 are 45 students, the students who view more than 60% of contents are 112 students.

IV. CONCLUSION

This paper proposed the two kinds of method to measure the achievement of learning using lecture contents, The method to measure the achievement of each student and the method to measure the achievement of all students. We are conducting an experiment to confirm the effectiveness of this method in Kagawa university.

ACKNOWLEDGEMENT

We appreciate the assistance from Photron Co., Ltd. and SRA West Japan, Inc. This work was supported by JSPS KAKENHI Grant Number 26730173.

REFERENCES

[1] MOOCs: http://moocs.com/[accessed: 2017.01.29]

[2] Jonathan Haber (2014) MOOCs (The MIT Press Essential Knowledge series), US,The MIT Press

[3] BIS (2013) The Maturing of the MOOC: Literature Review of Massive

[4] Coursera, https://www.coursera.org/[accessed: 2017.01.29]

[5] Masumi Hori, Seishi Ono, Shinzo Kobayashi, and Kazutsuna Ymaji, " Development of Open Education Platform Utilizing GakuNin and e-book ", IPSJ SIG Technical Report, Vol.2013-IOT-22 No.9, pp.1-8, 2013. (In Japanese)

[6] Takuya Saitoh, Toshihiro Hayashi, and Rihito Yaegashi, "The Lecture Contents with Index for Self Study and its System", Proceedings of International Conference on Information Technology Based Higher Education and Training 2012(ITHET2012), 6pages, 2012.

[7] Takuya Saitoh, Toshihiro Hayashi, and Rihito Yaegashi, " Self-Study Support System Using The Lecture Contents : Creation of Study Ontology from Syllabuses ", Proceedings of International Conference on Information Technology Based Higher Education and Training 2012(ITHET2012), 6pages, 2012.

[8] Learning Analytics - EDUCAUSE.edu, http://www.educause.edu/library/learning-analytics[accessed: 2017.01.29]

[9] Learning Management System:https://en.wikipedia.org/wiki/Learning_management_system[accessed: 2017.01.29]

[10] What is Joomla?:http://www.joomla.org/about-joomla.html[accessed: 2017.01.29]

[11] Ryosuke Takata, Naka Gotoda, Hiroshi Murai, Toshihiro Hayashi, and Rihito Yaegashi, "Development of the Function which Collects Viewing History in the Support System for Dividing and Viewing Lecture Contents", Proceedings of The Fourth International Conference on Informatics & Applications, pp.325-328, 2015

[12] Synchronized Multimedia Integration Language (SMIL 3.0), http://www.w3.org/TR/SMIL/[accessed: 2017.01.29]

ICT Operational Model and ICT Operational Pattern which Express Teacher's Operation in a Lecture

Naoya Okada *, Naka Gotoda †, Toshihiro Hayashi †, Norifumi Suehiro †,
Keizo Saisho *, Hiroshi Oota ‡ , and Rihito Yaegashi *
*Faculty of Engineering, Kagawa University,
Hayashicho 2217-20, Takamatsu, Kagawa 761-0396, Japan
Email: s13t213@stmail.eng.kagawa-u.ac.jp, {sai, rihito}@eng.kagawa-u.ac.jp
†Information Technology Center, Kagawa University,
Saiwaicho 1-1, Takamatsu, Kagawa 760-8521, Japan
Email: {gotoda, hayashi}@eng.kagawa-u.ac.jp, n-suehiro@ao.kagawa-u.ac.jp
‡UCHIDA YOKO CO.,LTD,
4-7, Shinkawa 2-Chome, Chuo-ku, Tokyo 104-8282, Japan
Email: ootahiroshi@uchida.co.jp

***Abstract*—It is an urgent task for the education institutes to use Information and Communication Technology (ICT) devices effectively. The education institutes not only introduce ICT devices, but also it is necessary to evaluate the effect of the introduced ICT devices. This paper proposes ICT Operational Model and ICT Operational Pattern which express teacher's operation in a lecture. This paper describes the outline of ICT Operational Model and ICT Operational Pattern. ICT Operational Model and ICT Operational Pattern can be used as the valuable information to evaluate the effect of the introduced ICT devices.**

***Index Terms*—ICT Operational Model; ICT Operational Pattern; ICT device**

I. INTRODUCTION

Kagawa University developed the Kagawa University type IT desk system (TDS) to support the effective enforcement of the class using ICT devices installed in the classroom in Kagawa University[1]. TDS can operate the ICT devices which were installed in the classroom by using the ICT device control system on the same interface. Figure 1 shows the TDS. Various kinds of ICT devices are stored in the TDS. Figure 2 shows the interface of the ICT device control system. The system is operated by iPad. All the ICT device operations are conducted through ICT device control system from iPad, and all operation logs are stored in the ICT device control system. Table 1 shows ICT devices installed in the TDS. TDS has been used in ten classrooms of Kagawa University. ICT devices play an important role in institutes, and therefore the effect of the introduced systems needs to be evaluated to keep or improve the performance of the institutes within the limited budgets and time. For example, many educational institutes including universities have introduced ICT devices to support effective on-site/remote teaching using multimedia contents, and some of them were evaluated by using limited methods such as questionnaire survey. TDSs which consist of various kinds of ICT devices have been developed and installed in classrooms, but their effect has not been evaluated so far, and also there are no valid methods to evaluate the effect systematically.

Figure 1. The TDS

In this paper, we created ICT Operational Model from the operation logs of the TDS using Operational Profile[1], [2] and ICT Operational Pattern from ICT Operational Model.

The Operational Profile that we used is the Extended Operational Profile[3]. Extended Operational Profile gave the sojourn times and the sojourn counts to the Operational Profile that is one of the modeling techniques of software and the information system. Sojourn times is using total times(minutes). Sojourn counts is total nunber of using.

Figure 2. Screen Image of the Interface of TDS

TABLE I. STORED ICT DEVICES IN TDS

Category	Device Name
Display device	Screen
	Projector
	Large Display
	Electronic White Board
Camera Device	Network Camera
Imaging device	Matrix Switcher
	Digital RGB Distributor
	ICT Control System
Sound Device	Speaker
	Powered Mixer
	Hand Microphone
	Tiepin Microphone
	2ch Receiver
Contents Showing Device	Blu-ray
	Visualizer
	Personal Computer(PC)
Etc	Lecture Recording System
	Video Conference system

```
2015-04-20 08:26:40,902 [pool-43-thread-1]
connection.TCPConnectionHandler$TCPCallableTask
(TCPConnectionHandler.java:312)
 DEBUG - Start to send command - %1PW01 1
```

Figure 3. The Operational Log in the ICT Device Control System

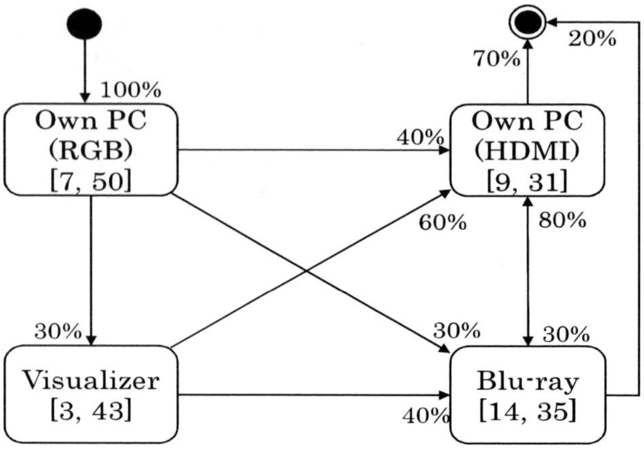

Figure 4. Extended Operational Profiles

TABLE II. THE KINDS OF OPERATION ORDER

Operation order	Content
%1PWAL	Turn on the projector
%1NAL	Switch the out put image
%1AUST	Switch the out put audio
%1BD	Control the Blu-ray
%1LR	Control the Lecture Conference System

This paper describes the outline of ICT Operational Model and ICT Operational Pattern. ICT Operational Model and ICT Operational Pattern suggest not only the certain effect to measure ICT-based teaching and plan for construction of ICT devices but also construction of learning program and learning environment using ICT devices. Besides, this result contributes to the curriculum design which utilized the ICT devices in the class and the development of the learning environment design.

II. ICT Operational Model and ICT Operational Pattern

In this section, we describes ICT Operational Model and ICT Operational Pattern. Operational profile is the model which added users' operate probability to finite state machine [1], [2]. For that reason, operational profile express functions that are used for a long time at once as "the function which is not often used". It is It was the problem so far. Fukutake [4] proposed new Operational Profiles (Extended Operational Profiles) which include users' sojourn times and sojourn counts in addition to users' operate probability. ICT Operational Model is expressed based on Extended Operational Profiles proposed by Fukutake. ICT device installed in TDS is controlled by the ICT device control system. Figure 3 shows the operational log in the ICT device control system. The ICT device control system works with the Web container, Tomcat. The parts below "start to send command" in Figure 3 show the operation order of the ICT device control system. Table 2 shows the kinds of operation order. Figure 4 shows a example of ICT Operational Model. It transits from Initial State to 「Own PC (RGB)」 with a probability of 100%. It transits from 「Own PC (RGB)」 to 「Visualizer」 with a probability of 30%. It transits from 「Own PC (RGB)」 to 「Blu-ray」 with a probability of 30%. It transits from 「Own PC (RGB)」 to 「Own PC (HDMI) 」 with a probability of 40%. 「Own PC (RGB)」 was visited seven times, and was stayed for the total of 50 minutes. ICT Operational Pattern is created from ICT Operational Model. ICT Operational Pattern indicates operational sequence, and ICT Operational Model and Pattern are created by hand.

III. Creation of ICT Operational Model and ICT Operational Pattern

In this section, we describes creation of ICT Operational Model and ICT Operational Pattern. ICT Operational Model was constructed from April 8, 2015 to April 30, 2015 in school of nursing 303 classroom in the faculty of Medicine.

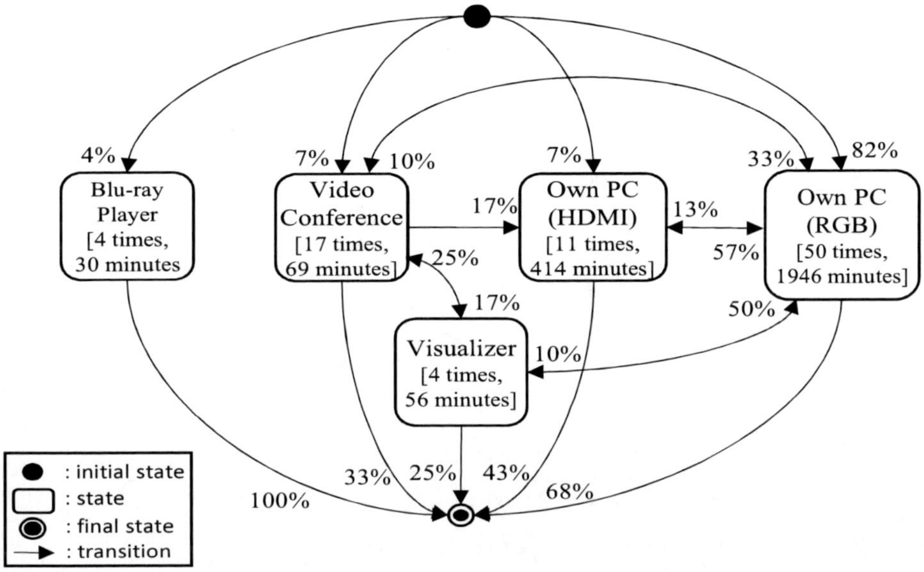

Figure 5. ICT Operational Model at the Nursing, 303 Classroom

TABLE III. ICT OPERATIONAL PATTERN AT THE NURSING, 303 CLASSROOM

number	Count of operation	ICT Operational Pattern
1st	17	Own PC (RGB)
2nd	3	Own PC (RGB) → Own PC (HDMI) → Own PC (RGB)
3rd	1	Own PC (HDMI) → Own PC (RGB)
4th	1	Own PC (RGB) → Own PC (HDMI)
5th	1	Video Conference → Own PC (RGB) → Video Conference → Own PC (RGB) → Visualizer → Own PC (RGB) → Visualizer → Own PC (RGB) → Visualizer
6th	1	Blu-ray
7th	1	Own PC (HDMI)
8th	1	Own PC (RGB) → Video Conference → Visualizer → Video Conference → Own PC (HDMI)
9th	1	Video Conference
10th	1	Own PC (RGB) → Video Conference

Figure 5 shows constructed ICT Operational Model. ICT Operational Model was generated from the operational logs of TDS. Twenty-eight classes used TDS in the school of nursing 303 classroom in the faculty of Medicine, and the time of all classes were 2516 minutes. It transits from 「Initial State」 to State 「Own PC (RGB)」 with a probability of 82%, State 「Own PC (HDMI)」 with a probability of 7% and, State 「Video Conference」 with a probability of 7%, State 「Blu-ray」 with a probability of 4%. It remains at State 「Own PC (RGB)」 fifty times for 1946 minutes. Own PC is used in the class of the 89% together with 「Own PC (RGB)」 and 「Own PC (HDMI)」 from 「Initial State」. Most of the classes did not use other ICT devices and finished the class using only 「Own PC」.

ICT Operational Patterns are created from ICT Operational Model by hand. We extracted a data of ICT device operations per lecture from ICT Operational Model. Table 3 shows the created ICT Operational Patterns. Ten patterns were generated from ICT Operational Model nursing 303 classroom. Using Only 「Own PC (RGB)」 is the most frequent pattern. It was used seventeen times. ICT Operational Model shows the tendency and sequence of teachers' ICT device operation. It indicates the certain effect to measure ICT based teaching.

IV. Conclusion

This paper proposes ICT Operational Model and ICT Operational Pattern which express teacher's operation in a lecture. This paper describes the outline of ICT Operational Model and ICT Operational Pattern. ICT Operational Model is the model which shows teachers' ICT device operation during lectures.

ICT Operational Model uses Extended Operational Profiles which include users' sojourn times and sojourn counts in addition to operational profiles. Also, this paper showed the construction of ICT Operational Model from the operational logs of TDS. ICT Operational Model and ICT Operational Pattern suggest not only the certain effect to measure ICT-based teaching and plan for construction of ICT devices but also construction of learning program and learning environment using ICT devices. ICT Operational Model and ICT Operational Pattern show the evaluation methods of software and information system. This research also can be applied to other software and information systems, as well as information systems for education. Now, we are developing the function which automatically creates ICT operational model and pattern from operational logs by using the result of this study.

ACKNOWLEDGEMENT

Funding from UCHIDA YOKO CO., LTD. is gratefully acknowledged. The authors would like to thank to staffs of Information Technology Center in Kagawa University.

REFERENCES

[1] R. Yaegashi et al., " ICT-based Teaching Support Desk System (IT kyotaku system) for Efficient Management of University Lectures — An Actual Practice According to the Cycle of Development and Operations —", Japanese Society for Information and Systems in Education, Vol.32, No.1, pp.84-97, Jan 2015.

[2] J. D. Musa, "The Operational Profile", Computer and system sciences, NATO ASI Series F, vol.154, pp.333-344, 1996.

[3] G. H. Walton, J. H. Poore, and C. J. Trammell, " Statistical Testing of Software Based on a Usage Model", Software Practice and Experience, vol.25, no.1, pp.97-108, 1995.

[4] H. Fukutake, L. D. Xu, R. Watanabe, T. Takagi, R. Yaegashi, " The Method to Create Test suite based on Operational Profiles for Combination Test of Status", Proc. of 16th International Conference on Software Engineering, Artificial Intelligence, Networking and Parallel/Distributed Computing (SNPD 2015), pp.623-626, June 2015.

Saudi Arabian Students' Attitudes to and Perceptions of Social Networking for Educational Purposes

Sulaiman Alqahtani
School of Information Systems
Curtin University
Perth, WA, Australia
S.alqahtani8@student.curtin.edu.au

Tomayess Issa
School of Information Systems
Curtin University
Perth, WA, Australia
Tomayess.Issa@cbs.curtin.edu.au

Theodora Issa
School of Management
Curtin University
Perth, WA, Australia
Theodora.issa@cbs.curtin.edu.au

Pedro Isaias
The University of Queensland
Brisbane, Australia
Pedro.isaias@uq.edu.au

***Abstract*— Web 2.0 applications, in the form of social networking sites, are increasingly being repurposed as academic tools in higher education institutions. In this context, social networking sites are used to support a number of key academic functions including the sharing of ideas between students and academic staff, the forming of dedicated study groups, the exchange of links and other academic objects and self-publication. While these tools are readily being adopted in mainstream Western contexts, little is currently known regarding whether – and how – social networking sites are used in other geo-cultural regions. This study sought to redress this research gap by investigating how often and in what ways Saudi Arabian students use social networking for learning purposes as well as how they perceive these instruments as educational instruments. The study was based on the analysis of results derived from focus group discussions with university students at four Saudi Arabian universities. The research found that Saudi Arabian students are aware of, and welcome, social networking sites and are starting to use them for academic purposes in the same way that university students do in more mainstream contexts. However, it is evident that, in Saudi Arabia, the utilization of these sites for teaching and learning purposes is not yet widespread, nor is it particularly sophisticated in terms of user knowledge of a range of social networking sites and their application to higher education. The study concluded that, due to students' enthusiastic reception of these sites, Saudi Arabia is well-placed to adopt them in a considered and organized manner, looking to global best practice usage. This study is part of a wider research project and the outcomes will be used as the basis of an in-depth survey which will be published in future research.**

Keywords; Web2.0; Social Network; Education; Saudi Arabia.

I. INTRODUCTION

Social networking sites, such as Facebook and Twitter, have developed under the umbrella of the interactive and collaborative platform known as Web 2.0[1]. Such applications offer users the opportunity to dynamically create and share self-generated content in communities defined by common interests and purposes. Whilst initially intended for social and leisure usages, these applications have penetrated a number of sectors such as business, healthcare and government, changing the landscape of human communication and interaction [2]. One sector that has particularly benefitted from the advantages offered by social networking sites is higher education where these applications have been put to use for educational purposes such as the establishment of academic groupings or networks, the dissemination of materials, the sharing of ideas and resources, and engagement with group-based collaborative projects [3]. World-wide, there has been a shift from informal and incidental usages of social media in education by students themselves to more purposeful and intentional incorporation of social networking into university courses, often at faculty-wide level. However, much of the research into the use of social networking in higher education has occurred within mainstream, Western contexts and little is known about how social networking is regarded and employed as an educational tool in non-mainstream contexts which may differ markedly in terms of pedagogical understandings, technological resources and cultural backgrounds. Saudi Arabia is one such non-mainstream context, and therefore does not offer a clear picture of how social networking is used and perceived as a pedagogical instrument. The aim of this study was to analyse data obtained from student focus groups in an attempt to determine their attitudes to and perceptions of the use of social networking for educational purposes.

In order to contribute to the body of knowledge about the use of social networking sites in the higher education sector in Saudi Arabia, this research addressed two main questions:

In what ways do Saudi Arabian students use social networking in learning activities?

What are students' attitudes to and perceptions of social networking for educational purposes?

The paper is structured into six sections: section I introduces the key themes aims and objectives of the paper, followed by Section II which describes how social networking has been used in higher education settings as both an informal and formal learning tool. Section III surveys the sparse literature on social networking in universities in Saudi Arabia while Section IV discusses the focus group as a research methodology as well as explains the approach used in this study. Section V reports the findings arising from the focus group sessions and Section VI extrapolates the key discussion points from the findings. Finally, the paper concludes by reiterating the main themes that have emerged from the research.

II. SOCIAL NETWORKING IN HIGHER EDUCATION

Higher education is considered to be a natural arena for the adoption of social networking technologies for two main reasons: firstly, the vast uptake of social networking by "Digital Natives" [4], or a post-1980 cohort born into a networked society, and secondly, the suitability of interactive technologies to serve the purposes of higher education where creating, sharing and disseminating ideas in academic communities is of primary importance. University students as a demographic tend to be technologically aware, bringing with them to university their established networking usages, habits and practices, as well as the capability to acquire new ones. Indeed, it is claimed that social networking is as "natural to education as the commute, the computer and everything else which students bring" [5].

Since the advent of social networking, an increasing number of studies have explored the intention to use, the rates and sectors related to usage, and the purposes and effects of usage of such sites by university students so as to learn more about how they communicate and interact by means of modern collaborative technologies [6]- [9].

In examining the purported purposes of social networking usage by university students, studies reveal that, apart from social and leisure uses, respondents use these tools for contacting peers and "talking about" academic work [6]-[9]. According to Selwyn [10], social networking is used by students as a means of discussing learning experiences, exchanging factual information with peers, and seeking moral support. Furthermore, there is a shift towards the formal incorporation of social networking sites by universities themselves, rather than simply leaving students to their own independent usages. A number of studies Saxena and Majumdar [11], Cuesta, et al. [12], Lahiri and Moseley [13], El Bialy and Jalali [14] attest to social networking as a formal method of student-student interaction and collaboration, student-instructor engagement, contribution and discussion of ideas, clarification of concepts, information posting (e.g., announcing assignments or events), information and resource-sharing (articles, course notes, video clips, links to webpages or blogs, photos) and self-reflection/publication [11]- [13], [15].

Research into the use of Facebook as an official educational tool, for example, confirms its powerful ability to create groupings or communities of users, acting as a dedicated shared space for the interactions of targeted students, often with university instructors or tutors as participatory or mediating interlocutors [11]-[13], [15]-[21]. While not as prolific as studies on Facebook within the higher education setting, research on Twitter confirms its serviceability as a convenient and cost-effective conduit for tapping into internal and external scholarly networks, allowing for immediate information sharing and updating [22]-[34]. Similarly, resource-sharing sites have been heralded for their relevance to higher education tasks, especially the use of social bookmarking sites as a means of annotating, categorising, exchanging and storing online documentary resources within the context of groups united by common academic pursuits [35]-[41]. Scholarly attention has likewise been paid to content-creation tools as learning accessories, such as blogging [42]-[47] and wikis [48]-[51]. In particular, studies of blogging and wikis as communication tools in tertiary settings emphasise their ability to enhance critical thinking, to develop a student "voice", as well as to facilitate collaborative group processes [52]-[58].

III. SOCIAL NETWORKING IN THE HIGHER EDUCATION SECTOR IN SAUDI ARABIA

While there is evidence that Saudi Arabian universities are making some use of social networking platforms, their usage appears to be largely restricted to communicative functions rather than educational engagement. University websites incorporate Facebook, Twitter and other Web 2.0 tools but only as a means of recruiting, informing and updating students and their parents [59], Ahmad, et al. [60] However, little published research is available to support enquiry into how Saudi college students perceive and make use of social networking as a learning tool and whether any usage is self-directed or a faculty directive [61].

Of the handful of studies that do exist, many focus on "e-learning" or distance learning technologies and classic Learning Management System [62] tools as opposed to more contemporary collaborative Web 2.0 instruments [59], [63]- [67]. Moreover, many of the more recent studies do not clarify the intended purposes of the applications. For example, a recent study at the University of Dammam found that respondents use the Internet accompanied by Facebook, Twitter and YouTube to support their studies without differentiating between students' independent, informal usage and the more formal university-driven incorporation of social networking sites in higher education [68]. In addition, while a study by Alwagait, et al. [69] explicitly references Twitter and Facebook usage by Saudi Arabian university students and suggests that using these sites does not adversely impact on GPA, it also does not clearly specify what these networking sites were being used for or whether indeed they were used for educational purposes at all. Generally, then, current research tells us little about whether and how social networking is actually used by students in university settings in Saudi Arabia.

In terms of barriers to uptake, Almalki [67] suggested that the main impediments to the penetration of social networking in universities in Saudi Arabia are the poor quality of internet connections in the country, and trust issues related to intellectual property and privacy. Another study concluded that the lack of wireless internet, poor maintenance of technology tools and the need for user training were the main barriers preventing the adoption of this technology by tertiary institutions [68]. Other obstacles cited by researchers are the lack of Arabic interfaces in social networking platforms, lack of Arabic user support documents and lack of online Arab content, as well as resistance to uptake due to traditional face-to-face, storytelling-focused and rote-based learning styles which are valued in this society [61], [70], [71]. Sultan, et al. [70] analysed a number of key cultural issues associated with the use of contemporary technologies for teaching and learning purposes in Saudi Arabia: one important question is how the deeply entrenched practice of "wasta" which is a personal influence through social connections, might fare when democratized digital forms of learning are used [70]. Another consideration is how well digital learning mechanisms align with typical Arab characteristics such as extreme politeness conventions and the avoidance of making critical comments to and about others. Moreover, Sultan, et al. [70] raise the question of how to equip Arab learners with global digital competencies such as the ability to filter content and make judgements about quality and trustworthiness of information within an education system that favours memorization and traditional examination success as measures of successful pedagogy. This is compounded by the dearth of Arabic open access content and the limited English possessed by Saudi citizens, making participation in an information culture extremely challenging. Against this background, this study aims to gauge current usage of social networking for educational purposes by Saudi Arabian students, as well as their attitudes to and perceptions of these sites.

IV. RESEARCH METHODOLOGY

Focus groups have been in use for several decades in various fields such as healthcare, marketing and numerous academic sub-disciplines within the social sciences. This is a qualitative method of collecting and analysing data, and is distinct in methodology from other qualitative techniques such as interviews and surveys [72]. Primarily, focus groups are intended to elicit data regarding the personal experiences and insights of individual members of the group in a relaxed and interactive environment. Each member of the focus group is encouraged to engage and converse with the moderator and other respondents [73].

In a typical focus group, the researcher facilitates the discussion rather than conducting individual interviews. Usually, a group will consist of five to twelve participants, and it is limited to this small number of participants to allow each participant to express an opinion about each question or statement, while providing the opportunity to agree or disagree with the opinions expressed by others in the group. Typically, the chosen participants are members of a particular group of interest to the research, and they are available. In this way, a focus group can help to indicate whether there is general agreement or consensus regarding a particular viewpoint. For this study, university students were selected because the research examines whether social networking should be incorporated into the university's educational regimen.

The usual procedure is to record the discussion and transcribe it. It is also important for the facilitator to ensure that everyone in the group has a chance to share his/her ideas and that any of the more assertive group members do not dominate the discussion [74].

Based on the guidelines mentioned above for using a focus group, four focus groups were conducted with Saudi Arabian university students who would be the target sample for the investigation into social networking at university. These four focus groups constituted the pilot study conducted prior to the subsequent more in-depth survey of students designed to provide a quantitative analysis of the different views and attitudes of the students. The findings from the focus group provided the basis for survey questionnaire.

The students were recruited by inviting interested students to participate on the grounds that they were social media users who actively used Facebook, LinkedIn, Twitter, or other popular social media platforms.

Each group comprised 7 to 10 students, with a gender balance so as to provide a representative sample of the student body at universities. The focus group discussions were conducted by the researcher in one of the lecture rooms on campus and the opinions and responses were recorded and transcribed. The universities were selected based on their classification as government or private universities, as well as their high ranking within the country [75].

TABLE I. FOCUS GROUPS

	Male	*Female*	*Total*
University A	8	-	8
University B	5	3	8
University C	5	4	9
University D	6	4	10

The focus group discussions covered several areas, namely, usage of social networking, purposes of usage, benefits of social networking, how best to incorporate social networking into the Saudi Arabian higher education sector, as well as the barriers to and drivers of social networking specific to Saudi Arabia. This study addressed only the student attitudes to and perceptions of social networking as an educational tool.

V. FINDINGS

The research found that the student participants in the focus groups actively used social media, especially Facebook and Twitter, and were very receptive to having it incorporated into the Saudi educational system. They felt that social media provided them with many benefits for both university work and entertainment, including using it to obtain information and communicating with other students as well as watching videos on their smartphones. They expressed a preference for professors providing them with course information online.

The students indicated that they frequently used different social media platforms, especially Facebook and Twitter. They used it for both work and in their social life, for entertainment, watching videos and communicating with other individuals. Students cited a number of benefits, including being able to do things such as finding information online more easily and quickly. Several mentioned using it for learning - looking up words or finding interesting articles. Another perceived advantage was that it allowed students to work from home, which saved them time commuting,

Some students were able to create groups to enhance their learning, sharing links to specific information and sharing this information with each other, which saved time as they did not have to do these tasks independently. For instance, one male student commented:

> *"We used it for both (work, entertainment, or learning). For example... (we used) video clips...on YouTube to learn more about a subject." (UniCM1)*

Another male student observed:

> *"We use it for learning about different things. Sometimes people share useful links that I save in my favorites for future used...The young men have formed a group and forums for intercommunication. They explain to one another and send messages through the sites." (UniCM2)*

Several students pointed out that social networking platforms enabled them to receive feedback and guidance from others. Commenting on these advantages, one male student stated:

> *"I have used SNS in one of the projects that I was working on...We used SNS to get feedback and the perception of people about our project, mostly after we have started the development and the operation stage...We viewed the feedback that we received from the people for the service we organized...and try to improve our service based on the feedback...until our project received high satisfaction from the users...So (SNS) was a quick point for communication with the people." (UniCM3)*

Some of the students indicated that they were able to learn more from each other in a time-efficient manner by posting questions and then obtaining answers from other students. Furthermore, this helped them because they were able to acquire more knowledge and insights from others. As one male student commented:

> *"We made an account on Facebook. Some Wikipedia issues were raised. Always the students and doctors were communicating with each other whether for homework or any other thing related to the subject." (UniDM1)*

Another male student observed:

> *"It was very nice (to use the SNS). If I have any question, I write it on Facebook. Next morning, I find the answer....Another student gives the answer. It was very beneficial." (UniDM2)*

A third respondent pointed out that he was able to obtain information from other students if he was not able to attend lectures; moreover, he could receive input from lecturers in regard to study materials. As he commented:

> *"I have obtained considerable benefits in entertainment and work, both. For instance, with respect to Whatsapp, if I could not go to the university, I would ask my groups on Whatsapp about what we had covered...Or take Twitter. If the lecturer would like a emphasize a certain point or request consulting references for a particular subject, he would say, for example, review that subject. It would be discussed further." (UniAM1)*

Another student simply observed:

> *"I use social networking sites, including Whatsapp and Twitter for both work and entertainment...as my colleague has maintained. In the case of absence,*

you may inquire about the subjects taught." (UniAM2)

A third echoed a similar experience in the following comment:

"As for social networking sites, I use Twitter, Snapchat, and Whatsapp. Whatsapp is, of course, for work and communication with friends if there was a lesson that I missed do to my absence...(And) lecturers do communicate with us. If a lecturer was absent for any reason he would inform us." (UniAM3)

Still other students pointed to the advantages of using social media for distance learning. It helped them with research project designs and provided them with answers to any problems they encountered along the way. It also enabled them to work at home which was very convenient and saved them time. As one male student commented:

"My program was distance learning...I used it in making questionnaires and obtaining answers (from Google). I followed Twitter summaries and cues." (UniBM3)

A female student concurred:

"It allows you to work from your house. I used Instagram for work for certain periods. It was extremely marvelous and beneficial. (UniBF2)

Another male student stated:

"If I would (use it) to search about any information or face a problem in using my mobile, I normally find the answer in the program, mainly in Twitter for solving the problems or obtaining other information." (UniBM1)

"In terms of the learning, it is beneficial. I use it for several things, (such as) for finding words and other things I feel are interesting." (UniDM3)

"We were a group. We agreed to prepare the graduation dissertation. All of our communications were maintained using Facebook." (UniBF3)

Some students also stated that they found it helpful to transfer written materials into electronic documents which could be shared, while hard copies documents could not be disseminated as efficiently. As one male student explained:

"The first thing to do is transfer the educational subjects into electronic, and then we introduced the social networking sites. It is not easy to introduce social networking sites when the learning is still paper-based." (UniBM1)

In some cases, the students were able to use social media for posting and promoting programs they had developed, such as video clips. As another male student explained:

"We were making films for the university...We planned to form a website onto which we downloaded educational video clips that we designed" (UniBM2)

Another advantage of the social media mentioned by many students was its speed, enabling them to do whatever they wanted to do very quickly. For instance, two male students offered these comments:

"As I work in the media, the most convenient use and most easy method for obtaining information and news is to access Twitter. It is very fast." (UniBM2)

"We can do things easily and faster anywhere." (UniDM3)

Similarly, the female students who participated in the focus groups used the social networking sites for both leisure and learning, though the female students stressed the use of social networking for entertainment and did not participate as much in the general conversation. As some of the female students commented:

"I mostly use it as a form of entertainment" (UniCF2).

The student was referring to Instagram, Twitter, and Facebook, wikis, and blogs.

"We have used Twitter and Instagram. The objective varies from person to another. Sometimes (it is) for leisure and some time to learn new things. (It) depends on the individual's interests." (UniCF1).

VI. DISCUSSION AND LIMITATIONS

As this research shows, the students in the focus group had had some favourable experiences with using major social networking sites for studying and learning purposes, most notably Facebook, Twitter, and WhatsApp. They especially liked the fact that these could be used quickly and easily as a means of keeping them connected with others. In general, in relation to their tertiary studies, the respondents used social networking sites for searching out and obtaining required academic information, connecting with others and forming study groups, learning about topics from video clips, and problem-solving by posting questions and receiving answers from other users. There was also some evidence of lecturers using social networking sites to post materials and to keep in contact with students, usually due to lecturer or student absence. The respondents also commented on the convenience of being able to use social networking sites from home. This positive orientation to using social networking as an educational tool suggests that, despite the barriers to uptake particular to Saudi Arabia, there is a high level of student acceptance of social media as an educational instrument and a desire to use it to facilitate the learning experience.

However, while the research reveals an enthusiasm for and a desire to use social networking for educational reasons, there is also evidence that most students independently use social media for personal reasons. While there is some suggestion that instructors engage with students via social networking platforms, it seems that there is limited formal inclusion of social networking sites in Saudi Arabian universities as a planned pedagogical aid. Hence, Saudi Arabia has not yet fully harnessed the benefits of social networking sites for teaching and learning purposes in higher education, with current usages being relatively unsophisticated and at an individual level of endeavor. It is also evident that Saudi Arabian students use a relatively narrow range of social networking sites, namely, Facebook, Twitter, WhatsApp, Snapchat and Instagram. Other applications which are advantageous to higher education, such as wikis, blogs and social bookmarking, were not mentioned by any of the respondents.

The significance of this study is that it indicates that there is great scope for Saudi Arabia to look to world-wide trends and developments so as to more formally incorporate social networking into its teaching and learning activities at a broader faculty or university-wide level using a range of interactive Web 2.0 tools.

This study had several limitations, namely, the small sample size as well as the restricted participation of females who were reluctant to share their views despite the best efforts of the researcher, in comparison to males. This can be attributed to cultural values in a predominantly patriarchal society. A further limitation was the limited knowledge of the participants who were unfamiliar with sophisticated usage of social networking as it applies to formal education. Moreover, the respondents had a limited awareness of the wide range of available social networking applications. Lastly, this study covers only a part of the focus group data as the rest of the data will be presented and discussed in future research.

VII. CONCLUSION

Social networking sites have a natural affinity with higher education due to their interactive and collaborative capacities. Universities world-wide have begun to actively tap into the potential of these sites as pedagogical tools in order to capture the interest and attention of millennium students. While there remain some barriers to the widespread uptake of this technology, Saudi Arabian universities are ideally positioned to harness the benefits of social networking sites in education due to the wide acceptance of these applications by students. Whilst usage is currently relatively incidental and unsophisticated, there is vast potential for Saudi Arabia to reap the benefits of these technologies by implementing them for teaching and learning purposes.

REFERENCES

[1] T. O'Reilly, "Web 2.0: Compact Definition?," ed, 2005.

[2] T. Issa and P. Kommers, "Social networking for web-based communities," Int. J. Cont. Engineering Education and Life-Long Learning, vol. 23, pp. 1-1, 2013.

[3] K. Seo, Using Social Media Effectively in the Classroom: blogs, wikis, twitter, and more: Routledge, 2012.

[4] M. Prensky, "Digital natives, digital immigrants," Gifted, pp. 29-31, February 2005 2005.

[5] M. Allen, "An education in Facebook," 2012.

[6] A. Kosik, "The implications of Facebook," Sharing the Commonwealth: Critical issues in higher education 9–10, 2007.

[7] C. Madge, J. Meek, J. Wellens, and T. Hooley, "Facebook, social integration and informal learning at university: 'It is more for socialising and talking to friends about work than for actually doing work'," Learning, Media and Technology, vol. 34, pp. 141-155, 2009.

[8] T. E. Bosch, "Using online social networking for teaching and learning: Facebook use at the University of Cape Town," Communicatio, vol. 35, pp. 185-200, 2009.

[9] K. F. Hew, "Students' and teachers' use of Facebook," Computers in Human Behavior, vol. 27, pp. 662-676, 2011.

[10] N. Selwyn, "Faceworking: exploring students' education - related use of Facebook," Learning, Media and Technology, vol. 34, pp. 157-174, 2009/06/01 2009.

[11] A. Saxena and P. Majumdar, "Use of Facebook in Higher Education: An extension of classroom learning," IMS Manthan (The Journal of Innovations), vol. 10, 2015.

[12] M. Cuesta, M. Eklund, I. Rydin, and A.-K. Witt, "Using Facebook as a co-learning community in higher education," Learning, Media and Technology, vol. 41, pp. 55-72, 2016/01/02 2016.

[13] M. Lahiri and J. L. Moseley, "Learning by Going Social: Do We Really Learn from Social Media?," International Journal of Learning, Teaching and Educational Research, vol. 11, 2015.

[14] S. El Bialy and A. Jalali, "Go Where the Students Are: A Comparison of the Use of Social Networking Sites Between Medical Students and Medical Educators," JMIR Medical Education, vol. 1, p. e7, 2015.

[15] S. El Bialy, A. Jalali, and A. Jaffar, "Integrating Facebook into basic sciences education: a comparison of a faculty-administered Facebook page and group," Austin J Anat, vol. 1, p. 1015, 2014.

[16] A. N. Çoklar, "Evaluations of Students on Facebook as an Educational Environment," Turkish Online Journal of Qualtitative Inquiry, vol. 3, pp. 42-53, 2012.

[17] R. Judele, D. Tsovaltzi, T. Puhl, and A. Weinberger, "Collaborative learning in Facebook: Adverse effects of individual preparation," in System Sciences (HICSS), 2014 47th Hawaii International Conference on, 2014, pp. 1616-1624.

[18] S. H. Sarapin and P. L. Morris, "Faculty and Facebook friending: Instructor–student online social communication

from the professor's perspective," The Internet and Higher Education, vol. 27, pp. 14-23, 10// 2015.

[19] M. Demirbilek, "Social media and peer feedback: What do students really think about using Wiki and Facebook as platforms for peer feedback?," Active Learning in Higher Education, June 10, 2015 2015.

[20] R. Wang, P. Scown, C. Urquhart, and J. Hardman, "Tapping the educational potential of Facebook: Guidelines for use in higher education," Education and Information Technologies, vol. 19, pp. 21-39, 2012.

[21] R. Gray, J. Vitak, E. W. Easton, and N. B. Ellison, "Examining social adjustment to college in the age of social media: Factors influencing successful transitions and persistence," Computers and Education, vol. 67, pp. 193-207, 2013.

[22] N. Saeed and S. Sinnappan, "Adoption of Twitter in higher education – a pilot study," Proceedings of ASCILITE - Australian Society for Computers in Learning in Tertiary Education Annual Conference 2011, pp. 1115-1120, 2011.

[23] G. Veletsianos, "Higher education scholars' participation and practices on Twitter," Journal of Computer Assisted Learning, vol. 28, pp. 336-349, 2012.

[24] S. A. Ferreira, C. Castro, and A. Andrade, "Morphology of cognitive communication 2.0 in Higher Education classroom," 2011, pp. 1-7.

[25] E. Kassens-Noor, "Twitter as a teaching practice to enhance active and informal learning in higher education: The case of sustainable tweets," Active Learning in Higher Education, vol. 13, pp. 9-21, 2012.

[26] T. B. Clarke and C. Leigh Nelson, "Classroom community, pedagogical effectiveness, and learning outcomes associated with Twitter use in undergraduate marketing courses," Journal for Advancement of Marketing Education, vol. 20, pp. 1-10, 2012.

[27] R. Junco, C. M. Elavsky, and G. Heiberger, "Putting twitter to the test: Assessing outcomes for student collaboration, engagement and success," British Journal of Educational Technology, 2012.

[28] T. Tsiakis, "Using Social Media as a Concept and Tool for Teaching Marketing Information Systems," pp. 24-44.

[29] C. Evans, "Twitter for teaching: Can social media be used to enhance the process of learning?," British Journal of Educational Technology, vol. 45, pp. 902-915, 2014.

[30] J. P. Carpenter and D. G. Krutka, "How and Why Educators Use Twitter: A Survey of the Field," Journal of Research on Technology in Education, vol. 46, pp. 414-434, 2014/10/02 2014.

[31] J. G. Suárez, C. T. Cervantes, and E. R. García, "Twitter as a resource to evaluate the university teaching process," Revista de Universidad y Sociedad del Conocimiento, vol. 12, pp. 32-45, 2015.

[32] J. Mankoff, R. Kravets, and E. Blevis, "Some computer science issues in creating a sustainable world," Computer, vol. 41, pp. 102-105, 2008.

[33] T. M. Stephens and M. E. Gunther, "Twitter, Millennials, and Nursing Education Research," Nursing Education Perspectives, vol. 0, p. null.

[34] Z. Bulbulia and J. Wassermann, "Rethinking the Usefulness of Twitter in Higher Education," 2015.

[35] M. Liu, L. Horton, J. Olmanson, and P.-Y. Wang, "An Exploration of Mashups and Their Potential Educational Uses," Computers in the Schools, vol. 25, pp. 243-258, 2008.

[36] D. Churchill, "Educational applications of Web 2.0: Using blogs to support teaching and learning," British Journal of Educational Technology, vol. 40, pp. 179-183, 2009.

[37] C. Greenhow, B. Robelia, and J. E. Hughes, "Learning, Teaching, and Scholarship in a Digital Age: Web 2.0 and Classroom Research: What Path Should We Take Now?," Educational Researcher, vol. 38, pp. 246-259, 2009.

[38] T. Farwell and R. Waters, "Exploring the use of social bookmarking technology in education- An analysis of students' experiences using a course-specific delicious," MERLOT Journal of Online Learning and Teaching, vol. 6, 2010.

[39] G. Edwards and B. F. Mosley, "Technology integration can be delicious: Social bookmarking as a technology integration tool," Educating Educators with Social Media, vol. 1, pp. 207-225, 2011.

[40] M. B. Zorica, I. O. Biskupic, T. Ivanjko, and S. Spiranec, "Students and privacy in the networked environment," 2011, pp. 1090-1094.

[41] T. Nashrawan, W. Jamie, and C. Andrew, "Social Bookmarking Pedagogies in Higher Education: A Comparative Study," International Journal of Information Systems in the Service Sector (IJISSS), vol. 1, pp. 24-36, 2014.

[42] K. Y. Lin and Y. F. Shen, "The nursing students' attitude toward using blogs in a nursing clinical practicum in Taiwan: A 3-R framework," Nurse Education Today, vol. 33, pp. 1079-1082, 2013.

[43] D. a. Powell, C. J. Jacob, and B. J. Chapman, "Using Blogs and New Media in Academic Practice: Potential Roles in Research, Teaching, Learning, and Extension," Innovative Higher Education, vol. 37, pp. 271-282, 2012.

[44] Y.-S. Chang and C. Yang, "Why do we blog? From the perspectives of technology acceptance and media choice factors," Behaviour & Information Technology, vol. 32, pp. 371-386, 2013.

[45] K. A. Mills and S. M. Ritchie, "E-motion diaries: blogging emotional responses to online learning in higher education," 2014.

[46] B. K. Pursel and H. Xie, "Patterns and pedagogy: Exploring student blog use in higher education," Contemporary Educational Technology, vol. 5, pp. 96-109, 2014.

[47] A. R. Stewart, J. M. Reid, and J. C. Stewart, "Students engaging in diversity: blogging to learn the history of jazz," Teaching in Higher Education, vol. 19, pp. 931-942, 2014/11/17 2014.

[48] H. Uzunboylu, F. Ozdamli, R. Ventura, and M. J. Quero, "Using Facebook in University Teaching: A Practical Case Study," Procedia - Social and Behavioral Sciences, vol. 83, pp. 1032-1038, 2013.

[49] C. Kummer, "Wikis in higher education," Saechsische Landesbibliothek-Staats-und Universitaetsbibliothek Dresden, 2014.

[50] M. Palomo-Duarte, J. M. Dodero, A. García-Domínguez, P. Neira-Ayuso, N. Sales-Montes, I. Medina-Bulo, et al., "Scalability of assessments of wiki-based learning experiences in higher education," Computers in Human Behavior, vol. 31, pp. 638-650, 2// 2014.

[51] A. Ioannou, S. W. Brown, and A. R. Artino, "Wikis and forums for collaborative problem-based activity: A systematic comparison of learners' interactions," The Internet and Higher Education, vol. 24, pp. 35-45, 1// 2015.

[52] B. Lamb, "Dr. Mashup; or, Why Educators Should Learn to Stop Worrying and Love the Remix," Educause Review, vol. 42, pp. 12-25, 2007.

[53] D. J. Skiba, "Nursing education 2.0: are Mashups useful for nursing education?," Nursing education perspectives, vol. 28, pp. 286-288, 2007.

[54] B. Taraghi, M. Ebner, and S. Schaffert, "Personal learning environments for higher education: A mashup based widget concept," pp. 15-22.

[55] S. Wheeler, "Learning Space Mashups: Combining Web 2.0 Tools to Create Collaborative and Reflective Learning Spaces," Future Internet, vol. 1, pp. 3-13, 2009.

[56] R. Ibrahim, "The Potential for Using Mash-Ups at a Higher Education," Research Journal of Information Technology, vol. 4, pp. 56-70, 2012.

[57] S. Bao, C. Zhang, and J. Wu, "A Mobile Learning Platform Based on Mashups for Foreign Language Learning," vol. 9, pp. 2599-2606, 2012.

[58] M. L. M. Kiah, B. B. Zaidan, A. A. Zaidan, M. Nabi, and R. Ibraheem, "MIRASS: Medical Informatics Research Activity Support System Using Information Mashup Network," Journal of Medical Systems, vol. 38, pp. 1-15, 2014.

[59] H. S. Al-Khalifa and R. A. Garcia, "The State of Social Media in Saudi Arabia's Higher Education," International Journal of Technology and Educational Marketing, vol. 3, pp. 65-76, 2013.

[60] P. Ahmad, A. Hussain, M. Aqil, T. C. Ahmad, M. Use, S. Arabia, et al., "Use of web 2 . 0 in Saudi Arabia Universities," Issn, vol. 3, 2013.

[61] M. Chaurasia, A. Asma, and A. Ahmed, "Opportunities and Challenges of Web 2.0 in Arab Education," in Global Learn, 2011, pp. 310-315.

[62] G. Helmstetter, Increasing Hits and Selling More on your Web Site USA: John Wiley & Sons, Inc. , 1997.

[63] A. A. Al Saif, "The motivating and inhibiting factors affecting the use of Web-Based Instruction at the University of Qassim in Saudi Arabia," 2005.

[64] A. R. Alenezi, A. Abdulkarim, and A. Veloo, "An Empirical investigation into the role of enjoyment, computer anxiety, computer self-efficacy and internet experience in influencing the students' intention to use e-learning: A case study from Saudi Arabian governmental universities," TOJET: The Turkish Online Journal of Educational Technology, vol. 9, 2010.

[65] J. Al-Otaibi, "The Saudi Universities students' use of Facebook- an applicable study," College of Arts, Riyadh, King Saud University, 2011.

[66] Y. Al-Saggaf, "The effect of online community on offline community in Saudi Arabia," The Electronic Journal of Information Systems in Developing Countries, vol. 16, 2004.

[67] A. M. Almalki, "Blended learning in higher education in Saudi Arabia: A study of Umm Al-Qura University," RMIT University, 2011.

[68] M. T. Al-Hariri and A. a. Al-Hattami, "Utilization of internet by health colleges students at the University of Dammam," Journal of Taibah University Medical Sciences, vol. 10, pp. 66-73, 2015.

[69] E. Alwagait, B. Shahzad, and S. Alim, "Impact of social media usage on students academic performance in Saudi Arabia," Comput. Hum. Behav., vol. 51, pp. 1092-1097, 2015.

[70] N. Sultan, S. Bunt-Kokhuis, C. Davidson, A. Sentini, and D. Weir, "E-Learning in the Arab Gulf: Responding to the Changing World of Education," in The GCC Economies, M. A. Ramady, Ed., ed: Springer New York, 2012, pp. 33-48.

[71] H. S. Al-Khalifa and R. A. Garcia, "The State of Social Media in Saudi Arabia's Higher Education," International Journal of Technology and Educational Marketing (IJTEM), vol. 3, pp. 65-76, 2013.

[72] M. D. Myers, "Quantitative Research in Information Systems - Section 2: Philosophical Perspectives," vol. 2013, 2013.

[73] R. Powell and H. Single, "Methodology Matters," Int J Qual Health Care, vol. 8, pp. 499-504, 1996.

[74] A. J. Veal, Research methods for leisure and tourism: A practical guide: Pearson Education, 2006.

[75] M. D. Slater, "Academic knowledge transfer in social networks," 2013.

Developing Students' Vocabulary Knowledge in Content Subjects: A Computational Linguistic Approach

Kirk Dowswell
College of Technological Innovation
Zayed University
Dubai, United Arab Emirates
email: kirk.dowswell@zu.ac.ae

Abstract— **Undergraduate students are exposed to discipline-specific lexis and concepts, particularly when studying in a second language. Current research suggests that most students find it difficult to fully comprehend academic reading material because they lack the requisite vocabulary, i.e., 5,000 to 8,000 word families for achieving 95% to 98% comprehension, respectively. It has also been suggested that teaching vocabulary explicitly is not an efficient use of classroom time. Thus, in order to enhance vocabulary acquisition and, ultimately, improve the reading comprehension skills of second language learners, this pilot study evaluated the use of a modified version of the Vocabulary Self-Selection Strategy (VSS+) as a self-directed learning tool. The study was conducted in an Arab higher education institution where undergraduate students studied Information Technology (IT) in English. It was anticipated that this unique intervention would improve vocabulary acquisition with minimal use of classroom teaching time. Results indicated that students were actively engaged with the wiki as a learning tool and there was a noticeable improvement in their vocabulary knowledge. Overall, the study has implications for teachers, as well as learners**

Keywords: data-driven learning; vocabulary self-collection strategy; vocabulary learning; involvement load hypothesis; teaching with wikis.

I. Introduction

The ability to read academic texts in English is one of the most challenging issues facing second language students studying at English-medium institutions (EMI). Many Emirati students who have studied in Arabic-medium schools are not equipped with these skills and thus find it difficult to obtain direct entry into these institutions. Consequently, many federal EMI's in the United Arab Emirates (UAE) require students who have not achieved an International English Language Testing System (IELTS) score of 5.0 attend pre-baccalaureate programs that focus on English academic literacy and language skills. Students can spend up to two years in these programs and can only progress by achieving the requisite IELTS score (5.0) and a pass in their final examination. IELTS broadly defines a Band 5 student as a modest user (IELTS, 2016).

Reading proficiency is assessed throughout these academic English courses and students are expected to have achieved a satisfactory level of academic literacy skills that will allow them to cope with the English language textbooks and content specific material encountered in their baccalaureate studies. At first glance, it would seem that most students do cope and have the language and academic literacy skills to meet subject requirements. However, feedback from content faculty and recent pre-graduation data in the institution where the study described in this paper took place, has revealed that over 60% of students who graduated in 2015, exited the institution with an IELTS level less than Band 6 on Reading. This indicates no or minimal improvement has been achieved by these students despite four years of subject specific study in the English language (Internal Dean's Council Report, December 21st, 2015).

IELTS broadly defines a Band 6 student as a competent user (IELTS, 2016) and Band 6.5 as the entry level demanded by many universities in the UK; this is largely considered the minimum level that a student should possess to cope with the rigors of academic study. Based on these definitions of language competence, many of the English as a Second Language (ESL) students studying at the institution where this study took place are struggling to cope with academic texts and are graduating at a level of less than 'competent'. Furthermore, the majority of these students are struggling with academic and technical language, once they have ceased to receive academic language support.

This situation stimulated several discussions at the institutional level about reading and the level of attainment, (as measured by the IELTS examination), that students need in order to function effectively and prompted the following questions:

1. Do ESL students studying at an EMI have sufficient academic literacy skills to be able to cope with their subject-specific reading material?
2. If not, what strategies can be employed to improve ESL students' academic literacy skills in content courses?

The present study addressed these questions by first conducting a short survey with the IT content teaching faculty, asking how they taught academic reading and content specific vocabulary in the classroom and what problems the lack of technical vocabulary knowledge caused their students. The majority of faculty indicated that a significant number of students did, indeed, face difficulties, however, a number of faculty felt it was not their place to rectify them (Internal College of Technological Innovation's Language Task Force Survey, January 2014). This inability of many content faculty members to consider the difficulties faced by their students in their subjects and the students' inadequate academic literacy skills led to the development of the next phase of this research project, described in this paper.

It was anticipated that by using contemporary text mining techniques to develop the students' academic vocabulary and by rethinking our approach to the development of academic literacy skills, particularly in the area of vocabulary acquisition, we should be able to reduce the difficulties faced by ESL students when studying content and allow them to utilize the higher order thinking skills needed to function in today's multi-literate society, as identified in Bloom's Revised Taxonomy [1]. By employing these techniques, coupled with the implementation of "Language Across the Curriculum" strategies, the aim would be to develop the students' Cognitive Academic Language Proficiency skills (CALP), [2] along with, what Volmer [3] calls, students' 'Conceptual Literacy' and 'Discourse Competence' skills.

In Section 2 of this paper, the literature review will address the issue of developing vocabulary knowledge. Section 3 will discuss the methodology used to develop the vocabulary and finally Section 4 of the paper will conclude with a discussion of the results and future implications for this pilot project.

II. BACKGROUND

Academic research, [4]. highlights the difficulties long-term (7 or more years of language instruction) second language learners have in reading academic texts. Difficulties they highlighted include those identified by Cummins [2] where students find it problematic to distinguish between spoken and academic language. The studies also provide some guidance on how these academic literacy skills, particularly vocabulary instruction, can be taught in content courses and thereby improve reading comprehension.

Research has demonstrated that there is a clear link between word knowledge and the ability to comprehend texts. This relationship was recently examined by Laufer and Ravenhorst-Kalovski [5] who not only suggested that increased vocabulary knowledge could lead to an improvement in reading comprehension, but also proposed two thresholds for text coverage and comprehension. This showed that for a student to understand 98% of a text, a knowledge of 8,000 word families is required and a knowledge of 4,000 to 5,000 word families for 95% coverage. This reinforces an earlier study by Hu and Nation [6] who proposed that for unknown vocabulary not to be a major hindrance to text comprehension, knowledge of roughly 98% of the lexis is required.

This awareness of the importance of academic discourse and, in particular, academic vocabulary is thus deemed necessary for students' success in university study. Consequently, it is paramount that content faculty be made aware of interventions that could enhance students' comprehension of academic texts. However, as the faculty survey revealed, many content teachers do not have the time or inclination to engage in strategies to improve their students' text comprehension. Therefore, many faculty rely on basic glossaries available in the course textbooks and assume that students will make use of these. To rectify this situation, the present study incorporated data driven techniques to develop subject-specific keyword vocabulary lists and then created an intervention based on an extended version of the Vocabulary Self-Collection Strategy Plus (VSS+) [7], the Involvement Load Hypothesis (ILH) [8] and a class wiki.

The VSS+ and wiki, when combined with the ILH formed an important part of the vocabulary retention strategy. The Involvement Load Hypothesis (ILH), [8] an idea that postulates that words processed with greater learner involvement are retained longer than those processed with a lower involvement load. The construct, labeled 'task-induced involvement', incorporates the cognitive components of 'Search' and 'Evaluation' and the motivational component of 'Need'. For example, the act of selecting a target word and finding its meaning demonstrates 'Need'. When followed by the action of searching for the definition and translating it into Arabic, the 'Search' process is fulfilled. Finally, the evaluation of the 'word sense' or context meets the 'Evaluation' criteria. Such activities warrant a high level of engagement from the student on the *Involvement Index* scale (i.e., Presence of factors: No factor=0, Moderate=1, and Strong=2). This study evaluated the level of vocabulary knowledge development between two groups of students: a control group following the same course with no intervention and a group engaging in the wiki tasks which, ranked high on the Involvement Index scale.

III. METHODOLOGY

The aim of this research was to develop and apply a pedagogical framework for the teaching and learning of IT content-specific vocabulary. It employed a quasi-experimental research design to test the impact of the VSS+ framework and it explored the following research questions:

1. Is there a significant difference between the VSS+ wiki intervention group and the control group that received traditional instruction?
2. What do the participants in the VSS+ wiki group think about the VSS+ wiki framework as a means of learning vocabulary?

A. Participants

A total of 8 male and 21 female university students majoring in Information Technology at an EMI university in the UAE participated in the study. The students, all ESL learners with Arabic as their first language, ranged in age from 20-30 years old. A control group of 11 female students were taught by a separate instructor and followed the traditional course of instruction. The intervention group consisted of two intact groups: one female class of 10 students and one male class of 8 students who were taught using the VSS+ by myself. Of the students participating in the intervention group, 17 completed a pre- and post-vocabulary knowledge (VKS) test as well as a questionnaire. From the control group, only 5 students completed the pre- and post-VKS test.

B. The Intervention - Selecting Appropriate Lexeis for the Content Course

Studies cited by Cobb [9] suggest that the first 2,000 most frequent words, coupled with the 570 word families in the

Academic Word List (AWL), can bring the coverage of an academic text up to approximately 90%. To increase comprehension to the minimum coverage of 95% the students will need to develop a word knowledge of 4,000 to 5,000 word families, [5].

The current debate on the benefits of rich vocabulary instruction, [10] as opposed to "genuine academic reading for the readers' own purposes, [11] has prompted educators to explore what intervention would be more successful with ESL students. However, evidence provided, [12] showed that Arab learners find vocabulary acquisition extremely challenging primarily because a limited number of words in English are borrowed from Arabic and also because the Arab teaching pedagogy is traditionally based on rote learning and minimal engagement in extensive reading activities. Based on this evidence, the present study employed 'rich' vocabulary instruction strategies in the style of the VSS+ intervention as these would be deemed useful for Arab ESL students.

Having decided on the method of intervention, it was necessary to compile academic words specific to the pilot content course, i.e., *IT in Global and Local Cultures*. There are numerous definitions of academic vocabulary but, [13] state that academic words can be categorized into two distinctive areas: general and discipline-specific words. General words are used across disciplines whereas discipline-specific words tend to be used in specific disciplines. As learning discipline-specific words does not always guarantee full comprehension of discipline-specific texts, it also advisable to incorporate scaffolding techniques to make the text more meaningful, [10]. Thus, a corpus of key academic words (general and discipline specific) was created using the *SketchEngine* application, [14].

The use of corpora in language teaching and learning, sometimes referred to as 'data-driven learning' a model created by Johns (1990), as cited in, [15] has greatly simplified the process of analyzing language and enabled the creation of frequency lists based on the course textbook. Once the lists were created and analyzed, keywords were chosen based on the following criteria: relevance to subject, academic word list and, finally, frequency level as per the Vocab Profiler, [16].

C. *Vocabulary Self-Collection Strategy*

The Vocabulary Self-Collection Strategy (VSS) is an approach that can be used for "general, basal reading or content area development", [17]. In this study, the focus was on content vocabulary development, with the main purpose being to develop students' understanding of subject-specific words and concepts. The instructional strategies used to achieve this involved specific instruction of the reading followed by the students selecting key terms that have been identified in the corpus analysis of the reading. The process, however, was slightly adapted to incorporate technology and use techniques similar to those adopted by, [7] with their VSS+ framework. After reading the text and discussing the major concepts in class, the students used a wiki to develop a subject glossary based on the vocabulary they selected. This allowed them to explore the words in much greater depth, as the template with hyperlinks enabled them to study the words in detail. (see Fig. 1)

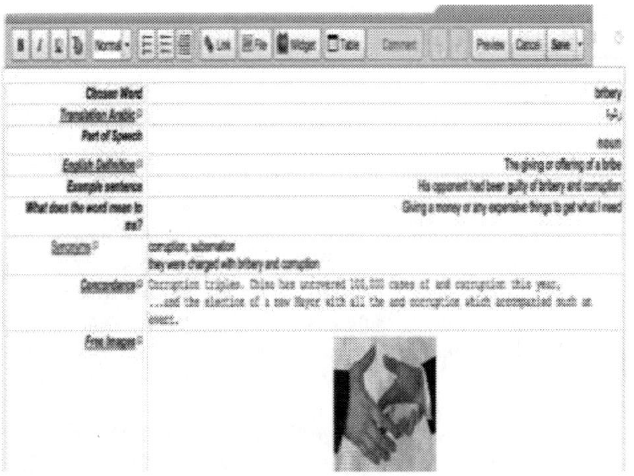

Figure I. Wiki Template Sample

The rationale for the use of the wiki was twofold. Firstly, it was expected that the students would be involved in specific activities that required reading the text, creating an easily available glossary and engaging in word focused tasks that encourage deep learning. Secondly, the word tasks were collaborative and loosely followed, [18] the six steps of vocabulary instruction. It is also generally recognized that what learners do with words is an important part of vocabulary retention and it is necessary for learning tasks to involve the components of "need, search and evaluation", [8] It was, therefore, postulated that the adaptation of the VSS+ /ILH intervention using the wiki framework discussed above would enhance content vocabulary acquisition.

As discussed above, the Vocabulary Self-Collection Strategy (VSS+) and Involvement Load Hypothesis (ILH) approaches, were used in conjunction with the class wiki tool. The intervention took place over a period of twelve weeks or six teaching units. The students in the intervention group were instructed on the use of the wiki as an autonomous learning tool. A vocabulary template was developed for the students to investigate the meaning of their selected lexeis (see Fig. 1). For each new topic covered in the course, students selected unknown vocabulary from the list of Key Words In Context (KWIC) words highlighted in the corpus or words they selected on their own from class readings. After reading the text and discussing the major concepts in class, the students used the wiki to develop a subject glossary based on the vocabulary they selected. Students in the class had the opportunity to edit the wiki entries as they saw fit. As an incentive, a small percentage of the final course grade was awarded for participation based on the number of wiki entries.

D. Data Collection Instruments & Proceedures

The following two vocabulary tests were administered as pre- and post-tests to both the intervention and the control groups:

- *X-Lex*: an online test of vocabulary breadth that assesses how many words a student knows. The students in the current study were presented with a set of words from five different frequency levels (1k to 5k) one at a time, in a context-free environment. They simply decided whether they knew the meaning of each word. Based on their responses *X-Lex* developed a profile of vocabulary knowledge for each frequency band and then suggested which level each should be placed in, [19]. The test was completed by 13 students from the intervention group and 11 students from the control group.
- Vocabulary Knowledge Scale, (VKS), [20] a test of students' knowledge of discipline specific vocabulary. This was adapted to test 130 prominent keywords extracted from the discipline specific corpus. The students in this study indicated their level of recognition of the words by selecting one of the options: a) I have never seen this word before; b) I have seen or heard of this word before; c) I think I can define this word; d) I am confident I can define this word. The test was completed by 18 students from the intervention group and 11 students from the control group.

The aim of the tests was to establish a vocabulary level for all students and to establish which of the 130 corpus keywords were known by both groups of students.

Additionally, at the end of the study, a questionnaire was used with the intervention group to assess the students' perceptions on the use of the wiki as an autonomous learning tool. The questionnaire consisted of 8 statements and asked participants in the intervention group to rate each statement on a 5-point Likert scale *(Agree, Strongly agree, Neither Agree nor Disagree, Disagree, Strongly Disagree)*. The questionnaire was administered at the end of the 12-week intervention and it was completed by 17 students.

IV. Results & Discussion

A. Pre- and Post-Test Comparisons

The first research question sought to investigate the effect of vocabulary instruction using the VSS+ with the intervention group and to compare the results with a control group who had received traditional vocabulary instruction.

The results were analyzed using a t-test and produced some interesting findings within the groups, but unfortunately limited information was obtained in the between-groups comparisons. This could be a result of the small amount of data available for the control group, many of whom failed to complete the post-test. It is planned to repeat the study with a much larger cohort of students and greater control over the testing proceedures.

The pre- and post-test scores were calculated with both the raw scores and the percentage scores. No significant difference was found between pre- and post-VKS, between the control and intervention groups. However, the t-test results showed that the intervention group performed significantly better with regards to their knowledge of vocabulary (see Table 1), which, suggests that the use of the VSS+ strategy and the wiki improved their vocabulary knowledge. Although the pilot study did not provide conclusive results, it is evident

TABLE I. T-Test results for Intervention group

VKS	Pre-Test (% of students)	Post Test (% of students)	Pre-Test (% of students)	Post-Test (% of students)		
	% Word recognition	% Word recognition	Mean	Mean	*t-test* score	*p* value
VKS 1(I have never seen this word before)	17%	10%	21.28	12.94	4.652	.000
VKS 2 (I have seen or heard of this word before)	9%	8%	11.89	10.67	.466	.647
VKS 3 (I think I can define this word)	12%	7%	15.00	9.00	2.848	.011
VKS 4 (I am confident I can define this word)	62%	74%	77.78	93.28	-9.520	.000

that using this method has the potential to enhance students' vocabulary and ability to comprehend academic texts.

Overall, the results of the VKS support the view that the wiki was a useful tool for teaching vocabulary, when using the VSS+ and ILH strategy because the students were actively engaged in the process. Not only did the students research the meaning and 'sense' of the vocabulary items they selected, but they also translated each word into Arabic and added a pictorial representation, where possible. Additional test results also revealed that there were no significant statistical differences between the male and female students. Finally, they were also engaged in the glossary review process, which, promoted collaborative learning and a sense of community within the class. All of the above would seem to support the conclusion that "What learners do with the word may be more important than how many times they encounter it.", [21].

B. Questionnaire

The second research question sought to discover what the intervention group thought about the class wiki and the VSS+ strategy, as a means of learning vocabulary. A questionnaire was used asking participants in the intervention group to rate a total of 8 statements on a 5-point Likert scale. The results of the questionnaire are shown in Table 2.

The feedback gathered from the questionnaire suggested that:

- Two thirds of the students in the intervention group found that a wiki is a useful vocabulary learning tool.
- 11 out of 17 students liked using the wiki as a way of exposing themselves to and learning new vocabulary.

TABLE II. QUESTIONNAIRE RESULTS (N=17).

Statement	SD	D	N	A	SA
1. The class wiki is a useful tool to practice new course vocabulary.	4	2	0	7	4
2. The class wiki has given me more exposure to new vocabulary.	4	0	2	5	6
3. I feel competent to peer review my classmates' wiki entries.	4	0	3	6	4
4. Peer review of the wiki entries has been useful for vocabulary learning.	4	0	3	7	3
5. I felt insecure to make corrections to other student's wiki entries.	3	6	7	1	0
6. I think my motivation to the subject has now increased.	3	2	3	3	6
7. The wiki has improved the sense of community in the class.	3	1	2	6	5
8. I would like to employ the wiki in all my courses.	4	3	4	2	4

Note: SD = Strongly Disagree; D= Disagree; N=Neutral; A= Agree; SA = Strongly Agree

- A further 10 students felt competent in peer reviewing their classmates' entries and felt that it was a useful learning exercise.
- Only one student felt insecure with editing other students' work.
- More than half of the students felt that their motivation increased and that it improved their sense of community in class.
- Just over one third of students would like to use a vocabulary wiki in all their classes.

By and large, the wiki proved to be functional as a teaching tool and was used throughout the semester for a variety of activities. It was particularly useful for collaborative activities, once the students had become used to the many features available. However, in the future, it would be advisable to employ the wiki solely as an online glossary that can be easily accessed and utilized, as a result of the finding that some initial difficulties were encountered when it was being used for other purposes.

The use of the wiki as the main technological interface appears to have been well received, with 11 out of 17 students indicating that is was a useful tool to learn vocabulary. However, the interface design was not as easy to manipulate as had been anticipated and valuable time was spent training students on the process for creating and editing the wiki glossary. The word template, although easy to use, required quite a few 'clicks' to achieve the end result and, thus proved to be frustrating for some students. As the activities were associated to the Involvement Load Hypothesis, [8] the students were required to click on a variety of links, to seek out the required information and then enter the results into the template, thus making the whole process quite time consuming.

V. CONCLUSIONS

The main purpose of this pilot study was to determine the effectiveness of the VSS + and ILH strategy, when used in conjunction with a wiki, as a means of enhancing the acquisition of content specific vocabulary by undergraduate Arab students studying at an EMI in the UAE. Each of the research questions sought to determine the level of effectiveness of this intervention. While the results from the first research question were not conclusive owing to the limited number of students in the control group completing the tests, the results for the intervention group indicated an improvement in vocabulary knowledge when the VSS+, wiki ILH intervention were used. The second research question addressed the students' attitudes to the VSS+, wiki and ILH as a means of developing their vocabulary. The questionnaire results indicated that the majority of students found the strategy and tools to be a useful method by which to learn new IT content specific vocabulary.

The present study has implications for both teachers and learners. The VSS+/Wiki/ILH framework could be easily adapted by content-specific teachers as a method for developing their students' vocabulary knowledge and concepts in their specialized courses. Although this a pilot study, these results indicate that this method of autonomous learning could have long term future implications that could be beneficial to many fields of study, wherein extensive knowledge and retention of vocabulary is required. The potential to share the framework and build it into course templates is also a possibility, as many universities now use learning management systems such as BlackBoard or Moodle that incorporate wikis in their course tools. With the help of free and readily available tools, the framework described in this paper, can help learners work collaboratively and further enhance their vocabulary knowledge.

At this point, it is useful to identify some of the factors that should be taken into consideration for the follow-up study. The development of the corpus in this study, although straightforward with the *Sketch Engine* application, could be created just as easily with the *AntConc* application that is freely available for all to use and has training videos readily available on *YouTube*. It would also be advisable to contact textbook publishers, well in advance, for a .txt version of the course textbook being used to create the corpus, as the option of scanning the whole textbook and creating the .txt file for use in the concordance is very time consuming, even when using specialized software. Finally, future studies should also analyze the long-term retention of the vocabulary, as it is subject specific and, unlike general vocabulary, it will not be recycled on a regular basis throughout the other subjects.

REFERENCES

[1] D.R. Krathwohl, "A revision of bloom's taxonomy: An overview," Theory into Practice, vol. 41 no.4, pp. 212-218, 2002.

[2] J. Cummins, "Cognitive/academic language proficiency, linguistic interdependence, the optimum age question and some other matters," Working Papers on Bilingualism, no. 19, pp. 121-129, 1979.

[3] H.J. Vollmer, "Language Across the Curriculum," Strasbourg: Council of Europe. [Online] Available from: https://www.coe.int/t/dg4/linguistic/Source/**Vollmer**_LAC_EN.doc 2006. 2015.11.21.

[4] Y. Freeman, and D. Freeman, "Academic language for English language learners and struggling readers: How to help students succeed across content areas." Portsmouth, NH: 2009.

[5] B. Laufer, and G. C. Ravenhorst-Kalovski, "Lexical threshold revisited: Lexical text coverage, learners; vocabulary size and reading comprehension." Reading in a Foreign Language, vol. 22, no. 1, pp. 15-30, 2010.

[6] M. Hu, and I.S.P. Nation, "Vocabulary density and reading comprehension." Reading in a Foreign Language, vol. 13 no. 1, pp. 403–430, 2000.

[7] T.D. Wolsey, L. Smetana, and D.L. Grisham, "Vocabulary Plus Technology." The Reading Teacher, vol 68, no. 6, pp. 449–458, [Online]. Available from https://www.learntechlib.org/p/15916, 2015.03.15

[8] J. H. Hulstiin, and B. Laufer, "Some empirical evidence for the involvement load hypothesis in vocabulary acquisition." Language Learning, vol.51 no. 3, pp. 539–558, 2001, doi:10.1111/0023-8333.00164.

[9] T. Cobb, "Range for texts v.3" Vocab Research Resources. [Online] Available from: http://www.lextutor.ca/cgi-bin/range/texts/index.pl, 2015.11.14.

[10] W. Nagy, and D. Townsend, "Words as Tools: Learning Academic Vocabulary as Language Acquisition." Reading Research Quarterly, vol 47, no. 1, pp. 91-108, January, February, March 2012. http://dx.doi.org/10.1002/RRQ.011

[11] S. Krashen, W. Nagy, and D. Townsend, "Letters to the editors." Read Research Quarterly, vol. 47, no. 3, pp. 233–234, 2012, doi:10.1002/rrq.018.

[12] B. Smith, "Arabic speakers." In M. Swan & B. Smith (Eds.), Learner English: A teacher's guide to interference and other problems. 2nd Ed. pp. 195-213. Cambridge: Cambridge University Press. 2001

[13] E.H. Hiebert, and S. Lubliner, "The nature, learning, and instruction of general academic vocabulary." In A. E. Farstrup & S. J. Samuels (Eds.), "What research has to say about vocabulary instruction" pp.106-129. Newark, DE: International Reading Association. 2008.

[14] A. Kilgarriff, P. Rychly, P. Smrz, and David Tugwell. The Sketch Engine. Proc EURALEX 2004, Lorient, France; pp. 105–116, [Online]. Available from: http://www.sketchengine.co.uk , 2015.3.05.

[15] A. O'Keeffe, and M. McCarthy, "The Routledge handbook of corpus linguistics." London: Routledge. 2010.

[16] T. Cobb, "VocabProfile Home" Vocab Research Resources. at [Online]. Available from: http://www.lextutor.ca/vp/ 2015.11.08.

[17] M.R. Haggard, "The vocabulary self-selection strategy: An active approach to word learning." Journal of Reading, vol. 26, pp. 203–207, 1982.

[18] R.J. Marzano, "Teaching basic and advanced vocabulary: A framework for direct instruction." Boston: Heinle. 2010.

[19] P.M. Meara, and J.L. Milton. "X_Lex. The Swansea Vocabulary Levels Test." Newbury: Express. 2003.

[20] T.S. Paribakht, and M. Wesche, "Vocabulary enhancement activities and reading for meaning in second language vocabulary development." In J. Coady & T. Huckin (Eds.), Second language vocabulary acquisition: A rationale for pedagogy, pp. 174-200, Cambridge, UK: Cambridge University Press. 1997.

[21] B. Laufer, and B. Rozovski-Roitblat, "Retention of new words: Quantity of encounters, quality of task, and degree of knowledge," Language Teaching Research, *2014 1362168814559797.*

Smartphones as a Support for the Language of Images in Continuing Professional Development

Laura Rayón
Faculty of Education
Alcalá University
Alcalá de Henares. Spain
e-mail: laura.rayon@uah.es

Yolanda Muñoz
Faculty of Education
Alcala University
Alcalá de Henares. Spain
e-mail: yolanda.munozm@uah.es

Ana María de las Heras
Pedagogy Department
UDIMA
Madrid. Spain
e-mail: anamaria.delasheras@udima.es

Antonio Bautista
Faculty of Education
Complutense University
Madrid. Spain
e-mail: bautista@edu.ucm.es

***Abstract*- In this paper, we advance some of the results of a study aimed at identifying the contributions of smartphones as a support for multiple systems of representation in continuing teacher training. The participants are three teachers of primary school. The still-image tools on smartphones enable the representation and communication of situations experienced in classrooms using photography. Taking photos of classroom situations that are considered difficult by these teachers, and later viewing these photos to help them reflect on what occurred in the classroom using photo-elicitation processes, enables us to evaluate the possibilities that smartphones offer to represent and communicate meanings, beliefs and ideas on problematic situations using images, while weighing up diverse alternatives for professional action. They further enable analysis of trends concerning the type of image captured and the meanings associated to them.**

Keywords-teacher education; photography; smartphones; photo-elicitation.

I. INTRODUCTION

We need to analyse two basic concepts to understand the functionality of smartphones to represent and communicate the situations experienced in classrooms through the language of images: smartphones as a means of communication based on audiovisual messages, and reflection on teaching practice mediated through photo-elicitation processes.

A. *Smartphones as a means of facilitating communication based on audiovisual messages*

The functions that smartphones offer us simultaneously allow producing audiovisual messages, editing, publishing, and dissemination on the virtual spaces. New forms of communication and social interaction in collective virtual spaces appear in people's lives daily. With this, image comes to the foreground to reveal people's subjective experience. In the same way as a text give us ideas, images give us information about events, people and things. But in particular, they are capable of generating meanings, personal interpretations associated with such representations. In this sense, a picture does not show us the world but different ways of seeing the world. This subjective dimension of images is important for Barthes [1] since it highlights the emotional dimension that photography promotes. He focuses his reflections on the sensations and emotions a photo produces. One's interest in the photo from such a perspective does not reside so much in its aesthetic beauty due to the composition of the elements it shows us, nor in the analogous reality it represents, but in its value in creating, communicating and transmitting the meanings that the photo contains.

The smartphones´ uses and systems of representation promote the visibility of our experiences and our personal perspectives. These devices enable us to share images and, with them, experiences and messages in real time through the different social networks and to reach any part of the world quickly, reliably and efficiently. The anonymous voice of the individual gains in prominence and, in our study, so do teachers' voices when faced with the dilemmas and problems of professional practice.

B. *Reflection on teaching practice through photo-elicitation processes.*

Teachers have a mediating role in teaching processes. This is why helping them understand the determinants of professional practice, helping them represent the situations they experience and allowing them to define the problems themselves, enables them to weigh up different choices of action and improve their teaching processes. This reflection on practice is key for developing any strategy for innovating and improving teaching. The modelling and transformational role of teachers, and consequently the need for autonomous development of their professional thought, justifies the need for teachers to carry out processes of reflection on their professional practice [2]. Many educators emphasize the critical role of learning through reflective practice in developing teaching capabilities [3] [4] [5].

The novelty in our study is placing a smartphone into teachers' hands so they can record and analyse the difficulties and dilemmas emerging in classrooms and educational centres, previously capturing there significant instants and moments in photos.

In this way, teachers can analyse, question, discuss and reflect on what happened in photo-elicitation sessions. This procedure consists of using photos to communicate people's life experiences [6]. It is a means of narration supported by images through which the thoughts, interpretations and meanings people place on the actions, objects or events represented in the photos are retrieved. The idea is to capture an image of reality to "see through others' eyes" (in this case, the teachers') aspects of this reality and their particular interpretations of the image captured [7].

In our case, given that during classroom activities it is difficult to reflect on professional problems and dilemmas, it is only later through photo-elicitation that the teachers become aware of their beliefs, theories, attitudes and values. This is because, based on the photos they take, they are asked about what the images represent and they provide a narration on what they are doing in class, what they could do and what would be advisable to do. This process forces them to analyse and make their problems and concerns explicit. When the teacher reflects on her practice, she constructs meanings over the realities within which she is working. She becomes involved with a process of observation, interpretation and construction of meanings. Essential processes in the "realization of their activity to the extent that the teacher inevitably makes many decisions, working with objectives and realities that can be interpreted, within complex, fluid settings: something that may not be so decisive in other professions" [8]. From this approach teachers are defined as a professionals who undertake their role in a personal way who give the profession a creative component.

What does a smartphone provide to help teachers record and reflect on these situations? What value does the language of images have in these analytical, questioning and discussion processes on what took place in classrooms and educational centres? What is the nature of the images that teachers take and what discourses do they articulate? We propose that the teachers take photos of situations and moments. This means we focus on the group of tools for taking still images that these devices have.

II. THE AIMS AND RESEARCH METHOD

The aims proposed to reveal how the language of images contributes to reflection on teaching practice are:

- Understanding how teachers use their smartphones to communicate using the language of images.
- Describing and make connections between the photos´ content and the teacher´s reflections that arise in the photo-elicitation sessions.

To meet these aims, we developed three types of procedures:

Photo-elicitation sessions. These sessions were conducted once every two weeks during three years. Before the sessions teachers take photos of events, tasks, dilemmas, conflicts, behaviours and so on that they consider most relevant and interesting in the life of their classroom and other spaces in the centre. The photos that each teacher takes are shown and participants comment on the reasons that prompted them to take each photo. After this, the members of the research group formulate questions or doubts on the content of images and the reasons given by the teacher. In this way, images "can offer researchers new and valuable routes to other people´s experiences, knowledge and values" [9].

Audio-reflection sessions. An audio recording is made of the photo-elicitation sessions with two research goals. Firstly, to analyse each teacher's narrations, and secondly, to codify the information provided to place it in context by analysing each photo's content.

Content analysis. To describe how the images and the meanings associated to these photos are used by teachers, according this method [10] [11], we grouped the photos according to their relationship between the internal narrative – what actually appears in the photos and the type of shot or composition – and their external narrative – what the image aims to communicate, the information recorded in the audio-reflection sessions [12]. To codify and sort both information types, we use NVivo 10 software, a programme that provides a flexible, multi-purpose work space, which allows us to create categories for analysis and to access information combining different types of records: text-based and still image, in our case. We understand that the most direct way of knowing these human experiences is to narrate them, rather than to quantify them. Our research strategy is based on the idea that each situation of photo-elicitation is equivalent to an open interview, which does not need a questionnaire, because the questions are oriented from the spontaneous manifestations of the teachers about images of moments in their classrooms.

III. CONCLUSION

Three fundamental aspects have stood out during our research:

Firstly, we verified how the language of images enables teachers to take photos easily to represent their ideas, concerns and problems in classrooms and educational centres. When an unexpected event occurs that activates their thought and a personal interpretation of that event, quick access to the camera app on smartphones makes it possible to record that moment, which is important to them, in a more efficient way than using a classic camera.

It may seem like an obvious question, but in the educational field, Smartphones, which have a great presence in our daily lives, are not as widely used in schools as video and photo cameras. The study is relevant because of the few existing experiences in which smartphones take center stage in the processes of reflection on the teaching practice. This allows them to be aware of their particular professional and ethical attitudes in response to specific problems. The important role that smartphones play in ongoing training and in improving professional practice of these three teachers is clear. For them, smartphones have gone from being a resource whose use was exclusively devoted to leisure, to becoming an important tool for professional development. In contrast to a typical camera, we carry our smartphones on us at all times, and that omnipresence is what helps when recording images. Since they are multi-functional, teachers also have other ways of recording ideas such as taking text and audio notes to record the reasons why they took the photos. Furthermore, in the images the teachers took, we confirmed that the spaces for reflection were not only in the educational centre or classroom; rather, having a device on them to record images allowed teachers to extend their reflective spaces beyond the school environment. Thus, they showed us photos taken in their personal space, such as photos taken at home and in leisure spaces. It is in these spaces that they can also retrieve the photos taken previously and calmly continue to build meanings and ideas. But in addition, smartphones allow to capture the immediacy. It also allows to capture the significant moment of an event or anecdote for the teachers, in a more effective way than if they used a camera of photos. The practical thinking of teachers is a difficult question to materialize. The events that are happening in the classroom do not allow the teacher to become aware of the ideas and theory that they use to respond to the problems that arise. The tactile functions of smartphones facilitate this task to make explicit that practical knowledge.

With regard to the second aim, we have seen that close-up photos – showing objects and things – are a type of record that predominates in their representations. We observed that the teachers constructed highly personal, intimate and, therefore, elaborate meanings, and they recognised that it would be difficult to express these without the support of the photos. The language of images appears to be a language for expressing ideas and thoughts that would be more difficult to communicate through written language. The meanings associated with the photos also reveal their ideological position. The use of images reveals a negotiation process regarding their identities as creative teachers who transform their professional practices and conditions, as opposed to a more uncritical and technical role in the teaching profession. In the processes of photo-elicitation the teachers discuss with the researchers alternative actions. These alternative actions are aimed at improving the problems detected. For example, one of the participating teachers is becoming aware of the problems of coexistence in her classroom during the process of photo-elicitation. Competitiveness among students emerges as their form of interaction. This process leads the teacher to implement a behavior modification project in her classroom.

A future line of work could be the inclusion of image and the processes of photo-elicitation such as a pedagogical strategy in initial teachers' curriculum. If the students use a multimodal language, they will improve their skills to observe and analyze critically their contexts and any educational situation.

ACKNOWLEDGMENT

A project subsidised by the Ministry of Economy and Competitiveness of the Spanish Government, within the R&D&i State Plan, reference EDU2014-57103-R.

REFERENCES

[1] R. Barthes, Camera lucida: reflections of photography. Barcelona: Paidós, 1990.

[2] M. Cochran-Smith. "Studying Teacher Education. What we know and need to know". Journal of Teacher Education, (56) 4, pp. 301-306, 2016.

[3] F. A. J. Korthagen and J. P. A. M. Kessels. "Linking theory and practice: changing the pedagogy of teacher education". Educational Researcher, 28 (4), pp. 4-17, 1999.

[4] J.J. Loughran. "Effective reflective practice: in search of meaning in learning about teaching". Journal of Teacher Education, 53 (1), pp. 33-43, 2002.

[5] A. E. Richert. "Inquiring about practice: using web-based materials to develop teacher inquiry". Teaching Education, 16 (4), pp. 297-310, 2005.

[6] D. Harper, "Talking about pictures: a case for photo elicitation". Visual Studies, 17 (1), pp.13-26, 2002.

[7] I. Kaplan and A. Howes, "Seeing with difference eyes: exploring the value of participative research using images in schools". Cambridge Journal of Education, 34 (2), pp. 143-155, 2004.

[8] J. Gimeno, El curriculum: una reflexión sobre la práctica, [The curriculum: a reflection on practice]. Madrid: Morata, 1988.

[9] S. Pink, Doing sensory ethnography, London: Sage, 2009.

[10] T. Van Leeuven and C. Jewitt, Handbook of Visual Analysis, London: Sage, 2001.

[11] J. Prosser, "Visual Methodology: Towards a More Seeing Research," in Handbook of Qualitative Research, N. Denzin and Y. Lincoln, Eds. London: Sage, 2011.
[12] M. Banks, Using Visual Data in Qualitative Research, London: Sage, 2008.

Speech Shadowing Support System in Language Learning

Carson Lee[1], Shinobu Hasegawa[2]
[1]School of Information Science,
[2]Research Centre for Advance Computing Infrastructure
Japan Advanced Institute of Science and Technology
Nomi, Japan
[1]crsnlee@jaist.ac.jp, [2]hasegawa@jaist.ac.jp

***Abstract*—Verbal communication is a major part of a language, but there are not many systems/solutions in the market that caters to self-learning of spoken language. Traditional classroom learning is affected by the cultural background of the learning environment, thus students from different backgrounds might end up speaking a different dialect or accent, and this might result in miscommunication. Speech Shadowing is an experimental technique where a subject repeats speech immediately after hearing it. However, it is a time consuming method as it requires 1-on-1 tutoring. In this paper, we present our approach to utilizing this method for a self-supported learning system and how to utilize technology to improve its efficiency over traditional speech shadowing methods.**

Keywords- Speech Shadowing; language learning; mobile learning

I. INTRODUCTION

The development of speech production throughout an individual's life starts from an infant's first babble and is transformed into fully developed speech by the age of five [1]. It is a type of cognitive skill, and thus, we cannot teach it the same way we would teach sciences or history, as cognitive skill learning is the learning of a skill or knowledge that is hard to symbolize.

Today, the English language is the de-facto lingua franca. Despite the widespread usage of English, there exists many variations of the English dialects, such as British English, Cockney English, American English, Engrish (generally refers to poor Japanese influenced English), Manglish (Malaysian English), and many more. The more formal dialects such as British English and American English are often used as the standard for major English proficiency test such as IELTS and TOEFL. Other dialects have evolved from their original one often due to cultural and environmental influences. For example, Manglish is a result of assimilating the many languages spoken in Malaysia into the English language. Another example would be Japanese English, where students often learn English the aid of furigana. There exist many consonants and vowels that are mutually exclusive in both language, and thus, a student who learns to speak English via furigana often end up having a hard time to be understood by non-Japanese English [2]. For example, a Japanese would often pronounce “eight” as “ei-to (エイト), fight as “figh-to (ファイト)”, or “the” as “za (ザ)”.

Another reason for doing this research is to reduce miscommunication due to different accents/dialects. Looking at the aviation industry, we can observe that many accidents have resulted from communication error. The nuances of a language can be complicated and the same word can carry multiple meanings. Depending on how it is delivered, the message conveyed might vary [3].

Furthermore, in this digital age, information can be disseminated very quickly through the internet and thus many people can spend their downtime (riding on a bus/train, waiting in line, etc.) to absorb more information via their mobile devices. This allows people to learn almost anywhere and anytime. However, some domains are not as easy to be learnt without the presence of an instructor or teacher. There are many applications that cater to language learning. However, the amount of smartphone applications that focuses on improving a learner’s speaking skill is also very limited. Most of these applications focuses on the reading/writing aspect, and the speaking aspect is usually very simple (such as pronunciation of a single word at a time). In teaching a student to speak a foreign language, most attention is devoted to the correct pronunciation of sounds and isolated words. Generally speaking, much less attention is paid to a correct production of intonation [4].

In this research, the aim is to utilize Speech Shadowing to improve verbal communication abilities according to a certain dialect/accent. The scope of this research will cover the development of a system to improve a user’s speaking skill in the English language via Speech Shadowing. In Section II, we will describe what speech shadowing is, and the problems faced by this method. The learning model that will be applied is discussed in Section III. At Section IV, we will describe our approach to solving the problems described earlier, and their algorithms. Section V will be the conclusion to this paper, summarizing it.

II. SPEECH SHADOWING

One way to improve a user’s speaking ability is via Speech Shadowing. Speech shadowing is an experimental technique where a subject repeats speech immediately after hearing it, usually through headphones to reduce noise and/or speech jamming. The reaction time between hearing a word and pronouncing it can be as short as 254ms or even 150ms [5]. While a person is only asked to repeat words, they also automatically process their syntax and semantics. Words repeated during the shadowing practice imitate the parlance of the overheard words more than the same words read aloud by that subject. We can also observe a similar behaviour in children as they begin to develop their speaking ability. They are often predisposed to imitate/shadow words and speech as a way to guide themselves to enter their cultural community [6]. Since children utilize this method to learn a language, it could be possible to utilize the same method for adults. In fact, learning the patterns of intonation is thought to take place unconsciously by mere imitation. That is, by listening to, and repeating model utterances the foreign-language learner has to acquire a proper intonation.

A. Traditional Speech Shadowing

In the traditional speech shadowing method, an instructor is needed to sit there to evaluate the student performing speech shadowing. Fig. 1 illustrates the usual steps for a speech shadowing session and they are as follows:

1) Playback of a speech/conversation recording

2) Student performs speech shadowing (repeats the heard speech with minimal delay as clearly and loudly as possible)

3) Instructor listens to the shadowed speech and provides evaluation/feedback to the student

4) The student attempts to improve based on the given feedback and retries the process on a later date.

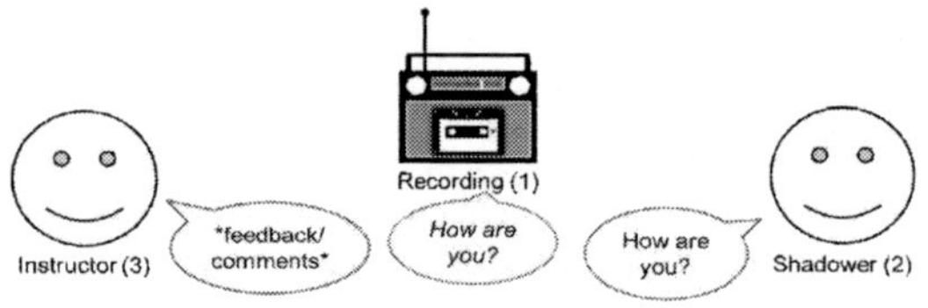

Figure 1. Traditional Speech Shadowing Session Setup

Due to the fact that one instructor can only focus on one student at a time during a speech shadowing session, the process becomes inherently expensive. The instructor should also be highly trained and/or be very experienced with the language and dialect that he is instructing on. This only adds to the cost of speech shadowing. Furthermore, because speech shadowing is still largely an experimental technique, there exists no formal feedback/evaluation method. Verbal and/or written feedback comments may be subjective and thus prove to be ambiguous at times. This makes it hard to keep track of past performance that could be used to help the student improve.

III. LEARNING MODEL

The learning model used in this research would be the Cognitive Apprenticeship Theory. It is the process where a master of a skill teaches it to an apprentice via 5 steps/stages, which is modelling, coaching, reflection, articulation and exploration [7].

- Modelling – Demonstrating the thinking process
- Coaching – Assisting and supporting student cognitive activities as needed (includes scaffolding)
- Reflection – Self-analysis and assessment
- Articulation – Verbalizing the results of reflection
- Exploration – Formation and testing of one's own hypothesis

The focus of this research will be modelling, coaching, and reflection, whereby the original speech would be the model, the scaffolding being the coach, and self-evaluation being the reflection.

Coaching would be done via scaffolding with the 4 elements being used to control the difficulty. The 4 elements would be discussed in Section IV.A. Initially the user would be given a questionnaire to judge their own level and a speech of appropriate difficulty will be given to the user to shadow without any scaffolding. After the initial rating, the user will then be given scaffolding suited to his level.

At this phase of the research, reflection would be self-evaluation. The user would be given some visual aids such as the audio waveform in order to evaluate his own performance and then he would answer a questionnaire. Feedback such as graphs will then be provided to show the user his current performance in various aspect of speech such as intonation, tempo, and pronunciation. The user can also track his past performances. These metrics would be fed back to the system in order to determine the coaching needed for the next shadowing session.

IV. OUR APPROACH

Due to the impracticality of the traditional speech shadowing for language learning on a larger scale, we propose a system that is able to replace the role of the instructor of the traditional method. At the same time, we want the system to provide a more tailored learning method for the student using it, so that he/she may learn and improve faster. The lack of an instructor also allows the student to learn independently, and due to the simplicity of our proposed system, the system can also be implemented on a mobile system, allowing students to learn anywhere and anytime. This will be approached by 2 methods

A. Speech Shadowing System

The system would contain recordings of speeches to be listened to, and the speeches will be sorted by difficulty levels according to their length, speed, and difficulty of the words or sentences. The system would also pickup and record the speech shadowed by the student so that it can be analysed to provide feedback and evaluation.

The difficulty level of the speeches will be determined by the following elements of speech:

- Length of speech
- Speed/tempo of speech
- Difficulty of words used
- Number of stresses/intonation in sentence

The reason the elements are chosen are explained as follows. The length of speech can directly affect the difficulty of the speech as it increases the cognitive load as it becomes longer. The speed and tempo of a speech also affects the difficulty of a speech as speech rate (the number of words spoken per minute) has been used extensively in the previous research of oral fluency [8] [9] [10]. Previous research also found that speech rate positively correlated with other measures of fluency, such as length of speech without pauses, hesitations, or repeats [11] [12]. Difficulty of words that appear is also taken into consideration as it can affect the understanding of a shadowed speech.

The number of stresses and intonation in a sentence can affect the difficulty of a speech because linguistic, syntactic and semantic information is more easily conveyed when a speaker produces the correct variations in pitch in a speech utterance [13]. Of all the elements of a target language, the intonation appears to be the most difficult to acquire [14]. First, because the intonation in infants is learned at a very early stage in the language-acquisition process [15], it is most resistant to change. Second, as a result of the fact that suprasegmental patterns are particularly deep-rooted, foreign language learners often superimpose the prosodic features of their mother language on the sounds of the foreign language. For this reason, foreign-language learners are often not aware of any differences in intonation between the mother language and the foreign language [4]. This makes the number of stresses in a sentence directly related to the difficulty of shadowing a sentence.

We propose that the system runs on a smartphone so that it can make the learning process more accessible as year-by-year digital media audiences are increasingly coming from mobile devices [16]. Setting up a headset is also easier and less costly compared to a desktop-based system as most smartphone owner would already have access to a headset. This also ensures students can learn on the go, although they should use the system in an isolated environment to avoid disturbing others.

An account would be created for progress tracking purposes. First time user of the system would take a standardised test and answer a short questionnaire to determine his/her initial level and proficiency (system initialization). The test would be a speech shadowing session without any support from the system. The difficulty of the speech would also be a predetermined medium level speech.

Under a normal use-case condition (post-initialization), students would login to the system and be presented with a list of recommended speeches to shadow, which are determined by the student's proficiency and level. The amount and type of scaffolding provided during a shadowing session is affected by the student's proficiency and level along with the difficulty of the speech attempted. Take for example Student A is rated by the system as a level 6 user (out of 10 possible levels, with 1 being lowest and 10 being highest) attempts a speech of difficulty level 2 (out of 5 difficulties with 1 being easiest and 5 being the hardest). Student A would get no scaffolding as his proficiency should be sufficient to attempt the speech with ease. However, if Student A attempts a level 5 difficulty speech, all scaffolding would be activated to help Student A with his shadowing attempt. In the optimal scenario, Student A should be attempting speeches with difficulty level that matches his own proficiency level, as the effect of learning via speech shadowing can be affected by having too much scaffolding.

TABLE I. USER LEVEL AND SPEECH DIFFICULTY LEVEL MATCHING

(User Level) / 2	Scaffolding	Notes
> speech level	No scaffolding	Scaffolding provided depends on user's proficiency on speech elements as well
= speech level	Partial Scaffolding	
< speech level	More / All Scaffolding	

Fig. 2 shows the types of scaffolding that is provided by the system:

1) Speech transcript
2) Pronunciation help
3) Highlighting sentence stress points
4) Speed control for recordings

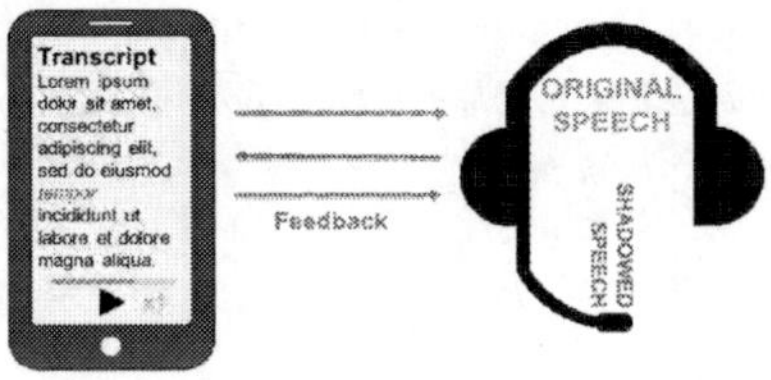

Figure 2. Scaffolding 1,3, and 4 being used in a shadowing session

Figure 2 provides an example of 3 types of scaffolding being used to coach the user. The Transcript is there to help the user know what exactly he/she is saying while the highlighted word is the part of speech where a stress is needed. A playback speed is also displayed and can be used to change the speed of the playback to help the user cope with higher difficulty speeches.

B. Performance Evaluation

In order to provide the student with a valuable feedback and evaluation without an instructor, a way to grade the speech shadowing session needs to be devised. Using 3 metrics, the user's performance can be measured more accurately and the training time needed can be shortened as the student knows what he has to focus on to improve. The 3 metrics that is used in this system are:

- Intonation
- Pronunciation
- Tempo

The user would evaluate the 3 metrics on his own by comparing his shadowed speech to the original recording. Using a simple questionnaire, the student would rate his own performance compared to the sample recording. The system will provide some visualisation of the data in order to make the process easier.

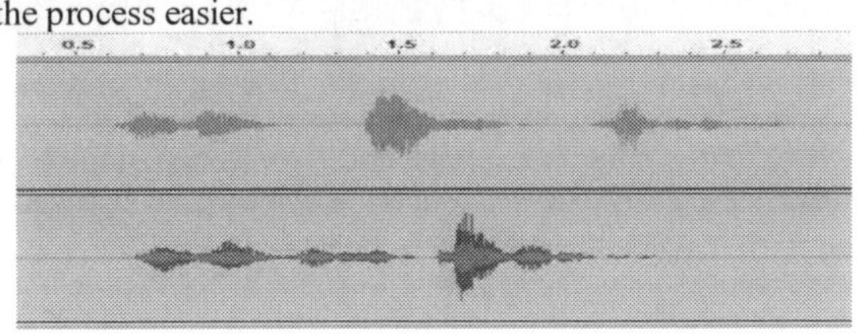

Figure 3. **Visualization** of intonation differece

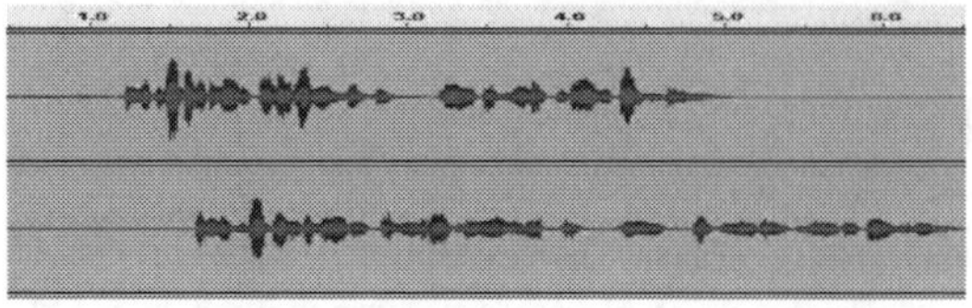

Figure 4. Visualisation of tempo difference

After the evaluation is done, the system would use the data to determine if a user has levelled up and thus have some of the scaffolding removed. The data would also be archived so that users can keep track of their past performance and pinpoint where their weakness is.

C. *Evaluation Algorithms – Determining user level*

1) Post system initialization

$$S_{cs} = (S_i \times W_i) + (S_t \times W_t) + (S_p \times W_p)$$
$$UL = \frac{S_{cs}}{10}$$
$$S_{pp} = S_{cs}$$

2) Next Iterations

$$S_{cs} = (S_i \times W_i) + (S_t \times W_t) + (S_p \times W_p)$$
$$UL = \frac{(S_{cs} + S_{pp}) \times W_{pp}}{10}$$
$$S_{pp} = \frac{S_{cs} + S_{pp}}{2}$$

TABLE II. USER LEVEL AND SPEECH DIFFICULTY LEVEL MATCHING

Variables	Definition
S_i	Score – intonation
S_t	Score – tempo
S_p	Score – pronunciation
S_{cs}	Score – current session
S_{pp}	Score – past performance
N_s	Total Number of Sessions
W_i	Weightage – intonation
W_t	Weightage – tempo
W_p	Weightage – pronunciation
UL	User Level

The variables are calculated after the user takes the standardised test during the system initialization phase.

V. CONCLUSION

In conclusion, speech shadowing could be a good method for learning and improving one's speaking proficiency. However, the traditional method of it is not suitable to implement on a larger scale. Therefore, we propose the idea of a speech shadowing support system so that we can overcome the constraint. By breaking down the elements in a speech, the system will be able to provide a more tailored coaching method to individual students. By further splitting up the user into different levels, the learning curve would not be as steep, making the task of learning much less daunting.

In future research, automated evaluation by the system will replace self-evaluation system and it would provide a more standardised method for evaluation and thus give better feedback for reflection. Just like in self-evaluation, the system would use intonation, tempo, and pronunciation to evaluate the user, and the result of the automated evaluation would be fed back into the system for the next session.

ACKNOWLEDGMENT

The work is supported in part by Grant-in-Aid for Scientific Research (C) (No. 26330395) from the Ministry of Education, Science, and Culture of Japan.

REFERENCES

[1] Kevin Shockley, L. S. Imitation in shadowing words. Perception & Psychophysics , pp. 422-429, 2004.

[2] Marslen-Wilson, W., Linguistic Structure and Speech Shadowing at Very Short Latencies. Nature Vol, pp. 244, 522-523, 1973.

[3] McMillan, David. Miscommunications in Air Traffic Control. Diss. Queensland University of Technology, 1998.

[4] Gerard W. G. Spaai and Dik J. Hermes, A Visual Display For the Teaching of Intonation. CALICO Journal, Volume 10 Number 3, 1993.

[5] Shudong, Wang, Michael Higgins, and Yukiko Shima. "Teaching English pronunciation for Japanese learners of English online." JALT CALL Journal 1.1 (2005): pp. 39-47.

[6] Trevor A. Harley and L. J., Decline and fall: A biological, developmental, and psycholinguistic account of deliberative language processes and ageing. Aphasiology, 2011.

[7] Dennen, Vanessa P., and Kerry J. Burner. "The cognitive apprenticeship model in educational practice." Handbook of research on educational communications and technology 3 pp. 425-439, 2008.

[8] R. Ejzenberg and H. Riggenbach, "The juggling act of oral fluency: A psycho-sociolinguistic metaphor," Perspectives on Fluency, Ann Arbor University of Michigan, pp. 287-314, 2000.

[9] Freed B. Riggenbach H. 'Is fluency, like beauty, in the eyes (and ears) of the beholder?', Perspectives on Fluency, Ann Arbor University of Michigan pp. 287-314, 2000.

[10] Lennon P. 'Investigating fluency in EFL: A quantitative approach,' , Language Learning, 1990, vol. 40, pp. 387-417, 1990.

[11] Freed, B.F., Segalowitz, N. and Dewey, D.P., Context of learning and second language fluency in French: Comparing regular classroom, study abroad, and intensive domestic immersion programs. Studies in second language acquisition, 26(02), pp.275-301, 2004.

[12] Segalowitz N , Freed B . 'Context, contact, and cognition in oral fluency acquisition,' , Studies in Second Language , 2004 , vol. 27, pp. 175 -201, 2004.

[13] Crystal, D. Prosodic Systems and Intonation in English. Cambridge: Cambridge University Press, 1969.

[14] Leon, P. R., and P. Martin, "Applied Linguistics and the Teaching of Intonation." The Modern Language Journal, 56, 3, pp. 139-144, 1972.

[15] Lieberman, P. (1967). Intonation, Perception and Language. Cambridge, MIT Press. ______, and S. B. Michaels, "Some Aspects of Fundamental Frequency and Envelope Amplitude as Related to the Emotional Content of Speech." Journal of the Acoustical Society of America, 34, pp. 922-927, 1962.

[16] comScore, Cross-Platform - Future in focus 2016.

ADPT++
Technology-Based Combined Strategy for Problem Solving

Claudia Martínez-Araneda, Marcia Muñoz
Computer Science Department
Universidad Católica de la Santísima Concepción
Concepción, Chile
e-mail: {cmartinez, marciam}@ucsc.cl

Matilde Basso-Aránguiz, Claudio Oyarzo-Vera
Civil Engineering Department
Universidad Católica de la Santísima Concepción
Concepción, Chile
e-mail: {mbasso, coyarzov}@ucsc.cl

Abstract — **The growth in student enrollment in the engineering programs, low student motivation and poor passing rates in first years' students in a Computer Science undergraduate program have demanded the incorporation of active learning strategies into the classroom in order to improve problem solving skills. This article describes a proposal and preliminary results of incorporating technology-based teaching strategies. The Analysis-Design-Programming-Testing (ADPT) teaching strategy was applied in the classroom, combined with a Flipped Classroom (FC) methodology. Preliminary results show clear benefits related to the availability of support media resources, increased time dedicated to solving problems in the classroom, and the creation of a collaborative and challenging classroom environment.**

Keywords-flipped classroom; ADPT, engineering education.

I. INTRODUCTION

In the last 10 years, Chile's social and educational context has generated an explosive growth in student enrollment in the engineering programs of the Universidad Católica de la Santísima Concepción (UCSC). This increase in the number of students has required optimizing the use of time in the classroom, and dedicating more time to student-centered activities supervised by an instructor.

This article presents a learning strategy that combines reverse teaching, also known as Flipped Classroom [1], and the Analysis-Design-Programming-Testing technique (ADPT) [2]. This teaching approach enables transferring part of the learning process to out-of-the-classroom activities by the use of videocasts (short videos allocated in a web-based platform), which introduce the theory and cognitive knowledge associated with the topic under study. In general terms, an instructor leads the in-classroom activities focusing on practical tasks designed to reinforce the theory and generate active and deeper learning in students.

Besides freeing in-classroom time by transferring the theoretical aspects of the course to out-of-classroom autonomous work, the use of videocasts allow students to recall those theoretical contents whenever and wherever they are.

The use of Information and Communications Technologies (ICTs) and the implementation of practical activities increased students' motivation and commitment to the assigned tasks. This new student disposition toward learning resulted in improved academic performance.

The remainder of the article is organized as follows: the next section presents the academic context where the proposed strategy for problem solving was applied. Section 3 describes the teaching and learning strategies supporting this work, which include Problem Based Learning (PBL), FC and ADPT. Section 4 shows a hybrid proposal that combines these technologies and the ADPT strategy which we have called ADPT++ (the name was chosen as a programming joke). Preliminary results are shown in Section 5. Finally, Section 6 presents our conclusions and outlines future work.

II. ACADEMIC CONTEXT

In 2011, the UCSC School of Engineering implemented a comprehensive curricular renovation of its five engineering programs based on the "Conceive, Design, Implement and Operate" (CDIO) initiative [3], which defines an educational framework for engineering programs helping identify program goals and associated learning outcomes, and promotes integrated curriculum design. Its main resources are the CDIO Syllabus and the CDIO Standards [4]. The CDIO Syllabus summarizes and organizes a set of engineering knowledge, personal and professional skills and attributes, and interpersonal skills. The 12 CDIO Standards serve as guidelines for educational program reform and evaluation, and provide a framework for continuous improvement. They address program philosophy (Standard 1), curriculum development (Standards 2, 3 and 4), design-build experiences and workspaces (Standards 5 and 6), new methods of teaching and learning (Standards 7 and 8), faculty development (Standards 9 and 10), and assessment and evaluation (Standards 11 and 12).

Among other issues, the curricular renovation addressed the problem of low motivation in first years' students by incorporating activities aimed at familiarizing students with their future professional role. Also, the new curricula incorporated the implementation of a student-centered teaching and learning approach, which was strongly supported through active learning methodologies (CDIO Standard 8), such as the strategies described in this work.

As a result of the curricular renovation, all engineering programs at UCSC were modified to include teaching methodologies based on problem solving and collaborative work. In these activities, students analyze different kind of engineering problems and design solutions following a structured approach according to their level of knowledge and training. and

III. Teaching and Learning Strategies

This section describes methodologies and strategies on which the proposal of this paper is based.

A. *Problem-Based Learning*

Problem-Based Learning (PBL) is defined as an active learning method in which teams of students learn by solving relevant problems and reflecting on their experiences [5]. Problems must involve a cognitive conflict, and must be challenging enough to motivate students to find a solution and, at the same time, must be complex enough so that their solution requires cooperation among all team members. The instructor must act as a facilitator, making the problem a real team challenge to be solved and thus preventing students from just dividing up the work. In this way, PBL not only helps students learn the specific subject of the course, but it also helps develop teamwork, autonomous learning, information searching from diverse sources, problem solving, decision making, oral and written communications, among others.

B. *Flipped Classroom*

At the beginning of the 21st century, methodological innovations known as "reverse classes" have been documented in the educational field in which what was taught in the classroom was now learnt outside of it, thus implying only a modification of the place where the activities were carried out [6][7]. Recent works define the Flipped Classroom (FC) [1][8][9] as a teaching/learning model that transfers the individual learning work to autonomous out-of-class activities and dedicates the in-class time to practical and cooperative activities that facilitate the acquisition, practice and application of the theoretical knowledge. This teaching model makes it possible for students to understand, analyze and apply information, enhancing the development of their cognitive skills [10][11][12]. From this perspective, this model considers learning at the center of the training process, with students taking an active and leading role and where instructors mainly guide and facilitate learning.

From a methodology implementation standpoint, Hamdan et al. [13] has identified a continuous process of learning assessment with an emphasis on permanent and on-time feedback to students as a key aspect to consider. Hence, flexible learning environments must be created that go beyond the traditional physical and time boundaries of a class [14]. On the other hand, Tucker [15] suggests the use of video for student learning outside the classroom and emphasizes the importance of integrating the contents seen in the videos with the activities to be developed in the classroom, so that they can effectively deepen and apply those contents.

As for the positive effect of the use of FC in the teaching and learning process, Brame [16] indicates that this strategy allows the student to have the educational material prior to the class and its revision at any time and place. In addition, the development of student-centered activities in the classroom encourages collaborative work, peer learning and greater student engagement in learning. Finally, it enables instructors to give feedback in real time, allowing them to recognize achievement, evaluate progress and thus take improvement actions. Although this methodological strategy has large benefits in the educational process, it is necessary to consider its limitations such as the low quality of videos, differences in students' autonomous work capacity, problems in the design of activities for classroom work and difficulties in synchronous and asynchronous communications between instructor and students, e. g., when fielding questions [17].

The Flipped Classroom methodology is applicable to different educational contexts, with evidence showing improvements in the classroom work environment and increased student motivation and involvement in their learning process [18]. Additionally, improvements in the learning outcomes achieved by the students have been documented [19][20]. At the same time, instructors and students both value positively the maximization of in-the-classroom time and the fostering of autonomous activities that leverage information and communication technologies [19][21].

C. *Analysis-Design-Programming-Testing strategy*

Analysis-Design-Programming-Testing (ADPT) is an active learning strategy based on a PBL approach. It is composed of the four stages of the classical software development method, also called the waterfall model [2].

Even though the ADPT method was proposed to support teaching computer programming, it includes generic elements of both PBL and collaborative learning methods. ADPT also encourages collaboration with other teams, can be applied to solving different kinds of problems, from well-structured simple problems to ill-structured relevant problems.

As shown in Figure 1, each team of students is assigned a problem to be solved using ADPT, and has to generate deliverable documentation for each stage. This process is guided and supervised by an instructor and teaching assistants. In this case, the learning outcomes are assessed through the results generated by the team for each of the stages. The analysis stage outcome is an analysis document including a description of inputs, processes, outputs, and constraints. The design stage has as output a flow diagram or pseudocode that represents the algorithm to solve problem. Next, the programming stage has as its deliverable the source code and finally, the test stage outcomes are a test plan and the results obtained of its application. Figure 1 shows the four ADPT stages and deliverables for each one.

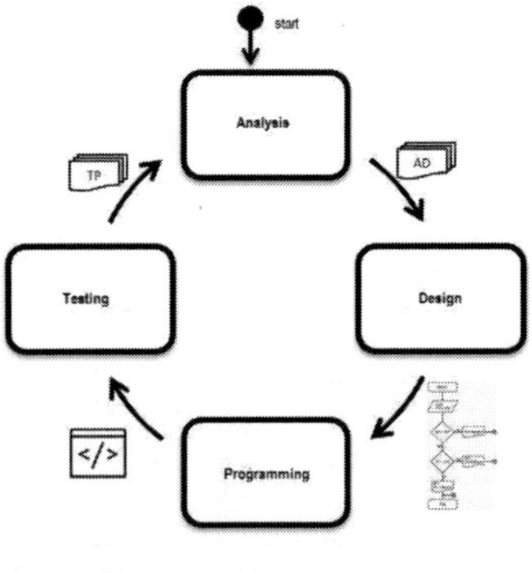

Figure 1. ADPT traditional sequence.

IV. ENHANCED ADPT STRATEGY: ADPT++

Even though other experiences that describe the implementation of Flipped Classroom strategies also encourage in-class active work [1][16], our proposal is of interest because we use this strategy to comply with the CDIO active learning standard and because there are few documents describing the implementation of flipped classroom strategies in the engineering domain, particularly in computer science, in Chile. This article presents an improved teaching and learning strategy that combines ADPT with the Flipped Classroom methodology, including elements of both PBL and collaborative learning methods. This strategy, called Enhanced ADPT or ADPT++, is described graphically in Figure 2.

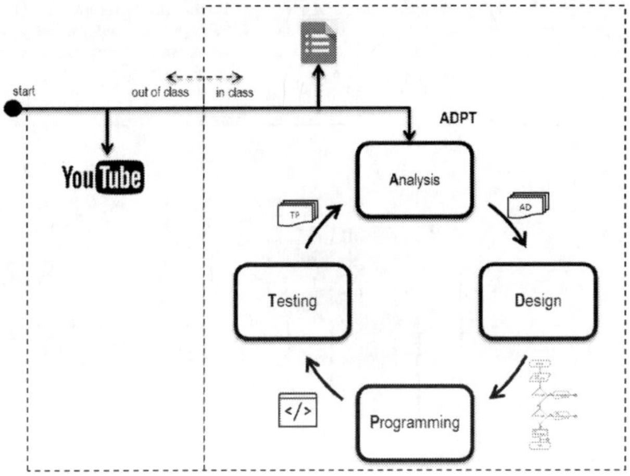

Figure 2. ADPT++ sequence.

The basic structure of this strategy involves the use of videocasts allocated in a Youtube channel which cover the theoretical fundamentals to be applied in classes. The cognitive learning outcomes associated to the contents of the videos are assessed by a formative test developed by means of a Google Forms tools at the beginning of each class. The purpose of this test is to detect whether students have previously viewed the videos and whether they were able to retain the minimum concepts needed to address the problem proposed in class. Then, the class focuses only on performing practical work based on the theoretical concepts presented in the video. Finally, the expected learning outcomes are assessed through the deliverables generated by the team for each of the stages of the ADPT method and through a perception survey.

Figure 3 details the four-step method used to guide the work involved in producing the videos and in designing the corresponding in-class didactic sequences.

Step 1 is performed by the lecturer responsible for the course with support from the program committee. Step 2 is supported by a technical crew which edits and customizes the video. Steps 3 and 4 correspond to the implementation and evaluation of the strategy. Steps 1 and 2 were performed one semester before the intervention with the students actually took place (Steps 3 and 4).

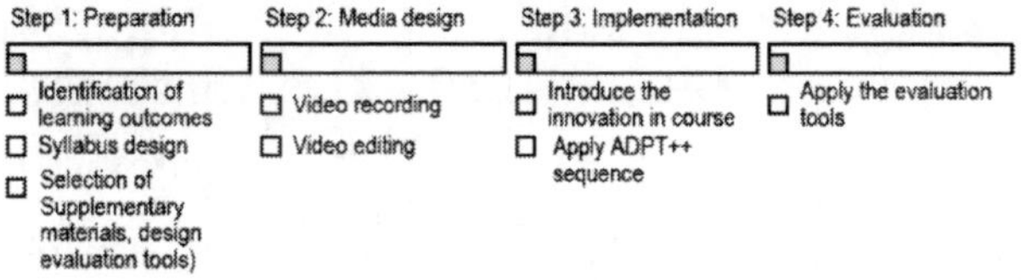

Figure 3. Workflow method.

This classroom strategy was applied to the Programming Lab I course during the Spring term of 2016 (from August to December). This course meets for 5 hours a week and corresponds to a second semester course in the Computer Science undergraduate program. The course was taught in two parallel groups of 24 and 29 students each.

In this course, students learn computer programming using basic tools and simple structured problems, and also develop teamwork skills. Table I presents the course's learning outcomes, associated to: (i) disciplinary knowledge and reasoning, (ii) personal and professional skills and attributes, and (iii) interpersonal skills.

TABLE I. CDIO SYLLABUS GOALS OF PROGRAMMING LABORATORY I

Disciplinary knowledge and reasoning	1 Fundamentals of algorithms, data structures and programming languages	
	1.1	Explains the different software development stages.
	1.2	Identifies inputs, outputs and constraints for a given problem.
	1.3	Designs a structured solution using an algorithmic representation technique.
	1.4	Builds an algorithmic solution using a structured programming language.
Personal and professional skills and attributes	2 Analyzes a problem by dividing it into identifiable parts, and propose solutions.	
Interpersonal skills	3 Can work in interdisciplinary teams.	

V. PRELIMINARY RESULTS

Student work was evaluated in two instances, first with a theoretical formative test and second with an active learning activity. The theoretical test results show if the students saw and understood the videocast before the class. The active learning activity in-class time, as in the ADPT strategy, consists of solving a problem in teams and generating the deliverables for the ADPT stages described in Section 3. This activity is assessed using two specially designed rubrics: (i) a ADPT process-product rubric, oriented toward assessing issues related to disciplinary knowledge (Table II), and (ii) a rubric designed to assess issues related to teamwork (Table III). Students grades were calculated assigning a weight of 80% to process-product performance and of 20% to teamwork performance, both evaluated using the rubrics shown in Table II and Table III, respectively.

TABLE II. ADPT++ PROCESS – PRODUCT RUBRIC

	Excellent (5 pts.)	Good (4 pts.)	Satisfactor y (3 pts.)	Poor (2 pts.)	Unaccepta ble (1 pts.)
A	Identifies 100% of the inputs, outputs and contraints of the problem.	Identifies most of the inputs, outputs and contraints of the problem .	Identifies some inputs, outputs and contraints of the problem.	Identifies few inputs, outputs and contraints of the problem.	Fails to identify inputs, outputs and contraints of the problem.
D	Designs the algorithms and test cases correctly 100% of the time.	Designs the algorithm and test cases correctly most of the time.	Partially designs the algorithm and test cases.	Designs the algorithm and test cases poorly.	Fails to design the algorithm and test cases.
P	Source code compiles 100% and documentatio n is complete.	Source code compiles 100%, but style and documentatio n must be improved.	Complete source code is observed but compilation fails.	Incomplete source code is observed.	No source code is observed.
T	Code passes 100% of test cases.	Code passes most (≥ 80%) of test cases.	Code passes ≥ 50% and < 80% test cases.	Code passes less than 50% test cases.	Code fails for all test cases.

Figures 4 and 5 show the preliminary results of the Programming Lab I course in terms of the student performance in Test 1 and Test 2, respectively. It is important to note that the ADTP strategy was first applied in 2013, while the ADTP++ strategy was only applied in 2016.

Results show an improvement in student performance starting in 2013, which can be seen in the shift of the score boxes toward higher scores. In 2011 and 2012, students failed to achieve the highest grades, unlike later years when the ADPT and ADPT++ strategies were applied. Low score outliers were found mainly when using ADPT++. This can be explained by noting that 20% of the students did not watch the video before class (Source: Google Analytics).

As shown in Figure 5, the score for Test 2 for 2016 (with ADPT++ strategy) was lower than the score for the 2013 to 2015 course versions (which applied the ADPT strategy). This may be due to the immaturity of our implementation, which still needs some work.

Both instructor perception and student feedback show an increase in student participation and motivation, which is consistent with the student reflective memos shown in [2].

TABLE III. ADPT++ TEAM WORK RUBRIC

	Excellent (5pts.)	Good (4pts.)	Satisfact ory (3pts.)	Poor (2 pts.)	Unaccept able (1 pts.)
Attitude (10%)	Positive attitude towards work.	Often has a positive attitude towards work.	Ocassional y has a positive attitude towards work.	Often demonstrat es negative attitude towards work.	Always demostrate s negative attitude towards work.
Development (10%)	Prepares and plans the work. Always supports the work of the team	Supports the work of the team.	Sometimes supports the work of the team.	Rarely supports the work of the team.	Never supports the work of the team.
Work quality (20%)	Always generates high quality work.	Almost always generates high quality work.	Generates work that ocassional y requires reviews.	Generates work that often requires reviews.	Generates low quality work.
Problem solving (40%)	Proposes solutions to the problems.	Refines solutions proposed by others.	Occasional ly suggests or refines solutions to problems.	Rarely contributes to solving problems.	Never contributes to solving problems.
Work with others (20%)	Always listens and keeps a good work environme nt.	Almost always listens and keeps a good work environme nt.	Occasional ly listens and keeps a good work environme nt.	Rarely listens and keeps a good work environme nt.	Never keeps a good work environme nt.

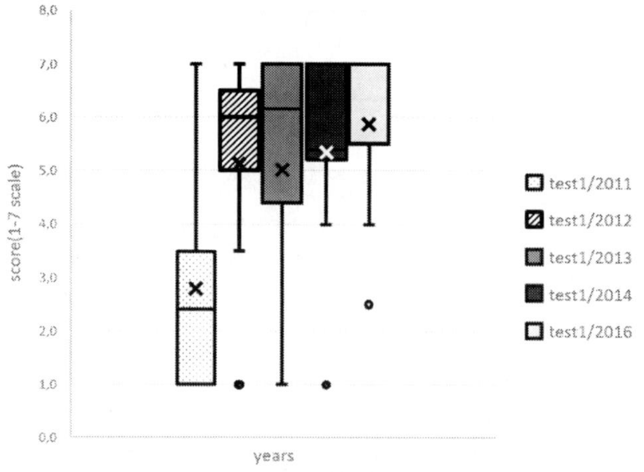

Figure 4. Scores for test 1 between years 2011 and 2016.

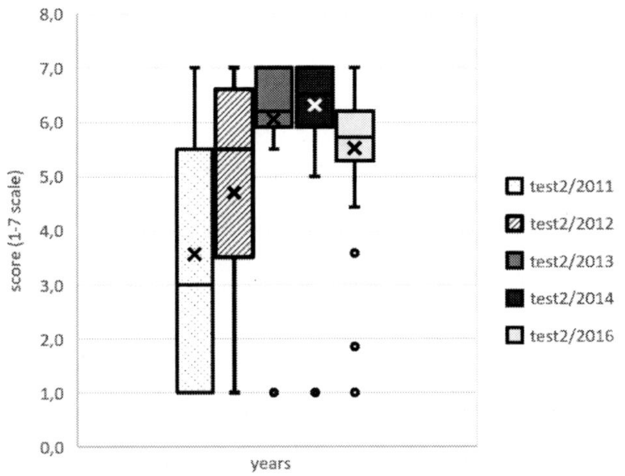

Figure 5. Scores for test 2 between years 2011 and 2016.

VI. CONCLUSIONS AND FUTURE WORK

This article presents a learning strategy that combines Flipped Classroom [1], and the Analysis-Design-Programming-Testing technique [2] called ADPT++. Our preliminary results lead us to believe that these methodologies help improve the students' learning of computer programming, in ways that go beyond just making better use of in-class time.

From the point of view of the students' commitment to their learning process, student participation in class increased. The inclusion of practical activities in class motivated their active participation and promoted collaborative learning. This strategy generated metacognition in students, making them aware of their learning process, and stimulated reflective work in the faculty regarding their teaching.

Aspects to be improved regarding the experience reported here are related to extending the use of this strategy to other courses. This will require specific training for faculty not familiar with this strategy. The implementation of appropriate spaces, equipment and a technical crew in charge of the production of videos are critical for the continuity and replicability of this experience. In addition, teaching assistants are needed to manage the videocast site, monitor the videos' rate of use, send out reminders and answer questions from users.

Our future challenges for this project are:

- To increase the number of courses and engineering programs applying this technology.
- To improve the quality of the videos, for example by incorporating checkpoints with short questions within videos to measure student comprehension of viewed contents.
- To create a training plan (workshop) to transfer our experience to other lecturers.
- To collect data to measure the impact of this strategy in students' performance and motivation.

ACKNOWLEDGMENT

This work was funded by Project FAD 11/2016 of the Universidad Católica de la Santísima Concepción, Chile.

REFERENCES

[1] J. Touron and R. Santiago, "Flipped Learning model and the development of talent at school," Education Journal, vol. 368, pp. 196–231, 2015.

[2] C. Martínez and M. Muñoz, "ADPT : An active learning method for a programming lab course in the Computer Science Program at UCSC," Proceedings of the 10th International CDIO Conference, Universitat Politècnica de Catalunya, Barcelona, Spain, June 16-19, 2014, http://www.cdio.org/node/6084 [retrieved August 2016].

[3] S. Loyer, M. Muñoz, C. Cárdenas, C. Martínez, and M. Cepeda, "A CDIO approach to curriculum design of five engineering programs at UCSC," Proceedings of the 7th International CDIO Conference, Technical University of Denmark, Copenhagen, June 20-23, 2011, http://ekrs.cdio.org/files/document/file/m5-loyer2011ucsc.pdf [retrieved August 2016].

[4] E. Crawley, J. Malmqvist, S. Ostlund, and D. Brodeur, Rethinking engineering education: The CDIO approach, Springer Sciences + Business Media, New York, 2007.

[5] H. S. Barrows and R. Tamblyn, Problem-Based Learning: An approach to Medical Education, Springer Publishing Company, New York, 1980.

[6] M. Lage and G. Platt. "The internet and the inverted classroom," The Journal of Economic Education, 31(1), pp. 11-11, 2000, http://goo.gl/qlo22v [retrieved January 2017].

[7] M. Lage, G. Platt and M. Treglia. "Inverting the classroom: A gateway to creating an inclusive learning environment," The Journal of Economic Education, 31(1), pp. 30-43, 2000, http://goo.gl/qjiJf9 [retrieved January 2017].

[8] J. Bishop and M. Verleger. "The Flipped Classroom : A survey of the research," ASEE National Conference Proceedings, Atlanta, 2013, https://peer.asee.org/22585 [retrieved January 2017].

[9] K. McDonald, K. and C. Smith. "The Flipped Classroom for Professional Development: Part I. Benefits and Strategies," The Journal of Continuing Education in Nursing, 44(10), pp. 437-438, 2013, http://goo.gl/MfvdkG [retrieved January 2017].

[10] J. Bergmann and A. Sams. "Flip your classroom: Reach every student in every class every day," International Society for Technology in Education, 2012.

[11] S. C. Kong. "Developing information literacy and critical thinking skills through domain knowledge learning in digital classrooms: An experience of practicing flipped classroom strategy," Computers & Education, 78, pp. 160-173, 2014, doi: http://dx.doi.org/10.1016/j.compedu.2014.05.009 [retrieved January 2016]

[12] S. C. Kong. "An experience of a three-year study on the development of critical thinking skills in flipped secondary classrooms with pedagogical and technological suppor," Computers & Education, 89, pp. 16-31, 2015, doi: http://dx.doi.org/10.1016/j.compedu.2015.08.017 [retrieved January 2017].

[13] N. Hamdan, P. McKnight, K. McKnight, and K. Arfstrom. The flipped learning model: A white paper based on the literature review titled "A review of flipped learning," 2013, http://www.flippedlearning.org/review [retrieved November 2016].

[14] N. C. Burbules, "Ubiquitous Learning and the Future of Teaching," Encounters on Education, 13, pp. 3-14, 2012, http://goo.gl/TJwpFj [retrieved November 2016].

[15] B. Tucker. "The Flipped Classroom," Education Next,12(1), pp. 82-83, 2012, http://goo.gl/7aGFgN [retrieved January 2017].

[16] C. Brame. "Flipping the classroom," Vanderbilt University, Center for Teaching, 2013, https://goo.gl/Wmxr0a [retrieved January 2017].

[17] N. Milman. "The Flipped Classroom Strategy: What Is it and How Can it Best be Used?," Distance Learning, 9(3), pp. 85, 2012, http://goo.gl/zgWacG [retrieved January 2017].

[18] Y. Chen, Y. Wang and N. Chen. "Is FLIP enough? Or should we use the FLIPPED model instead?," Computers & Education, 79, pp. 16-27, 2014, doi: 10.1016/j.compedu.2014.07.004 [retrieved January 2017].

[19] Observatory of Educational Innovation of Tecnológico de Monterrey, "Reverse Learning," Reporte Edutrends, 2014, http://goo.gl/aFiD55. [retrieved November 2016].

[20] R. Chiple and A. Ramos, "Accompaniment 100% in person for a 100% virtual mode," In P. Requeijo and C. Gaona (Eds.), Innovative Content in the Current University, pp. 189-204, 2014. Madrid, Spain: McGraw-Hill.

[21] E. Şengel, "To FLIP or not to FLIP: Comparative case study in higher education in Turkey," Computers in Human Behavior, 64, pp. 547-555, 2016.

EFL in Openness: A Project Based Language Learning with MOOCs and Online International Exchange

Yayoi Anzai
Kyushu University,
Innovation Center for Educational Resource (ICER),
Fukuoka, Japan
email: anzai.yayoi.450@m.kyushu-u.ac.jp

Abstract— **Open education has been getting much attention in various educational fields, and the language education is not an exception. It is a movement to enhance opportunities for learning, which empowered by the current technological revolution. In particular, the web has been employed in English as a foreign language (EFL) education to change a traditional classroom, and has created a community in which students are able to actively participate in, exchange ideas, and collaborate. By introducing two case studies, project based language learning with MOOCs and online international exchange, this paper explores new possibilities in Open learning and advocates the active use of ICT to foster English language learning.**

Keywords-English education; MOOCs; distance education; international exchange.

I. INTRODUCTION

Open education is a movement that expands educational opportunities. It relates to both methods and ideology. From the elite to minority, men to women, to education-benefitting areas to remote areas lacking access, it aims to expand opportunities for learning. There has been continued debate and trial and error amongst EFL teachers as to how best to remove the borders of the classroom, and approach English education from a global point of view that is also authentic. Due to development in Web technologies, it has become possible for learning to occur on a global scale, allowing for collaboration and sharing of knowledge and bringing about great changes in classroom structure [1]. The purpose of this paper is to report EFL instructional designs with open learning, and explores its potentiality.

Open Education's history can be classified into three generations, the first being about 40 years ago in Britain's Open University, which was introduced in print, radio, and television, the second being the impact of the Web (1.0 and 2.0) on the exchange of information across the world, and finally the Open Education of the 21st century- that is, the rise of the Open Educational Resources movement [2]. We can consider MOOCs to be a part of this. Bonk defines Open Education as something that anyone at any place and any time can undertake [3]. For example, Japanese students in Tokyo are able to listen to a lecture by a professor in the US in real time, using the internet. With variety of learning designs such as mobile learning and collaborative learning, Bonk outlines 10 main learning trends in education, describing them as 'openers' of education. The instruction in this paper was designed using one or more of these openers.

In Section 1, this study introduces how MOOCs can be integrated in a regular EFL classroom. In Section 2, the study introduces International exchange via ICT. These are the examples of EFL instructional designs which expanded opportunities for learning getting over the limitation of time and space. Realizing authentic language learning in global perspective without spending much money is a novel part of these EFL instructional designs.

II. CASE STUDIES

This section introduces two case studies, Project based language learning with MOOCs, and International exchange with ICT.

2.1. Project based language learning with MOOCs

Massive Open Online Courses (MOOCs) have its roots in a lecture delivered by Athabasca University's George Siemens and Canada's National Research Council's Stephen Downes's in 2008 titled 'Connectivism and Connective Knowledge' [4]. Now many of America's leading universities like Stanford and Harvard have been participating in MOOCs' platforms like Coursera and edX, and a dynamic Web technology-based educational environment enables students to participate in an online community synchronously or asynchronously. There is interaction between the instructor and the students, and among the students [5].

It is thought that one of the best ways to improve one's English is to study abroad, however that is not a realistic path for everyone to take. Furthermore, while texts like current affairs, essays, and stories are being used as teaching materials in textbooks, there are not many textbooks that deal with lectures from foreign universities. Subsequently, there has not been much exploration into how effective that material is for English education. So, this paper investigated the potential of the EFL instructional design with MOOCs as English teaching materials.

A pilot study was conducted in the first semester of 2013 at a Japanese university using a CALL. Their majors were International Economics and Politics. According to the results of a survey administered to the students, over 90% were unaware of MOOCs, so they were first introduced what MOOCs were. To help deepen the students' understanding, a statistics course offered by Princeton University through the popular platform Coursera was introduced, together with a discussion of Bonk's 'Instructional Ideas and Technology Tools for Online Success' that was delivered to an audience of over 4000 people in May 2012, and his articles about MOOCs [6][7]. The students were then split into groups of 3-4 people to complete the 'One Week Group Project'. They were asked to participate in a course of their choice for a minimum of one week, analyze the MOOC, and create a 20 minute presentation on their findings as it is seen Fig. 1.

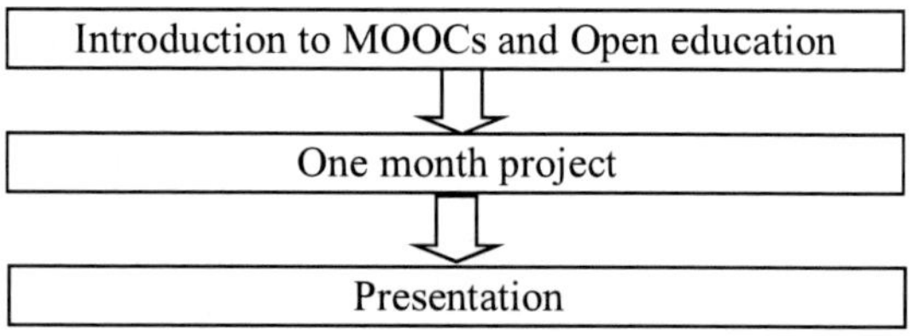

Figure 1. Structure of the EFL instruction

As a result, the students recognized usefulness of MOOCs to enhance English proficiency. This is reflected in responses to the question "Was MOOCs beneficial to improving your grasp of English?" as shown in Fig. 2 which details results of a survey conducted post-experiment. Positive responses were recorded across the board.

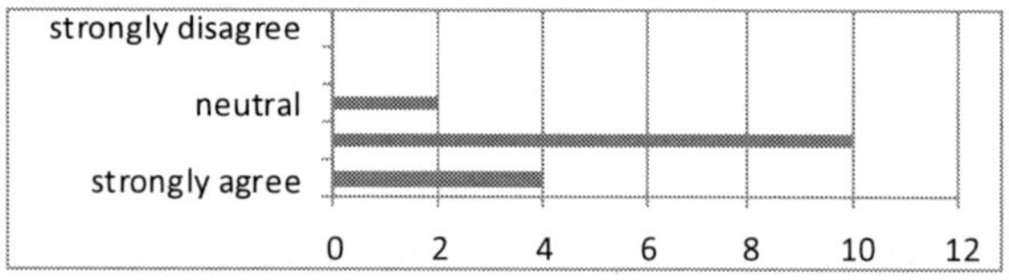

Figure 2. "Do you think MOOCs will enhance English proficiency?"

More concretely, firstly, there seems to be potential as preparation for study abroad. Since MOOCs broadcasts lectures from different universities, it is possible to use them to get used to American lecture styles, identify important vocabulary, practice reasoning, note-taking, and so on. Secondly, thanks to the learning communities around MOOCs, classes can move beyond being passive experiences to ones where students can provide their output. Students were surprisingly active in posting questions in an online community. The Internet, as a platform to get one's voice out into the world, would be good for improving one's courage and confidence in using English. It is important to consider that being able to get one's voice out online is vital for today's increasingly global society. Thirdly, students were not found to have technical issues with the introduction of MOOCs. The lesson was conducted in the CALL classroom, so the students, as "digital natives" [9] of the modern world who had been using computers and the Internet since birth, were already used to e-learning, which may have been a reason for the lack of stress. Fourthly, the students did not seem to experience any major language difficulties while participating in their MOOC. This may have been due to the fact that this class was targeted at students with intermediate to advanced English ability, and the subjects chosen in the MOOCs were easily understood subjects like music, health, and food. In addition, the lectures delivered were fairly visual. Fifth, it was observed that the final One Week Group Project presentations promoted critical thinking. As opposed to just reporting their findings in their presentations, some students had moved beyond that to evaluate the course structure and the pros and cons of learning with MOOCs. As such, this educational activity was a means to get the students to integrate their learning and think critically. This study's results unveiled the possibilities of MOOCs for English learning. MOOCs promises to be a new, appealing type of English study, in addition to stories, essays, news, songs etc.

2.2 International Exchange with ICT

A case study in using Web technologies for international exchange will be introduced in this section. In this class, Japanese and American university students conducted international exchange via writing. On the Japanese side, warm up activities were performed during the first semester of 2013. The aim of this class was to experience using English, a global language, as a communication tool. Our partner was the University of Kansas's English as a Second Language (ESL) class, consisting of students from China, South Korea, South-East Asia and the Middle East. Together, the classes jointly aimed to conduct an asynchronous international exchange, and utilize English as a communication tool.

Voicethread was the chosen tool for this exchange. The students from the University of Kansas's ESL class introduced the cities they would like to visit, and the Japanese students made comments and asked questions in English, to which the University of Kansas students responded. Fig. 3 is a screenshot from the international exchange. The students at the University of Kansas posted pictures of their favorite places together with their descriptions. Fig. 4 illustrates examples of this interaction. "Hi, I am A. I'm going to tell you about my hometown. My home town is a famous place in Saudi Arabia..." This student introduced his hometown, to which the Japanese student replied, "Hi, I am B from Japan. I have a friend from Saudi Arabia, so I want to visit there someday..." They read and responded with their own impressions.

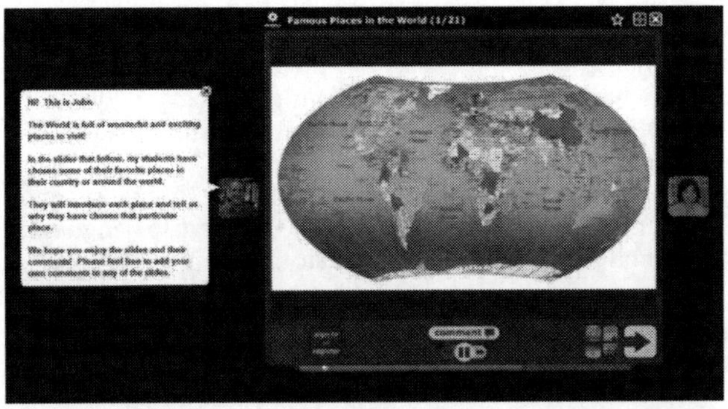

Figure 3. Greetings of an American and Japanese EFL instructors

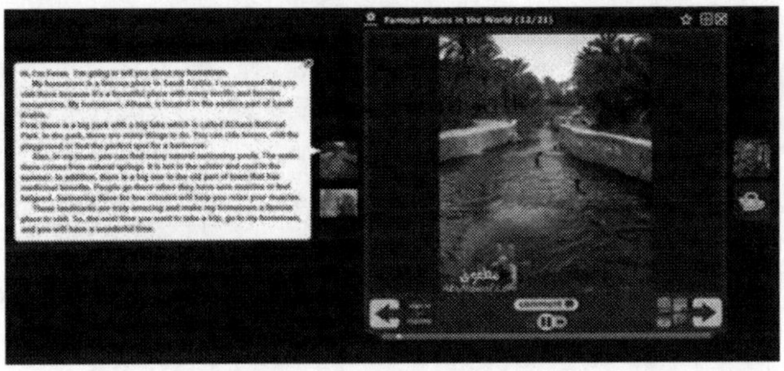

Figure 4. An example of the students' writing

English educators that employ ICT often desire international exchange as a means of crafting an authentic experience. Nowadays, there are many tools like Skype that can facilitate this. The Web tool used in this case is not complex either, being very simple to operate and requiring little set up before being able to be used in a class. Also in this type of international exchange, the difference in time zones are an issue, but the asynchronous style of contact meant that collaborative work was still able to be achieved. Both sides of the exchange could feel the presence of the other as they communicated. Due to concerns over student privacy, the students used icons instead of actual photos to represent themselves. That said, there is a gap between knowing that using English on the Web would allow one to communicate with people around the world, and actually being able to communicate with people around the world on the Web–in other words, having the awareness about something vs. actually experiencing something. Beyond studying English, it is also important to experience what it means to communicate in English.

III. CONCLUSION

These two case studies illustrate how ICT expanded opportunities for authentic English language learning. By using MOOCs, EFL learners can get access to quality educational contents as well as having interactions with learners around the globe. The same hold true for the International exchange. This interaction among learners is the strong characteristic of language learning with current technologies.

Taking into account second-languages and spoken foreign languages, it is estimated that 1.4-1.5 billion people in the world are English speakers [8]. In addition, the number of people who use English on the Internet are thought to be even higher, highlighting the importance of being able to communicate in the language. The English educators of today now face a world where technology they would not have dreamed of as a child is available, and they are aiming for a more authentic classroom experience by introducing technology into the classroom. As is seen, the incorporation of ICT in English education in universities has the possibility to traverse the boundaries of time and physical distance created by the walls of the traditional classroom, and allow participation, interaction, and collaboration in a global community. We can open the English classroom to the world with computers and mobile technologies. How this is incorporated into each English class will depend on the aims and curriculum design of each individual class, as well as creativity of the EFL teachers.

ACKNOWLEDGMENT

This study was partly supported by a Grant-in-Aid for Scientific Research (C), JSPS KAKENHI Number 26350332 from April 2014-March 2017 with representative researcher: Dr.Yayoi Anzai.

REFERENCES

[1] Y. Anzai, "Digital trends among Japanese university students: Podcasting and wikis as tools for learning," In C. J. Bonk, M. M. Lee, and T. Reynolds, (eds.), A Special Passage Through Asia E-Learning Chesapeake, VA: AACE, pp. 547-552, 2009.

[2] A. Kanwar, and V. Balaji, Three generation of open education: future implications. Paper presented at World Innovation Summit for Education, Doha, Qatar. Available from http://dspace.col.org/bitstream/handle/11599/1223/2010_Kanwar_Three_Generations_Transcript.pdf?sequence=1&isAllowed=y 2017.02.04

[3] C. Bonk, The World is open. San Francisco: Jossy-Bass, 2009.

[4] S. Downes, Free learning, 2011. Retrieved from http://www.downes.ca/files/books/FreeLearning.pdf 2017.02.03.

[5] Y. Anzai, What about MOOCs for language education? In Proceedings of World Conference on E-Learning in Corporate, Government, Healthcare, and Higher Education 2013, Chesapeake, VA: AACE, pp. 557-561, 2013.

[6] C. Bonk, Want some MOOC with your TV dinner? Available from

http://www.evolllution.com/distance_online_learning/want-some-mooc-with-your-tv-dinner-part-1/ 2017.02.03
[7] C. Bonk, (2013). Want some MOOC with your TV dinner? Available from http://www.evolllution.com/opinions/want-some-mooc-with-your-tv-dinner-part-2/ 2017.02.03
[8] M. Prensky, Digital natives, Digital immigrants, 2001. Available from http://www.marcprensky.com/writing/Prensky%20-%20Digital%20Natives,%20Digital%20Immigrants%20-%20Part1.pdf 2017.02.03.
[9] D. Crystal, D., English worldwide, In Hogg, R., and Denison, D. (eds.) A history of the English language, Cambridge: Cambridge University Press, pp. 420-439, 2006.

Towards Automatic Coding of Collaborative Learning Data with Deep Learning Technology

Chihiro Shibata
School of Computer Sciences
Tokyo University of Technology
Tokyo, Japan
email:shibatachh@stf.teu.ac.jp

Kimihiko Ando
Cloud Service Center
Tokyo University of Technology
Tokyo, Japan
email:ando@stf.teu.ac.jp

Taketoshi Inaba
Graduate School of Bionics, Computer and Media Sciences
Tokyo University of Technology
Tokyo, Japan
email:inaba@stf.teu.ac.jp

***Abstract*— In Computer Supported Collaborative Learning (CSCL) research, gaining a guideline to carry out appropriate scaffolding by analyzing mechanism of successful collaborative interaction and extracting indicators to identify groups where collaborative process is not going well, can be considered as the most important preoccupation, both for research and for educational implementation. And to study this collaborative learning process, different approaches have been tried. In this paper, we opt for the verbal data analysis; its advantage of this method is that it enables quantitative processing while maintaining qualitative perspective, with collaborative learning data of considerable size. However, coding large scale educational data is extremely time consuming and sometimes goes beyond men's capacity. So, in recent years, there have also been attempts to automate complex coding by using machine learning technology. In this background, with large scale data generated in our CSCL system, we have tried to implement automation of high precision coding utilizing deep learning methods, which are derived from the leading edge technology of machine learning. The results indicate that our approach with deep learning methods is promising, outperforming the machine learning baselines, and that the prediction accuracy could be improved by constructing models more sensitive to the context of conversation.**

Keywords-CSCL; leaning analytics; coding scheme; deep learning methods.

I. INTRODUCTION

A. Analysis of collaborative process

One of the greatest research interests in the actual Computer Supported Collaborative Learning (CSCL) research is to analyze its social process from a social constructionist viewpoint, and key research questions are as follows: how knowledge and meanings are shared within a group, what types of conflict, synchronization and adjustment of opinions occur, and how knowledge is constructed from discussions. And answering to these questions enables to develop more effective scaffolding methods and CSCL system and tools.

In earlier researches at initial stage of CSCL, the focus was on each individual within a collaborating group, and the main point of interest had been how significantly a personal learning outcome was affected by characteristic types of a group (such as group size, group composition, learning tasks, and communication media) [1]. However, it gradually became clear that those characteristics are complexly connected and intertwined with each other, and showing causal relation to a specific result was extremely difficult. From the 1990s, the interest in CSCL research had moved away from awareness of the issue on how a personal learning is established within a group, to attempting to explain the process by clarifying the details of group interactions when learning is taking place within a group [2].

However, attempting to analyze collaborative process goes beyond merely shifting a research perspective; it also leads to fundamental re-examination of its analytical methodology. In other words, this involves a shift from quantitative analysis to qualitative analysis. Naturally, there are useful data among quantitative data saved within CSCL system, such as the number of contributions within a group, the number of contributions by each group member, and in some cases contribution attributes obtained from system interface (sentence opener), but those are very much a mere surface data. The most important data for analysis are contributions in chats, images/sounds within tools such as Skype, and various outputs generated in the process of collaborative learning; for analysis of those, ethnomethodologies such as conversation analysis and video analysis have been invoked [3] [4].

However, those researches by their very nature tend to be in-depth case studies of collaborative activities with a limited number of groups and have the disadvantage of not at all being easy to derive a guideline that has a certain level of universality and can be applicable in other contexts.

Therefore, researches have been carried out using verbal data analysis method that carry out coding from a perspective of linguistic or collaborative learning activities on a certain volume of language data generated in collaborative learning and analyzing them [5][6][7]. The advantage of this method is that it enables quantitative processing while maintaining qualitative perspective, with collaborative learning data of considerable size as the subject, while coding them manually is an extremely time consuming task which goes sometimes beyond men's capacity. For example, Persico et al. developed a technological tool which helps the tutors to code the contributions in chats and displays quantitative information about the qualitative information and coding data [8]. However, given that the coding procedure itself remains manual in most existing studies [9][10], there is an insurmountable limit in front of big data. Hence, we seek an automatic coding technique for a large scale collaborative learning data with deep learning methods.

B. *Educational data and Learning Analytics*

With the progress of educational cloud implementation in educational institutions, data generated in Learning Management System (LMS), e-learning, Social Network Service (SNS), Massive Open Online Course (MOOC) and others are increasing rapidly, and a new research approach called Learning Analytics (LA) that tries to gain knowledge that would lead to support of learning and educational activities by analyzing those educational big data is becoming more active [11][12]. Big educational data obtained from CSCL system integrated in educational cloud at a campus, such as conversation data, submitted documents and images/sounds of learning activities, will certainly become a subject for analysis in the near future: therefore, it is believed that we are coming into a time when it is necessary to seriously examine a new possibility of collaborative learning research as LA. Due to such background, in this research we have reconstructed CSCL system that has been operating in a campus server for the last five years as a module within Moodle, which is a LMS within the campus cloud, and have already structured an environment that can be operated within the campus and collect/analyze collaborative learning data.

C. *The goal and purpose of this study*

The goal of our research is to analyze large-scale collaborative data from LA perspective as described above and discover the mechanism of activation and deactivation of collaborative activity process which could not be gained from micro level case studies up to now. Furthermore, this research, based on its results, aims to implement supports in authentic learning/educational contexts, such as real-time monitoring of collaborative process and scaffolding to groups that are not becoming activated.

In this paper, as the first step towards this goal, we present work in progress, which attempts to develop an automation technique for coding of chat data and verifies its accuracy. To be more specific, a substantial volume of chat data is coded manually, and has a part of that learnt as training data in deep learning methods, which are derived from the leading edge technologies for machine learning; afterwards, automatic coding of the raw data is carried out. For validation of accuracy, the effectiveness of using deep learning methods is assessed by comparing accuracy against Naive Bayes and Support Vector Machines, which are baselines of machine learning algorithm used in existing studies that carried out automatic coding by machine learning.

D. *Structure of this paper*

This paper is structured as follows. In Section II, we present the related work. The Section III describes our datasets and coding scheme. The approach with deep learning methods for automatic coding is discussed in Section IV. Then, our experiment and results from our evaluation are described in Section V. Section VI concludes the paper.

II. Related Work

Since deep learning can often outperform existing machine learning methods, such as SVMs, it has been applied in various research areas, such as image recognition and natural language processing [13]. Text classification is an important task in natural learning processing, for which various deep learning methods have been exploited extensively in recent studies. A structure called a CNN has been applied for text classification using word- or character-level modeling [14][15]. LSTM [16] and gated recurrent units (GRUs) [17] are popular structures for RNNs. Both structures are known to outperform existing models, such as n-grams, and are thus widely available as learning models for sequential data like text. RNNs are also applied to text classification in various ways [18][19]. For instance, Yang et al. used a bidirectional GRU with attention modeling by setting two hierarchical layers that consist of the word and sentence encoders [18].

In the field of CSCL, some researchers have tried to apply text classification technology to chat logs. The most representative studies would be Rosé and her colleagues'works [20][21][22]. For example, they applied text classification technology to a relatively large CSCL corpus that had been coded by human coders using the coding scheme with 7 dimensions, developed by Weinbeger and Fisher [21][23]. McLaren's Argunaut project took a similar approach: he used online discussions coded manually to train machine-learning classifiers in order to predict the appearance of these discussions characteristics in the new e-discussion[24]. However, it should be pointed out that all these prior studies rely on the machine learning techniques before deep learning studies emerge.

III. Data and Coding Scheme

In this section, we explain how we collected our dataset and what coding scheme we adopted to categorize the dataset.

A. Data Description

Our dataset obtained through chat function within the system, comes from conversations among students while carrying out online collaborative learning in university lectures using CSCL, which had been previously developed by the researchers of this study [25].

This CSCL is used without face to face contact; therefore, these data are all from occasions when unacquainted and separated students formed groups within lecture halls at the campus. And within the system all names of students are shown in nicknames, so that even if students knew each other they would not recognize each other.

The overview of CSCL contributions data used in this research is shown in Table 1. The number of lectures is seven and all classes of these lectures form groups of three to four; in fact, there are a lot of data that we could not process by coding them in this research. Learning times vary depending on the class, from 45 to 90 minutes. In total, the dataset contains 11504 contributions; there are 202 groups from all the classes, with 426 participating students; since students attend multiple classes, the number of participating students are smaller than the product of number of groups and number of students in a group.

Table 2 shows a conversation example of chat. This is a conversation example of three students.

TABLE I. CONTRIBUTIONS DATA USED IN THIS STUDY

Number of Lectures	7 Lectures
Member of Groups	3-4 people
Learning Time	45-90 mintutes
Number of Groups	202 groups
Number of Students	426 students

TABLE II. CONVERSATION EXAMPLE (TRANLATION FROM JAPANESE)

Talker	Contents
D	Where do you want to change?
E	That's right ··· I guess, first of all, we definitely need to change the question, and then, what about the well-formed formula?
D	How is it that changes only the third line of the question?
D	Regarding the well-formed formula, it's the final part after ⊃.
E	That's good idea.
F	I agree. How do we want to change that?

B. Coding scheme

In accordance with our manual for code assignment, one code label is assigned to one contribution in a chat. There are 16 types of code labels as shown in Table 3, and one of those labels is assigned for all cases.

All labels in our dataset are coded by two people; the coincidence rate between the labels assigned was 67%. However, when we reviewed the resultant coding data, it was discovered that there were duplicated labels for some contributions, and some labels had variances depending on the coder; therefore, after conferring among us, we unified labels and re-coded the contributions. The resultant number of labels assigned is shown in Table 3. Concordance rate is 82.3% and this is a high concordance rate with 0.800 Kappa coefficient, and we consider this to be sufficiently practical for use as an educational dataset in deep learning methods. Fig. 1 shows the frequencies of the labels in the dataset. Nine labels describe more than 90% of occurrences; label occurrences appear to have a long-tail distribution. The main purpose of this study is to learn and infer these labels from posted contributions.

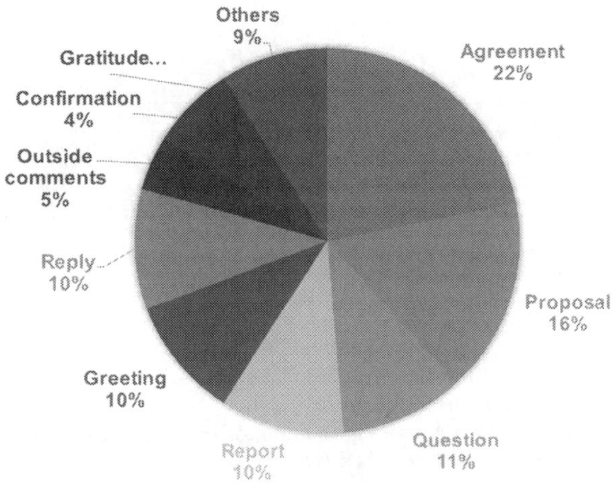

Figure 1. Ratio of each conversational coding labels

IV. APPROACH -- DEEP LEARNING

In recent years, deep learning technology has led to dramatic developments in the field of artificial intelligence. Deep learning is a general framework of learning methods that use neural networks with millions of weight parameters. The weights in neural networks are optimized so that their output coincides with labels in the given data. With the recent development of parallel computing using Graphics Processing Units (GPUs) and optimization algorithms, machines are able to learn large numbers of parameters from large datasets at realistic costs.

To try automatic coding, we adapt three types of deep neural network (DNN) structures: a convolutional neural network (CNN) -based model and two bidirectional Long short-term memory (LSTM) -based models, LSTM and Sequence-to-Sequence (Seq2Seq). The first and second models take only a single contribution as input and cannot refer to context information in the conversation. Conversely, the Seq2Seq model can capture context information by using a pair of sentences as its input, which represent source and replay contributions.

A. CNN-based model

The CNN-based model uses the network architecture proposed by Kim et al. (Fig. 2). Before training, all words in

TABLE III. List of labels

Tag	Meaning of tag	Contribution example	Number of times used
Agreement	Affirmative reply	I think that's good	5033
Proposal	Conveying opinion, or yes/no question	How about five of us here make the submission?	3762
Question	Other than yes/no question	What shall we do with the title?	2399
Report	Reporting own status	I corrected the complicated one	2394
Greeting	Greeting to other members	I'm looking forward to working with you	2342
Reply	Other replies	It looks that way!	2324
Outside comments	Contribution on matters other than assignment contents Opinions on systems and such	My contribution is disappearing already; so fast! A bug	1049
Confirmation	Confirm the assignment and how to proceed	Would you like to submit it now?	949
Gratitude	Gratitude to other members	Thanks!	671
Switchover	A contribution to change event being handled, such as moving on to the next assignment	Shall we give it a try?	625
Joke	Joke to other members	You should, like, learn it physically? :)	433
Request	Requesting somebody to do some task	Can either of you reply?	354
Correction	Correcting past contribution	Sorry, I meant children	204
Disagreement	Negative reply	I think 30 minute is too long	160
Complaint	Dissatisfactions towards assignments or systems	I must say the theme isn't great	155
Noise	Contribution that does not make sense	?meet? day???	143

the data are converted to word vectors. Word vectors are often obtained by pre-training using another external dataset. In this study, we implemented two types of word vectors: 1) vectors obtained by applying word2vec (the skipped gram model with negative sampling) to all Japanese text in Wikipedia, and 2) randomly initialized vectors that are tuned simultaneously with the CNN.

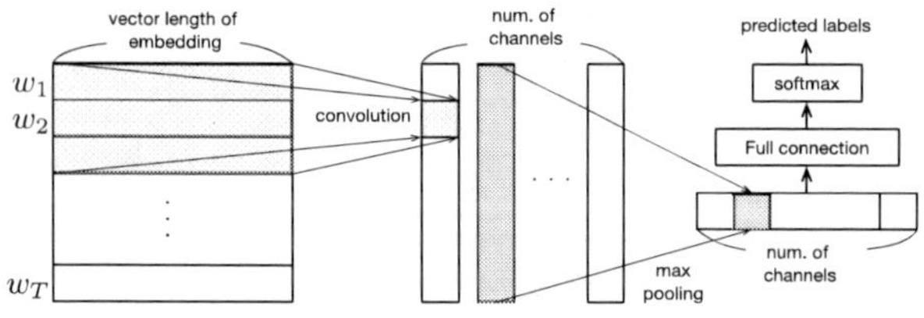

Figure 2. CNN-based model

B. Bidirectional LSTM-based model

An LSTM is a recurrent neural networks (RNNs) that is carefully constructed so that it can capture long-distance dependencies in sequential data. Generally speaking, an RNN consists of input vector x_t and output vector y_t for each time t. To obtain the output $y_{\{t\}}$, the previous output vector $y_{\{t-1\}}$ is fed to the neural network along with the current input vector x_t. The LSTM has another hidden vector, c_t, called the *state vector* in addition to the input and output vectors. While the state vector is also output from the neural network, it is computed to track long-distance relations through a function called a *forget gate,* which is designed to decide whether the state vector should be changed. We feed word vectors into the two-layer LSTM network sequentially in both the forward and reverse directions. After all words in a contribution are input, both output vectors are concatenated and fed into the two-layer fully-connected network and the softmax layer to obtain classification results. Fig. 3 illustrates this architecture.

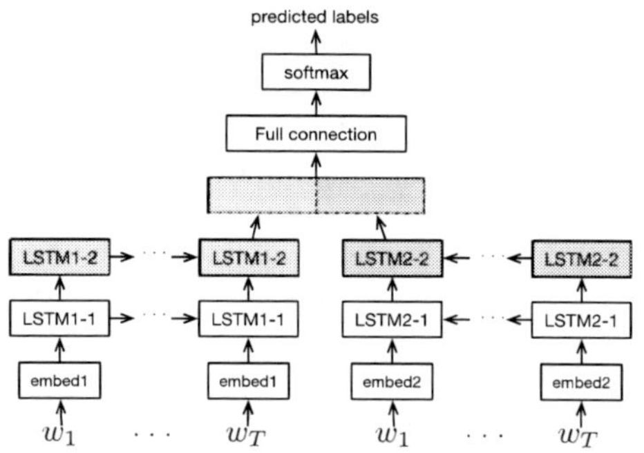

Figure 3. Bidirectional LSTM-based

C. Bidirectional Seq2Seq-based model

Each contribution is a part of a conversation; therefore, to classify labels more accurately, we must account for conversational contexts. To do this, we convert all contributions in conversations into pairs of *source* and *reply* contributions. Even if a user posts a contribution that does not explicitly cite another, we assume that it cites a previous contribution. We also suppose that the first contribution of each conversation cites the empty string. To construct a model that regards the source contribution as a conversational context and the reply as a representation of the user's intention, we use the Seq2seq framework. Seq2seq

[26] was originally proposed as a neural model using RNNs for machine translation, and later applied to other tasks, such as conversational generation [27]. It consists of two separate LSTM networks, called the encoder and decoder. We use two-layer LSTM networks for both the encoder and decoder. Words are sequentially fed in both the forward and reverse directions. Output vectors from decoders are concatenated and fed into the two-layer fully-connected network and the softmax layer (Fig. 4).

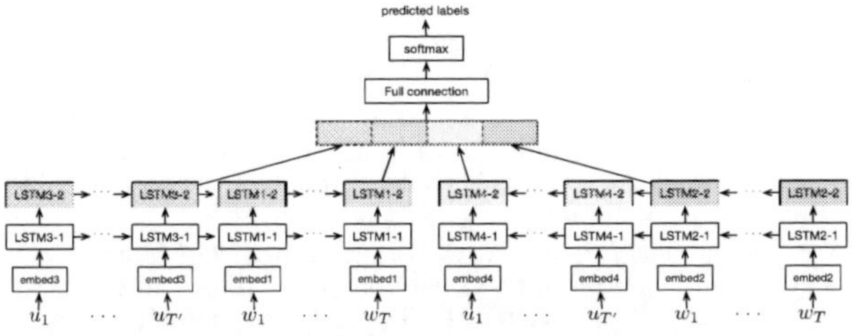

Figure 4. Bidirectional Seq2Seq-based model

V. EVALUATION

For each contribution, we trimmed sentences beginning with the symbol ">," which were automatically generated by the system. Since all the data consist of Japanese text, morphological analysis was needed. We split texts into words using a tool called MeCab. Replacing low-frequency words with "unknown," the vocabulary size was decreased to approximately 4,000. Each contribution was given two labels annotated by different people; we removed contributions that were assigned two different labels. We used 90% of the remaining 8,015 contributions as training data and 10% as test data. The accuracy of the learning result for each model is measured with the test data.

A. Baseline Methods

For comparison, we used three classifiers; Naive Bayes, a linear support vector machine (SVM), and an SVM with a radial basis function (RBF) kernel. We also used two types of feature sets: unigrams only and unigrams and bigrams. For the SVM classifiers, in order to improve the classification accuracy, input vectors were obtained by normalizing zero-one vectors whose elements represent occurrences of unigrams or bigrams.

B. Model Parameters and Learning

Model parameters, such as the vector sizes of layers, are determined as follows. Both the size of word embedding and the size of the last fully connected layer are 200 for all models. We set the patch size of the convolutional layer in the vertical direction to 4 and the number of channels to 256 for the CNN-based models. We set the size of both LSTM layers to 800 for the LSTM and Seq2Seq models.

Models are learned by stochastic descent gradient (SDG) using an optimization method called Adam. To avoid overfitting, iteration was stopped at 10 epochs for the LSTM-based methods and 30 epochs for the CNN-based methods. Due to the fluctuation in accuracy results between epochs, we took the average of the last 5 epochs to measure the accuracy of each model. To prevent overfitting, dropout was applied to the last and second-last fully connected layers.

C. Experimental Results

Table 4 shows the accuracies of the three DNN models and baseline methods. Overall, the DNN models outperform the baselines, even as the SVMs maintain their high performance. Among baseline methods, the SVM with the RBF kernel achieved the highest accuracy. For the CNN-based models, using word vectors trained using the Wikipedia data slightly enhanced accuracy. For LSTM-based models, bidirectional processing yielded slightly higher accuracy than single-directional processing.

There was no significant difference in the accuracies of the CNN model using Wikipedia and the bidirectional LSTM model. Both of these methods outperformed the best of SVMs by 1–2%.

Seq2Seq model outperformed other methods clearly; the best of SVMs by 5-6% and other DNN models by 3-4%.

TABLE IV. PREDICTIVE ACCURACIES FOR BASELINES AND DEEP-NEURAL-NETWORK MODELS

Naïve Bayes		SVM(Linear)		SVM(RBF Kernel)	
unigram	uni+bigram	unigram	uni+bigram	unigram	uni+bigram
0.554	0.598	0.642	0.659	**0.664**	0.659

CNN		LSTM		Seq2Seq	
with wikipedia	w.o. wikipedia	single-direction	bidirection	bidirection	bidir. w. interm.
0.686	0.677	0.676	0.678	**0.718**	0.717

The kappa coefficient for the bidirectional LSTM model was 0.63, which is sufficiently high. However, to automatically comprehend and judge the activities of users from only the labels inferred by machines, the kappa coefficient must be improved. By using the Seq2Seq model, which is able to capture the contextual information from the source or the adjacent contribution, the kappa coefficient was improved to 0.723.

Hereafter, we analyze the misclassification of each label individually. The precision and recall for each label are shown in Table 5. Of the ten most frequent labels, the precision of "Greeting" predictions were highest (F1: 0.94) and that of "Agreement" was the second highest (F1: 0.83). "Question" was also predicted with high accuracy (F1: 0.77). These results are consistent with our intuition, as both seem to be easy to infer from the contributions themselves, without knowing their context. In contrast, as Table 5 shows, the label "Reply" was hard for our model to predict. That performed worst with respect to the recall, tending to be misclassified as an "Agreement", "Proposal" or "Report," as shown in the confusion matrix (Fig. 5). This can be solved if richer context in neighboring contributions is used as input to classifiers in addition to the source contribution.

VI. CONCLUSION AND FUTURE WORK

As the first step to analyze collaborative process of big educational data, we tried to automate time-consuming

TABLE V. PRESITION AND RECALL FOR EACH LABEL (RESULT OF BI-DIRECTIONAL LSTM)

	Presition	Recall	F1-value
Agreement	0.85	0.81	0.83
Proposal	0.73	0.74	0.73
Question	0.75	0.8	0.77
Report	0.64	0.62	0.63
Greeting	0.94	0.94	0.94
Reply	0.62	0.46	0.53
Outside comments	0.17	0.47	0.25
Confirmation	0.58	0.74	0.65
Gratitude	0.67	0.67	0.67

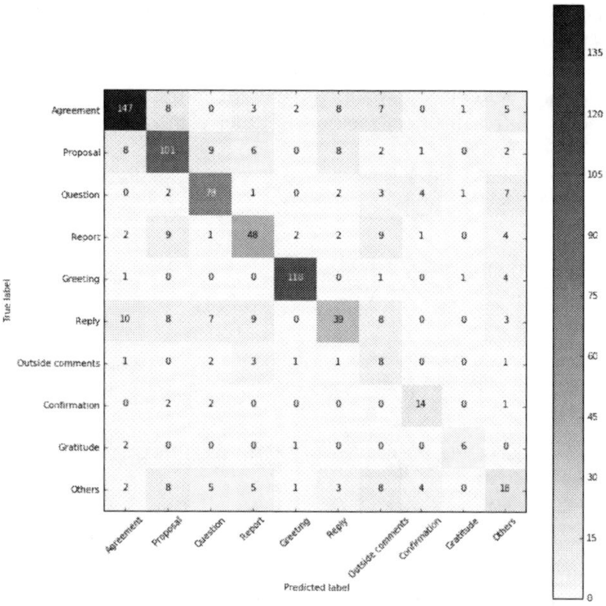

Figure-5. Confusion matrix for the Seq2S2q model.

coding task by using deep learning methods. The result was promising; our approach, particularly, Seq2Seq model outperformed other methods clearly; the best of SVMs by 5-6% and other DNN models by 3-4%. It seems that this model could obtain almost the same predictive accuracy with other coding schemes than ours, for the reason that our coding scheme is sufficiently complex with 16 labels, based not on the surface information, but on the contextual significance of each contribution.

As for the future research directions, we may have two approaches to pursue. The first approach concerns coding scheme. Our scheme, based on speech acts, was sufficiently complex, but not global. To capture the collaborative process more precisely, it will be necessary to construct a coding scheme which is more sensitive to details of interaciton and social cognitive process of learning. The second approach is about DNN models. To improve prediction accuracy, it may be effective to introduce an attention model to our DNN models. In addition, the context of conversation should be considered. To capture context more precisely, it may be necessary to construct more complex models that take multiple preceding contributions as input vectors.

ACKNOWLEDGMENT

This work was supported by JSPS KAKENHI Grant Number 26350289 and 16K01134.

REFERENCES

[1] G. Stahl, T. Koschmann, and D. Suthers, "Computer-supported collaborative learning," In The Cambridge handbook of the learning science, K. Sawyer, Eds. Cambridge university press, pp.479-500, 2014.

[2] P. Dillenbourg, P. Baker, A. Blaye, and C. O'Malley, "The evolution of research on collaborative learning," In Learning in humans and machines: Towards an interdisciplinary learning science, P. Reimann and H. Spada, Eds. Oxford: Elservier, pp. 189-211, 1996.

[3] T. Koschmann, "Understanding understanding in action," Journal of Pragmatics, 43, pp435-437, 2011.

[4] T. Koschmann, G. Stahl, and A.Zemel, "The video analyst's manifesto (or The implications of Garfinkel's policies for the development of a program of video analysis research within the learning science)," In Video reseach in the learning sciences, R. Goldman, R. Pea, B. Barron and S. Derry, Eds. Routledge, pp.133-144, 2007.

[5] M. Chi, "Quantifying qualitative analyses of verbal data : A pratical gauide," Journal of the Leanrnig Science, 6(3), pp.271-315, 1997.

[6] A. Meier, H. Spada, and N. Rummel, "A rating scheme for assesseing the quality of coputer-supported collaboration processes," International Jounala of Computer Suppported Collaborative Learning, 2, pp.63-86, 2007.

[7] H. Jeong, "Verbal data analysis for understanding interacitons," In The International Handbook of Collaborative Learning, C. Hmelo-Silver, A. M. O'Donnell, C. Chan and C. Chin, Eds. Routledge, pp.168-183, 2013.

[8] D. Persico, F. Pozzi, and L. Sarti, "Monitaring collaborative activities in computer supported learning," Distance Education, 31(1), pp.5-22, 2010.

[9] L. Lipponen, M. Rahikainen, J. Lamillo, and K. Hakkarainen, "Patterns of participation and discourse in elementary students'computer-supported collaborative learning,", Learning and Instruction, 13, pp.487-509, 2003.

[10] S. Schrire, "Knowledge building in asynchronous discussion groups: Going beyond quantitative analysis," Computer & Education 46, pp.49-70, 2006.

[11] 1st Internationa Conference on Learning Analytics and Knowledge. [Online]. Avaiable from: https://tekri.athabascau.ca/analytics/ 2016.11.29

[12] B. R. Schaun and P. S. Inventado, "Educational data mining and learning analytics," In Learning Analytics, J. A. Larusoon and B. White, Eds. Springer, pp.61-75, 2014.

[13] Y. LeCun, Y. Bengio, and G. Hinton, "Deep learning," Nature, 521(7553), pp.436--444, 2015.

[14] Y. Kim, "Convolutional neural networks for sentence classification," arXiv preprint arXiv:1408.5882, 2014.

[15] X. Zhang, J. Zhao, and Y.LeCun. "Character-level convolutional networks for text classification," In Proceedings of the 28th International Conference on Neural Information Processing Systems (NIPS2015), pp.649-657, 2015.

[16] S. Hochreiter and J. Schmidhuber, "Long short-term memory," Neural Computation, 9(8), pp.1735--1780, 1997.

[17] J. Chung, C. Gulcehre, K. Hyun Cho and Y. Bengio, "Empirical Evaluation of Gated Recurrent Neural Networks on Sequence Modeling," arXiv preprint arXiv:1412.3555, 2014.

[18] Z. Yang, et al., "Hierarchical Attention Networks for Document Classification," In Proceedings of the 2016 Conference of the North American Chapter of the Association for Computational Linguistics(NAACL2016), Human Language Technologies, 2016.

[19] D. Tang, B. Qin, and T. Liu, "Document modeling with gated recurrent neural network for sentiment classification," In Proceedings of the 2015 Conference on Empirical Methods in Natural Language Processing(EMNLP2016), pp.1422–1432, 2015.

[20] C. Rosé, et al., "Towards an interactive assessment framework for engineering design project based learning," In Proceedings of DETC2007, 2007.

[21] C. Rosé, et al., "Analyzing collaborative learning processes automatically: Exploiting the advances of computational linguistics in computer-supported collaborative learning," International Journal of Computer Supported Collaborative Learning, 3(3), pp.237-271, 2008.

[22] G. Gweon, S. Soojin, J. Lee, S. Finger and C.Rosé, "A framework for assessment of student project groups on-line and off-line," In Analyzing Interactions in CSCL: Methods, Approaches and Issues, S. Putambekar, G.Erkens and C. Hmelo-Silver Eds. Springer, pp.293-317, 2011.

[23] A. Weinberger and F. Fischer, "A frame work to analyze arugmetative knowledge construciton in computer-supported learning," Computer & Education, 46(1), pp.71-95, 2006.

[24] B. McLaren, O. Scheuer, M. De Laat, H. Hever and R. De Groot, "Using machine learning techniques to analysze and support mediation of student e-discussions," In Proceedings of artificial intelligence in education, 2007.

[25] T. Inaba and K. Ando. "Development and Evaluation of CSCL System for Large Classrooms Using Question-Posing Script." International Journal on Advances in Software, 7(3&4),pp.590-600, 2014.

[26] D. Bahdanau, K. Cho, and Y. Bengio, "Neural machine translation by jointly learning to align and translate," arXiv preprint arXiv, pp.1409.0473, 2014.

[27] O. Vinyals and Q. V. Le, " A Neural Conversational Mode," arXiv preprint arXiv:1506.05869, (ICML Deep Learning Workshop 2015), 2015.

The Web MIDI API in On-Line Applications for Music Education

Luca A. Ludovico

Laboratorio di Informatica Musicale
Dipartimento di Informatica
Università degli Studi di Milano
Email: luca.ludovico@unimi.it

***Abstract*—This work discusses a recent browser technology known as the Web MIDI API to design and release browser applications for music. This application programming interface (API), still under development by the Audio group of the World Wide Web Consortium (W3C), provides support to the Musical Instrument Digital Interface (MIDI) protocol, enabling web applications to interface with MIDI input and output devices on the client system and send and receive MIDI messages. The paper critically analyzes advantages and drawbacks currently presented by the Web MIDI API in the context of web-based music education. In the final part of this work, a case study will be discussed.**

Keywords–MIDI; Web applications; Music education; Web MIDI API.

I. Introduction

In computing, a *web application* – or *web app* – is a client-server software application in which the client or user interface runs in a web browser. Web applications are very popular, since they offer a number of advantages: they are cross-platform, easy to update, often free, and they should not require ad hoc installations. The distribution of web applications is immediate and their audience potentially includes all users owning a network-attached device equipped with a web browser. These characteristics are very important for educational applications too. For instance, portability and compatibility are at the base of the *Bring Your Own Device* (BYOD) paradigm, whose advantages, risks and perspectives in the educational field have been discussed in [1], [2], [3]. As stated in [4], the most important quality criteria for the success of web applications include reliability, usability, security, availability, scalability, maintainability, and time-to-market. Most of these aspects must be considered also in the design and implementation of applications for students.

The Musical Interface for Digital Instruments (MIDI) is a well-known and widely-adopted protocol to exchange messages among compatible music devices. Even if nowadays MIDI could seem out of date and naive to non-experts – suffice it to recall that the maximum bitrate of the protocol is 31.25 kbps and the structure of messages is composed by 7-bit packages – it is still largely supported by professional music and audio equipment. Some recent initiatives are bringing new life to the format. In this sense, it is worth citing: the recent reorganization of the official web site [5], with updated contents, a new graphical layout and a *News* section; the release on the marketplace of innovative music controllers, such as the *ROLI Seaboard Grand*, able to extend the potential of the original MIDI protocol still preserving full compatibility [6]; and finally, the establishment of interest groups which join academia and industry in order to apply MIDI to new contexts and meet recent technological requirements. In this light, the World Wide Web Consortium (W3C) launched an initiative aiming to design and implement the so-called Web MIDI API. This specification defines an Application Programming Interface (API) supporting the MIDI protocol, enabling web applications to enumerate and select MIDI input and output devices on the client system and send and receive MIDI messages [7]. As stated in the official W3C page, the Web MIDI API is intended to enable non-music MIDI applications as well as music ones, by providing low-level access to the MIDI devices available on the users' systems. Further details will be provided in Section IV.

The goal of this paper is to match the advantages of web applications in the music education field with the flexibility and power of the MIDI protocol for music reproduction. The point of intersection of these two worlds lies in the technology known as the Web MIDI API. The early development stage of the API, the limited support currently offered by browsers and the consequent lack of available applications make this promising field relatively novel.

The paper is structured as follows: Section II will discuss web resources for music teaching and learning; Section III will provide an overview of the MIDI protocol and its applicability to music education; Section IV will give details about the Web MIDI API initiative; Section V will present a critical analysis of this approach concerning the design, development and release of web applications; finally, Section VI will discuss the case study of an on-line application for music coding.

II. Web Resources for Music Teaching and Learning

Computer-based technologies can help music education from many points of view, ranging from teaching strategies to new approaches to composition and performance, from assistive technology and music therapy to K-12 listening skills development [8]. In recent times, the pervasiveness of network technologies and the availability of high-speed connections have resulted in a rise of meaningful Internet-based music resources. Just to mention some examples:

- The official web sites of important institutions – see the digitalization project of the *Bach Archiv Leipzig* [9], the music section of the *Beic Digital Library* [10], and the archive of the *Teatro alla Scala* [11], to name but a few – nowadays offer high-quality materials to Internet users. The mentioned examples cover heterogeneous aspects of music, including scores [12], audio recordings [13], and heterogeneous opera-related contents [14] respectively. These materials are of great interest for the community of experts, scholars and music students, but they cannot be easily reused in an educational context, due to both technical limitations and copyright issues;

- There are collections of downloadable music resources, often based on the efforts of community members. In this light, two relevant examples are the *Internet Archive*, a site that retrieves digitized content from the web including music scores and audio files [15], and the *IMSLP/Petrucci Music Library* [16], a popular platform to share public domain music [17];
- Other on-line initiatives providing non-interactive resources for music education and dissemination, including static web pages, video tutorials, etc. For example, the YouTube official channel of the Philharmonia Orchestra – London (UK) collects in the *Instrument Guides* section a number of videos aiming to present musical instruments to young people.

Many studies discussed the integration of web-based material into music teaching, documenting phases of integration that include supplemental links to resources, web-based teaching sequences, and various media to support course content [18]. All the mentioned initiatives are potentially useful for music teaching and learning, nevertheless, in order to achieve effective educational results some additional features would be desirable. The ideal web interface should not only grant high-quality and certified resources, achieve cross-platform compatibility, and be always available, but it should also support an active and customizable experience of music contents, present multi-modal interactivity, and foster peer-to-peer and student-teacher interactions.

Keeping these goals in mind, we can provide a non-exhaustive state of the art on recent on-line initiatives that embody such a vision. An example of web platform containing high-quality materials for music education is *DREAM – Digital Resource Exchange About Music* [19], a virtual space for exchanging information about digital learning tools [20]. Another relevant example is *EMIPIU – Enhanced Music Interactive Platform for Internet Users* [21], a web environment that adopts the IEEE 1599 standard to encode music in all its aspects according to a multi-layer structure and presents an advanced web player to enjoy such contents in a synchronized way [22]. As an evidence of its pedagogical valence, the same technology has been employed in the on-line version of a music textbook for children published by Pearson [23]. Finally, let us mention the *Chrome Music Lab* [24] a set of simple on-line tools that let anyone explore how music works. This initiative is a collaboration between musicians and coders, and its core technology lies in the freely available *Web Audio API* [25].

In our opinion, a more detailed survey about web applications currently available for music education would go beyond the scope of this work.

III. MIDI and Music Education

The *Musical Instrument Digital Interface* (MIDI) is an industry standard music technology protocol that connects products from many different companies including digital musical instruments, computers, tablets and smartphones. The MIDI specification describes the protocol, the digital interface and low-level hardware aspects, such as ports, cables and connectors.

The original protocol was designed and released in the 1980's. Despite significant enhancements over the years, the MIDI specification officially remains at version 1.0 [26]. Later extensions include the Standard MIDI File format, MIDI Show Control, MIDI Time Code, and MIDI Machine Control. Nowadays the activities of the MIDI Manufacturers Association (MMA) are focusing on new transfer protocols, such as MIDI over USB and over wireless.

MIDI is used everyday around the world by musicians, DJs, producers, educators, artists and hobbyists to create, perform, learn and share music and artistic works. Advanced and innovative interfaces to make music through MIDI are constantly under development, as shown during the Annual General Meeting of the MMA occurred at the 2016 Winter NAMM Show. The importance of MIDI as a commonly-accepted and widely-adopted standard is also demonstrated by the libraries available for the main programming languages, such as the *C# MIDI Toolkit* for C#, the package *javax.sound.midi* for Java or the *MIDI Toolbox* for Matlab [27].

The MIDI data stream is a unidirectional asynchronous bit stream at 31.25 kbps. The interface on a MIDI instrument will generally include three different connectors, labeled MIDI IN, MIDI OUT, and MIDI THRU. The data stream is usually originated by a MIDI controller or by a MIDI sequencer. A *MIDI controller* is a device which is played as an instrument, and it translates the performance into a MIDI data stream in real time as it is played. Examples include not only keyboards, but also electronic drums, wind controllers and guitar-like MIDI devices. A *MIDI sequencer* is a device which allows MIDI data sequences to be captured, stored, edited, combined, and re-played. The MIDI data output from a MIDI controller or sequencer is transmitted via the devices' MIDI OUT connector. The final recipient of the data stream is commonly a MIDI sound generator or sound module, which will receive MIDI messages at its MIDI IN connector, and respond to these messages by playing sounds. Further information can be retrieved from the official documentation.

It is worth underlining that MIDI does not transmit audio signals; instead, it sends event messages about musical notes, controller signals for parameters, such as volume, vibrato and panning, cues and clock signals to set the tempo, and system-specific MIDI communications. In other terms, MIDI itself does not make sound, rather it encodes the exchange of messages generated by a MIDI chain and to be interpreted by synthesizers in order to produce sound. The pros and cons of this key aspect of MIDI will be discussed in Section V.

A MIDI device can be a piece of hardware (controllers, synthesizers, etc.), a virtual/software tool, or a part of a software environment. From a logical point of view, the simplest MIDI chain presents a message generator – like a keyboard controller – and a message consumer – like a synthesizer. There are devices that integrate both functions in a unique product, as shown in Figure 1. Obviously, more complex layouts can be created through the concatenation of multiple devices, e.g., controllers, sequencers and sound modules, as shown in Figure 2.

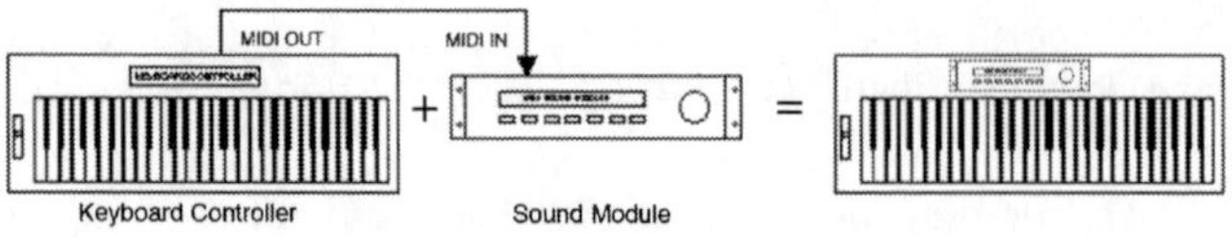

Figure 1. An example of minimal MIDI chain: a keyboard controller connected to a sound module.

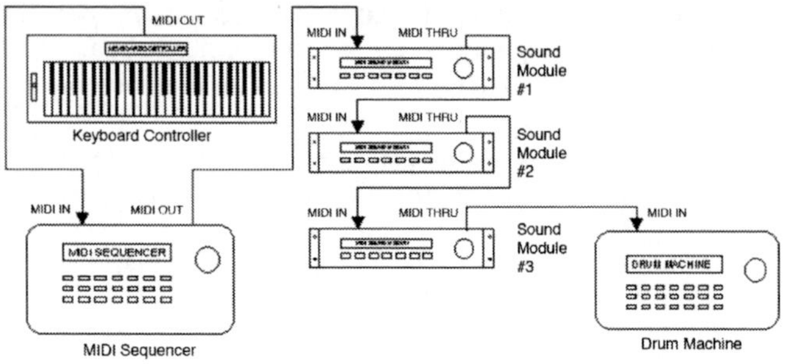

Figure 2. An example of non-trivial MIDI setup in daisy-chain configuration.

Thanks to the huge support offered by most keyboard controllers and to the availability of software counterparts for physical equipment, MIDI can be easily adopted in any educational environment. For instance, in the proposals detailed below, a network-attached computer will be sufficient to experience MIDI-based activities oriented to music education. According to some experts, MIDI can even bring a paradigm shift in music teaching and learning (see [28] and [29]). Among a number of didactic applications of the protocol, it is worth mentioning:

- the production of easy, low-cost, on-the-fly audio renderings of potentially complex music pieces, in contexts of instrument performance [30], vocal training [31], and assisted composition [32];
- the accompaniment for music lessons and individual instrumental practice [33];
- the support offered to real-time distributed music performances, mainly due to the lightweight exchange of MIDI messages, as documented in [34] and [35];
- new possibilities of music expression and interaction for people affected by various kinds of disability, thanks to ad-hoc MIDI-compatible controllers. A relevant application of MIDI to therapy and special education can be found in [36], which presents the use of MIDI devices in order to enable students with physical and learning disabilities to participate to a festival of popular music.

For a more detailed discussion of the advantages and drawbacks of MIDI in music education, please refer to [37] and [38].

IV. The Web MIDI API

In Section II we have cited a number of heterogeneous web applications for music education, and in Section III we have explored the applicability of MIDI-based approaches to this field. Now the question is how to couple the advantages of on-line solutions with the potential of MIDI, and the answer lies in the Web MIDI API [7].

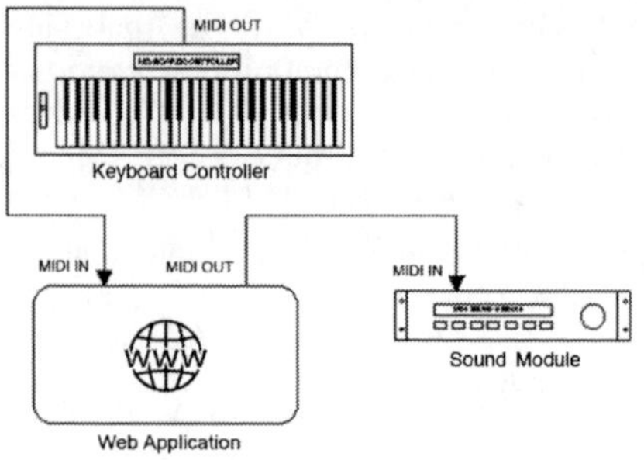

Figure 3. An example of MIDI chain formed by a web application that is piloted by a keyboard and controls a sound module.

This specification defines an API to support the MIDI protocol within web applications, so that applications can enumerate and select MIDI input and output devices on the client system and send and receive MIDI messages. In accordance with the MIDI philosophy, also the API is not designed to describe music or controller inputs semantically; rather, it is intended to reproduce the mechanisms of MIDI input and output interfaces, enabling direct access to devices that respond to MIDI (e.g., controllers, synthesizers, lighting equipment, other pieces of software, etc.). For the sake of clarity, please note that the Web MIDI API is not a way to play Standard MIDI files (SMFs) in a browser; this function should be performed by a future extension of the HTML5 `<audio>` tag instead.

The Web MIDI API puts the web application in communication with other parts of the physical or virtual MIDI chain by sending and receiving standard MIDI messages. In this way, the web application becomes a new MIDI-compatible actor connected to the MIDI chain, as intuitively shown in Figure 3. The API aims to enable a brand new class of applications on the web that can respond to MIDI controller inputs, even with no music purposes. Examples may range from MIDI-controlled video games to interfaces for the music expression by users with disabilities. All these approaches can result in the design and implementation of interactive browser-based educational products.

From a practical point of view, adopting the Web MIDI API in a web page requires to embed ad-hoc JavaScript code. The first steps is searching for MIDI available resources on the client system by invoking the `requestMIDIAccess()` method. Then, it is possible to select the input/output devices to be connected, if any. For an application that has to produce sound, this implies to pick at least the default MIDI synthesizer. Finally, the application can listen to MIDI messages as well as user actions in input, process them and finally send MIDI messages in output. The `send(data,timestamp)` method of the `MIDIOutput` interface enqueues the message(s) to be sent to the corresponding MIDI port, provided that the `data` parameter contains one or more valid and complete MIDI messages. It is also possible to specify when the data should be sent to the port; if the `timestamp` parameter is not present, is set to zero or to a time in the past, data are to be sent as soon as possible.

V. Critical Analysis

Before HTML5, the performance of audio files in a web page could occur only through a plug-in – e.g., Macromedia Flash or Windows Media Player – or non-standard HTML syntax such as <bgsound>, an Internet Explorer element associating a background sound with a page. These custom solutions caused incompatibilities between implementations and across different browsers, implying different behaviors of the same page when visited by different users and unwanted installations of third-party plug-ins.

The introduction of the <audio> element in HTML5 specification solved these issues. The idea was to provide web designers and programmers with a standard way to embed into web pages audio in MP3, Wav, and Ogg format. Nowadays, the <audio> element is largely supported by web browsers, as shown in Figure 4.

Consequently, at present there are standard approaches to sonify web pages through background music and to play audio content on demand. Nevertheless, in some cases a solution based on pre-recorded sound files is neither efficient nor effective. Let us consider those applications where audio is produced in response to a specific user action, and sound parameters (pitch, loudness, duration, timbre, etc.) should change accordingly. For the sake of clarity, the sonification of a button click can be easily implemented by loading a default sound file, whereas a web interface to explore multiple music-scale models performed by different instruments would require a considerable number of recordings; and the situation would become even more critical in the case of an interactive application (e.g., a touch-sensitive keyboard with multi-timbral synthesis) where user actions are unpredictable. In those music-oriented applications where sound parameters may change considerably and are difficult to predict since they depend on users' choices and behaviors, MIDI can play an important role.

Among the advantages offered by a MIDI-based approach, we can mention:

- A production of sound samples completely demanded to a MIDI synthesizer, with no need to pre-record audio fragments with all the variants required (e.g., different pitches, durations, timbres, etc). This implies also the possibility to use the full range of General MIDI patches for multi-timbral synthesizers, and to modify sounds through all the supported Control Change commands;
- A very light and compact client-server exchange of music data, since MIDI does not transmit audio signals, rather it sends commands to trigger audio events;
- The possibility to embed web applications into MIDI chains, by connecting them with other MIDI-compatible real (hardware) or virtual (software) devices;
- Provided a basic knowledge of the MIDI protocol, the easiness of use by programmers, even if the adoption of the HTML5 <audio> element is very straightforward as well.

Element	Google Chrome	Internet Explorer	Mozilla Firefox	Apple Safari	Opera
<audio>	4.0	9.0	3.5	4.0	10.5

Figure 4. The main browsers supporting the HTML5 <audio> element. The numbers below specify the first browser version that offers full support.

	Google Chrome	Android browser	Opera
Web MIDI API	4.9	5.3	42

Figure 5. Browsers supporting the Web MIDI API. The numbers below specify the first browser version that offers full support.

Of course, there are also some annoying drawbacks to take into account:

- MIDI is not an audio format, consequently the resulting sound quality on different systems is unpredictable since it largely depends on the characteristics of the sound module in use;
- MIDI is not a music-notation format, so it can be employed to encode scores only in non-professional applications or in simplified contexts, such as most children-oriented music games;
- The Web MIDI API requires a MIDI chain to produce sounds, namely the presence of either a hardware or a software synthesizer;
- The Web MIDI API has not reached the status of standard yet, and at the moment of writing it is supported only by the browsers listed in Figure 5.

The first two drawbacks listed above are connected to the choice of MIDI as a way to represent music symbols and produce sounds; conversely, the last two are directly linked to the current characteristics of the Web MIDI API. Experience shows that the success of web applications resides in multiplatform support, cross-browser compatibility and no need to perform ad hoc installations, whereas at present the Web MIDI API seems to go the opposite way: it requires the adoption of a specific subset of browsers and the availability of physical MIDI devices attached to the client – an uncommon situation for most users – or, more likely, the installation of software emulators.

Some of these problems will be hopefully solved when the API becomes a standard. In the meanwhile, to get round the problem it is possible to distribute applications wrapped in ready-to-use software packages that embed all the required installations, resources, and configurations. For example, Docker [39] is an open-source project wrapping up in a so-called *container* all the resources needed in order to run one or more processes. This isolation concerns both hardware (CPU, memory, file system, etc.) and software (libraries, tools, code, and so on). After the public deployment, the package launched on a client behaves like a virtual machine.

VI. Case Study: A Web Application for Music Coding

In order to foster artistic creativity and analytical skills in young students, we designed, implemented and released a publicly-available web environment for *music coding*. Music

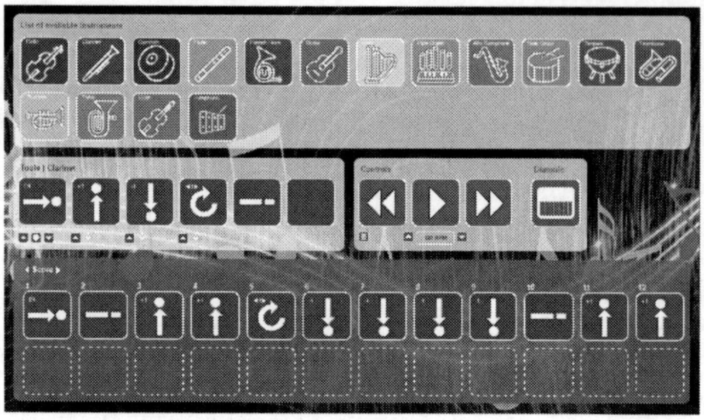

Figure 6. A web interface for music coding where music is generated through the Web MIDI API.

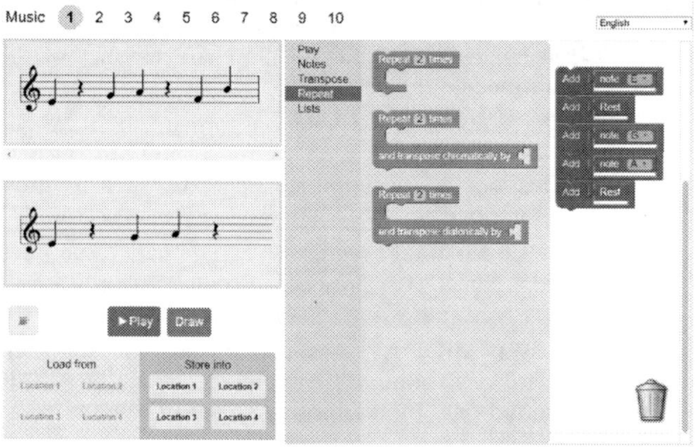

Figure 7. An evolution of the web application for music coding, based on Google Blockly and deployed as a Docker package.

coding can be seen as an evolution of *creative coding* [40], where the latter is applied to music education and its goals embrace not only personal creativity, but also the analysis and comprehension of music processes.

The web environment – to this end – proposes a simplified subset of music operators involving mainly rhythmic and melodic aspects of music. Examples include `Play(p)`, i.e., "Play a given pitch", `Transpose(v)`, i.e., "Modify the previous pitch according to a number of ascending/descending steps", and `Tie()`, i.e., "Extend the duration of a note".

In addition to a short list of music operators, the interface also presents a palette of musical instruments to choose from. The reasons that led to multi-timbral support are manifold: making music creation and reproduction more engaging, supporting the study of harmony and the listening of polyphony through different timbres, introducing young students to the characteristics of orchestral instruments, etc.

Due to the young age of expected users, music operators and musical instruments are represented through playful and colored icons, as shown in Figure 6.

This is not the place to provide further details about the user interface, nor to discuss the validity of its pedagogical approach. For those interested in deepening these topics, a detailed discussion can be found in [41] and [42]. Rather, in this context we are interested in the way music is produced in response to user choices: in fact, sound performance has been demanded to the Web MIDI API.

The choice of the Web MIDI API against other standard solutions, such as sampled sounds, is motivated by a number of factors. First, the multi-timbral support combined with the possibility to play a wide range of pitches would have required the generation of approximatively 2000 sound samples. MIDI syntax easily solves this issue thanks to:

- the parametric values of Note On events, which make pitch (and even velocity) easy to set;
- the use of different MIDI channels properly configured through Program Change messages in order to support different timbres.

Furthermore, the MIDI numeric representation of music parameters allows to easily compute a music tune coming from an algorithmic process. Let us recall that the interface has been conceived to foster music coding, thus notes are not necessarily expressed in an imperative way (e.g., "Play C4"), but they can result from the application of a number of music operators (e.g., "Play C4", "Transpose a major third up and play", "Repeat the last note"). In this sense, the MIDI approach intrinsically simplifies the computation of music parameters that drive sound performance.

Such a web application for music coding is publicly available at http://coding.lim.di.unimi.it. Please note that the Web MIDI API requires a compatible browser – e.g., Google Chrome – and the connection to a MIDI sound module to work.

Recently, we made the interface evolve releasing a new version in form of a Google Blockly game. Blockly [43] is a library for building visual programming editors which uses interlocking, graphical blocks to represent code concepts like variables, logical expressions, loops, and more. In our context, blocks have been linked to music concepts, e.g., music operators and basic score elements, as shown in Figure 7. For the reasons above, also this application adopts the Web MIDI API as a base for the sound engine. In order to solve the cross-platform and installation issues mentioned in Section V, we decided to make the Blockly-based implementation available to schools and other interested institutions as a Docker package.

VII. CONCLUSION

Thanks to its well-known characteristics, the web can be a great means to design, implement and distribute valid and engaging educational tools, and the field of music is no exception. In recent years we have seen the release of a large number of web applications focusing on music, including playful approaches to learn a musical instrument, professional ear-training apps, on-line viewers/players for music archives, and so on. Within this multi-faceted scenario, MIDI – a format dating back to the 80's but still widely adopted by the community of professional musicians – has shown signs of great vitality.

In this paper we have analyzed the applications of MIDI to web frameworks for music-education, an intersection made possible by the Web MIDI API. At the moment of writing, this W3C initiative is still under development, and the support offered by web browsers is very limited. Nevertheless, we consider the Web MIDI API very promising, and many implications in education – e.g., by interfacing the web app with external MIDI controllers – have yet to be explored.

REFERENCES

[1] K. W. Miller, J. Voas, and G. F. Hurlburt, "BYOD: Security and privacy considerations," It Professional, vol. 14, no. 5, 2012, pp. 53–55.

[2] R. Afreen, "Bring your own device (BYOD) in higher education: opportunities and challenges," International Journal of Emerging Trends & Technology in Computer Science, vol. 3, no. 1, 2014, pp. 233–236.

[3] P. Bruder, "Gadgets go to school: The benefits and risks of BYOD (bring your own device)," The Education Digest, vol. 80, no. 3, 2014, p. 15.

[4] J. Offutt, "Quality attributes of web software applications," IEEE software, vol. 19, no. 2, 2002, pp. 25–32.

[5] "MIDI.org," http://www.midi.org/, accessed: 2017-02-22.

[6] J. Flanagan, "Sensitive piano keys let pianists create new sounds," New Scientist, vol. 219, no. 2925, 2013, p. 22.

[7] C. Wilson and J. Kalliokoski, "Web MIDI API," W3C, working draft, Dec. 2016, https://webaudio.github.io/web-midi-api/.

[8] P. R. Webster, Computer-based Technology and Music Teaching and Learning: 2000–2005. Dordrecht: Springer Netherlands, 2007, pp. 1311–1330.

[9] "Bach digital," https://www.bach-digital.de/, accessed: 2017-02-22.

[10] "BEIC - Biblioteca musicale," http://www.beic.it/it/articoli/biblioteca-musicale/, accessed: 2017-02-22.

[11] "Archivio La Scala," http://www.teatroallascala.org/archivio/, accessed: 2017-02-22.

[12] U. Wolf, "Bach-autographen online. kooperationsprojekt bach-digital angelaufen urz liefert kompetenz und rechenpower," Universität Leipzig, Journal, vol. 4/2008, 2008, p. 24.

[13] A. Baratè, L. A. Ludovico, and G. Haus, "Integration of audio resources into a digital library: The BEIC case study," International Journal of Digital Curation, vol. 10, no. 2, 2015, pp. 48–57.

[14] G. Haus and L. A. Ludovico, "The digital opera house: an architecture for multimedia databases," Journal of Cultural Heritage, vol. 7, no. 2, 2006, pp. 92–97.

[15] "Internet Archive: Digital Library of Free Books, Movies, Music & Wayback Machine," https://archive.org/, accessed: 2017-02-22.

[16] "IMSLP/Petrucci Music Library: Free Public Domain Sheet Music," http://imslp.org/, accessed: 2017-02-22.

[17] P. M. Hash, "Internet resources for historical research in music education," Journal of Historical Research in Music Education, vol. 31, no. 1, 2009, pp. 3–5.

[18] N. Barry, "Integrating web based learning and instruction into a graduate music education research course: An exploratory study," Journal of technology in Music Learning, vol. 2, no. 1, 2003, pp. 2–8.

[19] "DREAM — Digital Resource Exchange About Music," http://dreammusictool.ca/, accessed: 2017-02-22.

[20] R. Upitis, K. Boese, and P. C. Abrami, "Demonstrating DREAM: A digital resource exchange about music." International Association for Development of the Information Society, 2015.

[21] "EMIPIU," http://emipiu.di.unimi.it/, accessed: 2017-02-22.

[22] A. Baratè, G. Haus, L. A. Ludovico, and G. Presti, "Advances and perspectives in web technologies for music representation," DigitCult - Scientific Journal on Digital Cultures, vol. 1, no. 2, 2016, pp. 1–8.

[23] S. Erotoli and V. Vacchi, C'è musica per tutti. Vol. A-B. Pearson, 2014.

[24] "Chrome Music Lab," https://musiclab.chromeexperiments.com/, accessed: 2017-02-22.

[25] P. Adenot, C. Wilson, and C. Rogers, "Web Audio API," W3C, working draft, Dec. 2015, https://www.w3.org/TR/webaudio/, accessed: 2017-02-22.

[26] M. M. Association, "The complete MIDI 1.0 detailed specification version 96.1," La Habra: MIDI Manufacturers Association, 1996.

[27] T. Eerola and P. Toiviainen, MIDI Toolbox: MATLAB Tools for Music Research. Jyväskylä, Finland: University of Jyväskylä, 2004. [Online]. Available: www.jyu.fi/musica/miditoolbox/

[28] G. Jordahl, "Teaching music in the age of MIDI," Classroom Computer Learning, vol. 9, no. 2, 1988, pp. 78–85.

[29] J. Zhu, "MIDI and music teaching in colleges of multimedia system application," in Key Engineering Materials, vol. 474. Trans Tech Publ, 2011, pp. 1926–1930.

[30] M. Ajero, The effects of computer-assisted keyboard technology and MIDI accompaniments on group piano students' performance accuracy and attitudes. ProQuest, 2007.

[31] C. Yun and W. Fu, "On the feasibility of employing MIDI in vocal music teaching," Journal of Mianyang Normal University, vol. 4, 2010, p. 038.

[32] S. Reese, "MIDI-assisted composing in your classroom," Teaching music, 1995, pp. 199–206.

[33] F. Kersten, "Using MIDI accompaniments for music learning at school and at home: MIDI and other computer technologies can help students build their musical skills in the classroom and at home," Music Educators Journal, vol. 90, no. 4, 2004, pp. 44–50.

[34] D. Gang, G. V. Chockler, T. Anker, A. Kremer, and T. Winkler, "TRANSmidi: a system for MIDI sessions over the network using transis," in Proceedings of the International Computer Music Conference. Citeseer, 1997, pp. 283–286.

[35] D. Akoumianakis, G. Vellis, I. Milolidakis, D. Kotsalis, and C. Alexandraki, "Distributed collective practices in collaborative music performance," in Proceedings of the 3rd International Conference on Digital Interactive Media in Entertainment and Arts, ser. DIMEA '08. New York, NY, USA: ACM, 2008, pp. 368–375. [Online]. Available: http://doi.acm.org/10.1145/1413634.1413700

[36] B. Cole, "MIDI and communality," Organised Sound, vol. 1, no. 01, 1996, pp. 51–54.

[37] T. E. Rudolph, Teaching music with technology. GIA Publications, 2004.

[38] X. Guo, "The application and research of computer MIDI technology in music education," in International Conference on Social Science and Technology Education (ICSSTE 2015), 2015, pp. 236–241.

[39] "Docker," https://www.docker.com/, accessed: 2017-02-22.

[40] K. Peppler and Y. Kafai, "Creative coding: Programming for personal expression," Retrieved August, vol. 30, no. 2008, 2005, p. 314.

[41] L. A. Ludovico and G. R. Mangione, "Music coding in primary school," in Smart Education and Smart e-Learning, ser. Smart Innovation, Systems and Technologies, R. J. Howlett, L. C. Jain, and V. Uskov, Eds. Springer International Publishing, 2015, pp. 449–458.

[42] A. Baratè, L. A. Ludovico, and G. R. Mangione, "A web framework to develop computational thinking through music coding," in Proceedings of the 2nd International Conference on New Music Concepts (ICNMC 2016), M. Della Ventura, Ed. Milano, Italy: ABEditore, 2016, pp. 157–167.

[43] "Google Blockly," https://developers.google.com/blockly/, accessed: 2017-02-22.

A Web-based Petri Nets Application To Teach Music Analysis and Composition

Adriano Baratè

Laboratorio di Informatica Musicale
Dipartimento di Informatica
Università degli Studi di Milano
Email: adriano.barate@unimi.it

Abstract—**Music Petri nets are a mathematical formalism suitable to express the results of musicological analysis. Being able to infer the structure of a music piece and to represent it through Petri nets is not a trivial task, even for an expert of musicology who is skilled in computational thinking. From this point of view, a computer-based tool can be useful both in the learning phase and in the *a-posteriori* assessment of the achieved results. After providing the theoretical bases about Petri nets, this paper will describe a web application for music education and dissemination, able to integrate and synchronize the results of music analysis with music-related media content within a single on-line framework.**

Keywords–Music; Web; Petri Nets; Analysis; Composition.

I. Introduction

Musicology is the part of the humanities that studies music as a branch of knowledge. Nowadays, the scholarly analysis and research-based study of music can benefit from technology under a number of perspectives, ranging from the technical reproducibility of sound to its preservation through ad-hoc file formats and musical databases, from advanced computing techniques to infer music characteristics to the exploitation of intangible cultural heritage through computer interfaces.

Computational musicology is defined as the study of music with computational modeling and simulation [1]. This discipline is not related only to the use of computers and technological devices, but also to the adoption of statistical and mathematical methods. In this sense, mathematical formalisms aimed at representing music structures and their relationships deserve a particular mention.

The analytical activity that brings to a formal description of music can respond to different goals, including:

- *comprehension*, when the analysis of already existing pieces aims at a deep understanding of their structures and of the music processes the composer had in mind;
- *re-synthesis*, when the final goal is an automatic, computer-driven, or hand-made (but aware) generation of new music materials based on the discovered models.

As explained below, a promising formalism to explain musical processes is the one based on the adoption of Petri nets. Even if Petri nets have been conceived in a context different from information theory, they proved to be a valid means to describe concurrent, asynchronous, and parallel processes, and these features make them suitable to music analysis as well.

Unfortunately, for a student – even trained in music and skilled in computational thinking – the task of carrying out the analysis of a music piece through Petri nets is not trivial: first, such a formalism requires the development of specific analytical skills; moreover, checking the validity of the achieved results is not easy, especially without a way to link the unveiled structures with the original music content. For this reason, we have created a set of computer-based tools for the editing, step-by-step execution and synchronized multimedia performance of Petri nets.

In particular, this work focuses on the design and implementation of a web application for music education and dissemination, where the results of music analysis through Petri nets are integrated and synchronized with an advanced media player thanks to the IEEE 1599 technology.

The paper is structured as follows: Section II will introduce the key concepts about Petri nets, Section III will focus on their musical interpretation, Section IV will discuss the issues related to the teaching of Music Petri nets to university students, Section V will describe a web prototype to facilitate learning and result assessment, and finally Section VI will provide some clarifying examples.

II. A Short Introduction To Petri Nets

A Petri Net is an abstract and formal model aiming to represent the dynamic behavior of a system with asynchronous and concurrent activities [2]. It can be defined as a directed bipartite graph, in which the *nodes* may represent *transitions* (i.e., events that may occur) and *places* (i.e., conditions). Transitions are linked to places, and vice versa, by directed *arcs*, that describe which places are pre- and/or post-conditions for which transitions. Please note that arcs never run between places or between transitions.

Places in a Petri net may contain a discrete number of marks called *tokens*. Any distribution of tokens over the places will represent a configuration of the net called a *marking*. The upper limit of tokens that a given place can host represents its *capacity*.

A transition in a Petri net may fire if it is enabled, i.e., there are sufficient tokens in all of its input places and there is sufficient room in all of its output places to host newly generated tokens. When the transition fires, it consumes the required input tokens, and creates tokens in its output places. Please note that tokens are not moved from an input to an output place, but consumed in the former and created in the latter.

Arcs are weighted, and the so-called *arc multiplicity* defines how many tokens should be consumed/created in the corresponding input/output place respectively.

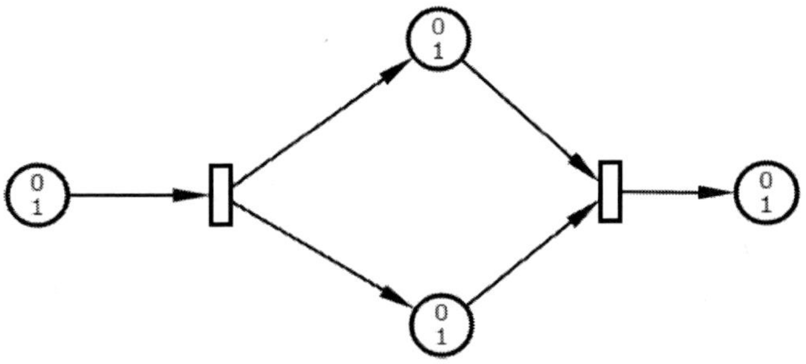

Figure 1. An example of Petri net including 4 places (with no initial marking and capacity set to 1) and 2 transitions.

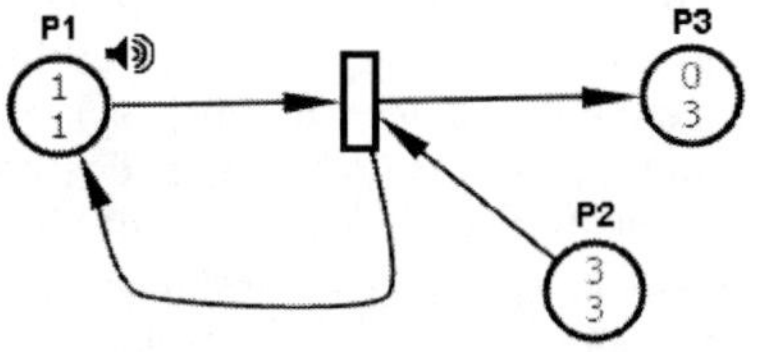

Figure 2. An iterative structure to play the music fragment contained in P1 for $n+1$ times, with P2 having an initial marking $n=3$.

A firing is atomic, in other words it is a single non-interruptible step. Moreover, unless an execution policy is defined, the execution of Petri nets is non-deterministic: when multiple transitions are enabled at the same time, any one of them may fire. Petri nets have an exact mathematical definition of their execution semantics, with a well-developed mathematical theory for process analysis [3].

Thanks to their characteristics, Petri nets are well suited for modeling the behavior of distributed systems. The modeled processes can include choice, iteration, and concurrent execution [4].

Petri nets are usually represented through a graphical formalism, where transitions are symbolized by bars or rectangles, places by circles, and arcs by lines with an arrow head. A conventional way to indicate the current place marking and its capacity is to inscribe in the circle an upper and a lower number respectively. A complete example of graphical representation is shown in Figure 1.

III. Music Petri Nets

A specific extension of Petri nets has been created for music applications. In this implementation, called Music Petri Nets (MPNs), places can be associated to music objects to be played when a token is received, and transitions can contain musical operators that alter the music objects of input places and put these modified objects into output places. A music object may be anything that could have a musical meaning, e.g., a single note, a fragment of music, a control signal, etc. Music operators apply transformational algorithms, such as transpositions, inversions, and time stretching. It is worth underlining that in MPNs not all places are necessarily associated to music objects, nor the transitions to musical operators: in this case, these entities are used for mere net evolution, in accordance with their original function in Petri nets. For example, an iterative structure like the one shown in Figure 2 can be adopted to play a music fragment multiple times. This example presents place P1 carrying a musical content and P2 acting as a counter and reserved for net evolution.

MPNs have been applied both to the analysis of already existing pieces of music [5] and to composition and musical expression [6]. In the former case, that is more relevant for our present goals, one factor that clearly influences the analytic power of MPNs is the intrinsic structure of the piece to be described. A composition that mainly contains well-defined music fragments – repeated as they are or after applying some modifications and presenting clear mutual relationships – can be easily mapped onto a limited number of connected structures. The resulting MPN would be compact and effective in the representation of the whole piece structure, as it often happens for counterpoint. Conversely, it would be very difficult to effectively describe a jazz improvisation through this formalism, even after an accurate *a-posteriori* analysis.

IV. Teaching Music Petri Nets

Even if presented to the scientific community in a number of conferences and scientific works, MPNs are deeply rooted in the research activities of the Laboratory of Music Informatics (LIM, Laboratorio di Informatica Musicale) of the University of Milan.

The department of Computer Science of this university offers a degree course in *Music Informatics* that gathers about one hundred freshmen per year. One of the courses that all students have to attend is *Computer Science for Music* (*Informatica applicata alla musica*), where they face technologies and formalisms both from a theoretical and from a practical point of view. In particular, half course (48 hours) is delivered in a computer-equipped classroom. Each lesson lasts approximatively 3 hours, and – after a teacher-led initial part – students are left time for exercises under the supervision of an expert.

In the context of the *Music Informatics* degree, MPNs are seen as a professionalizing subject that may help students investigate the musical processes and provide a formal representation for them. For all we know, this is the only graduate program in the world where MPNs are taught.

This topic is traditionally explained to students in the space of 4 lessons lasting 3 hours each, initially focusing on the theoretical aspects and then increasingly shifting the emphasis towards teacher-guided exercises. At the end of this cycle of lessons, the students should be able to:

1) analyze a piece of music and infer its structure in terms of relationships among musical objects;
2) convert this schema to a MPN model;
3) use the mentioned MPN model to create new music pieces, altering the model itself in different ways, e.g., modifying its initial marking or topological characteristics.

The first lessons focus on how traditional Petri nets works, so the basic structures can be presented with no reference to their meaning from a musical perspective. An example of these structure-oriented exercises is shown in Figure 3. After some clarifying examples and assignments, ad-hoc music excerpts can be analyzed (see Figure 4). In the last lessons, students are invited to use the learned concepts to create new music structures.

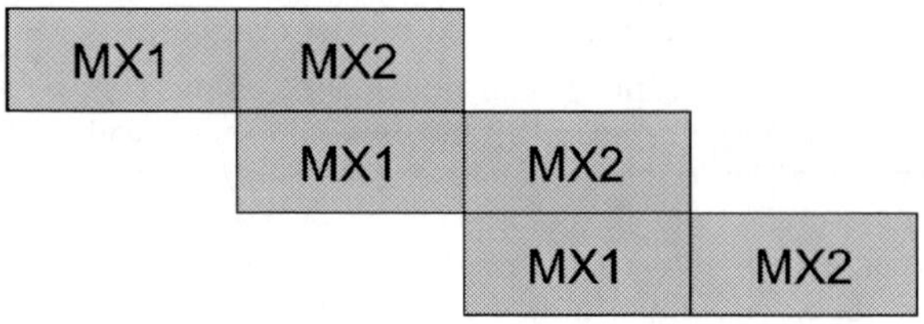

Figure 3. An exercise with a structure presented as an abstract schema.

Figure 4. An exercise with a music piece to be analyzed and represented as a MPN.

The homework assignment for the final exam is to analyze a music excerpt and to provide a MPN formalization of it. There are no constraints about the scores to analyze: music works may belong to any genre and come from any culture, geographical area, and historical period. Moreover, analysis can occur at different degrees of abstraction and detail: as a matter of fact, some students focus on the macro-structural analysis of a complete music piece, other students on a limited number of measures but achieving a very high degree of detail.

In order to foster students' comprehension of this non-trivial subject and to facilitate their tasks, a software tool called *ScoreSynth* – aiming at the representation and step-by-step execution of MPNs – has been released. *ScoreSynth* allows to draw a Petri net of arbitrary complexity, to fix its initial marking, to assign musical fragments to places, and to let the net evolve evaluating its step-by-step behavior, finally achieving the generation (or the reconstruction) of a music score. The interface of *ScoreSynth* is shown in Figure 5.

The student satisfaction towards this free application is quite high, nevertheless *ScoreSynth* presents a number of known limitations:

- it produces a score from a logical point of view, but it cannot perform it;
- the resulting Petri net is not integrated with graphical (score) and audio (performance) contents;
- it requires a specific training to be used;
- consequently, it is mainly an editor rather than a tool to show the expressive power of MPNs to non-experts;
- it works off line, running on a client system;
- it has been developed only for Microsoft Windows^{TM}.

In order to solve the mentioned issues, the idea was to shift towards the web-based solution presented in the next section.

V. A Web-based Approach

Before introducing the web-based approach to the visualization, editing, and execution of MPNs, it is worth recalling that the LIM lab has recently worked on an international standard called IEEE 1599, a format that aims to provide a comprehensive description of a music piece in all its aspects. IEEE 1599 is an XML-based standard that can embed multiple and heterogeneous descriptions of a single music piece, all mutually synchronized: metadata, score symbols, graphical content, audio content, and even structural information. Further details are provided in the official documentation [7] and in ad-hoc scientific publications [8]. Moreover, this format has proved to be very effective in a number of music-oriented educational contexts, as discussed in [9].

A detailed discussion about IEEE 1599 would shift the focus from the aims of the present work. For our purposes, it is sufficient to recall that an IEEE 1599 document could host one or more Petri nets coming from a multi-level analysis, link the discovered music objects to music symbols and to their multimedia representations encoded in the document itself, and finally allow a synchronized visualization of all these contents.

Since a web player for IEEE 1599 is already available on the web, the idea was to augment its functionalities by adding the possibility to view and interact with Petri nets. The original web player is integrated in the EMIPIU portal, whose Music Box section demonstrates the potentialities of IEEE 1599 through a number of significant and heterogeneous musical examples. This web application is fully compliant with W3C standards and independent from the hardware and software characteristics of the local system in use. EMIPIU (Enriched Music Interactive Platform for Internet User) is a publicly-funded international scientific cooperation carried out by the Laboratorio di Informatica Musicale (LIM) - Università degli Studi di Milano and the Laboratoire d'Informatique, de Robotique et de Microélectronique de Montpellier (LIRMM) - Université Montpellier. The portal includes project details, official documentation and a community area to exchange opinions, share materials and request clarifications on technical issues.

As mentioned above, for the purposes of this work the most interesting section is the Music Box area, containing the media player that implements advanced navigation and synchronization of music-related contents. The base URL of

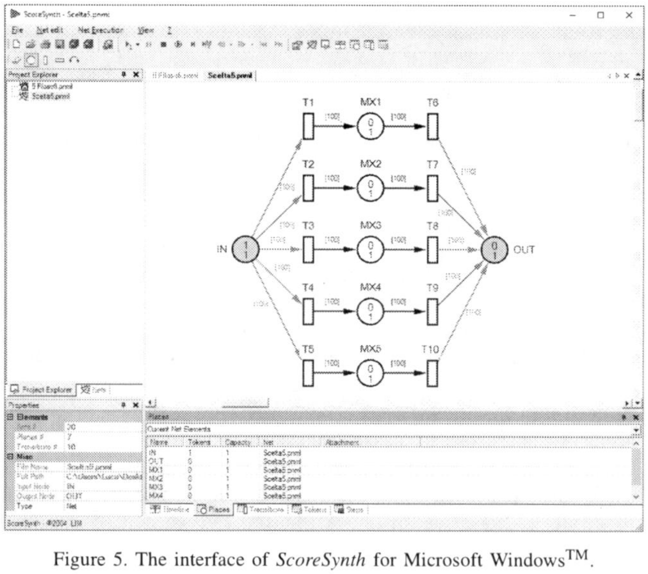

Figure 5. The interface of *ScoreSynth* for Microsoft Windows^{TM}.

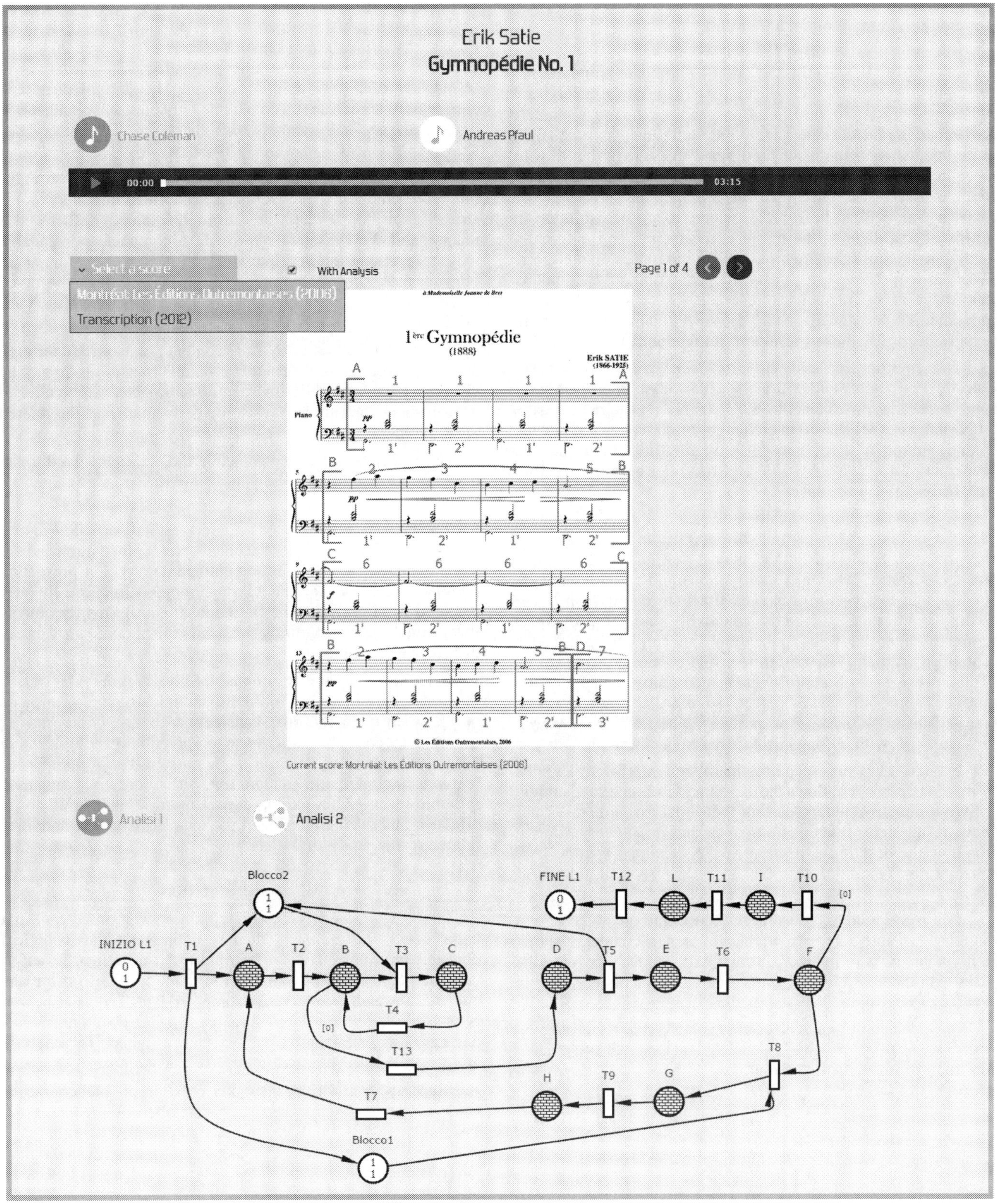

Figure 6. The web interface for MPNs analysis integrated with score and audio.

the portal is http://emipiu.di.unimi.it/.

Recently, the standard IEEE 1599 player has been integrated with a MPN section. In order to produce the additional materials needed by the player, two new tools have been developed. The first one is used to associate the music objects contained in places to the corresponding fragments of the IEEE 1599 file, whereas the second tool maps the state of the MPN to specific timings of the music piece. In this way, when an audio track is played within the IEEE 1599 player, the corresponding Petri net model can be shown, synchronizing its evolution in terms of markings as the music is advancing, and optionally showing the music fragments associated to places on the score. The entire process (i.e., analysis, generation of the model, and mapping of fragment correspondences in the IEEE 1599 document) helps students check their work, and allows them to experience the achieved results in an interactive environment.

The environment still supports *ScoreSynth* as a way to encode Petri nets, but it provides also high interoperability with other systems thanks to the Petri Net Markup Language (PNML), an XML-based interchange format conceived for the representation of Petri nets [10]. PNML documents can be generated also by *ScoreSynth*, and they can be imported into the IEEE 1599 web player.

This approach intrinsically solves most issues listed in Section IV. First, the audio rendition(s) of the Petri net model is demanded to the IEEE 1599 player, that is also responsible for the operation known as *score following*, that is the process of listening to a performance and tracking the position in the score. Besides, as it regards availability and cross-platform compatibility, the web application can run on any device equipped with an HTML5 browser and connected to the Web. The downside of this approach is that, currently, the application can be used only as a viewer, so the Petri net must be created using *ScoreSynth* or another PNML editor. However, an evolution with editing functions is under development.

Finally, it is worth recalling that a web interface integrated with a media player allows the exploitation of the great amount of work done by students during their final assignments. Until now, results have remained on paper, and it was very difficult to show the descriptive power of MPNs to non-experts.

VI. EXAMPLES

The web-based approach described in the previous section supports an integrated experience of music content together with its analysis formalized through MPNs, thus providing the user with the possibility to gain a deep understanding of music processes scaffolded by multimedia.

In this section, we will discuss a case study focusing on the *Gymnopédie No. 1* by Erik Satie. The example is available on line at http://satie.lim.di.unimi.it.

Please note that in this context we are not interested in the process that generated a specific musicological analysis. This kind of activity may achieve different results, depending on the music features to analyze, the target degree of abstraction and – obviously – the skills and aims of the expert. For instance, the example we will mention carries two different analyses, which is perfectly consistent with the "multi-instance" approach of IEEE 1599 towards the content of any layer: potentially, multiple scores, multiple audio performances, and multiple analyses as well.

The interface is a variant of the web player for IEEE 1599 documents, with the presence of a Petri net viewer under the score. A drop-down menu allows to select which analysis to follow out of many (in this case, the IEEE 1599 document carries only 2 analyses). A check box enables the visualization of related cues and symbols over the score. The interface is shown in Figure 6.

This viewer supports subnets too, a useful device to make the representation more compact by embedding a complex structure inside. Subnets are formally defined in Petri nets theory, and they essentially provide a compact and readable way to represent the multiple levels of abstraction of a net. In our interface, subnets are graphically rendered through grayed places and they can be double clicked in order to explore their hidden content.

The places that carry musical content are identified through a loudspeaker icon. When the in-going transitions fire, they virtually launch a music fragment. Such places can be clicked to alter their marking and force the performance of the related music content.

As the performance is advancing, the places involved in the execution are highlighted in yellow and their marking changes accordingly.

The *Gymnopédie No. 1* is a good testbed for MPN theory and applications. In fact, even if this composition is far from Renaissance or Baroque contrapuntal style, it presents a number of clearly identifiable music objects, that are literally repeated or slightly variated; compositions of smaller objects form higher-level structures (i.e., musical phrases) that are in turn repeated, and so on.

In conclusion, this example – fully working via web – illustrates the possibility to investigate the structure of a piece of music through multiple analyses, each one composed by multiple layers. The experience of potentially complex and very articulated information is facilitated by a number of features, including the integration with score following and multiple-level subnet exploration. This tool has proved to be effective and even engaging in the learning/teaching activities related to the study of MPNs.

VII. CONCLUSION

In this work we have presented a new web-based tool that helps *Music Informatics* students understand musicological concepts and music analysis through Petri nets, thus fostering computational thinking skills. Even if models still have to be encoded through *ScoreSynth* or another PNML editor, now it is possible to embed them into IEEE 1599 documents, thus having a single integrated environment to check the analysis and to provide an intuitive multimedia experience.

Since the introduction of this solution in the course of *Computer Science for Music*, the number of errors in the assignments for the final exam has significantly decreased, and student satisfaction has raised, as the author of a musicological analysis can now see (and show to others) the result of his/her efforts.

As it regards future work, we are planning the development of a complete web-based solution that permits to analyze music pieces, design MPNs models, connect IEEE 1599 documents, and publish the result in an integrated player available on line.

REFERENCES

[1] E. Coutinho, M. Gimenes, J. M. Martins, and E. R. Miranda, "Computational musicology: An artificial life approach," in Artificial intelligence, 2005. epia 2005. portuguese conference on. IEEE, 2005, pp. 85–93.

[2] C. A. Petri, "Introduction to general net theory," in Net theory and applications. Springer, 1980, pp. 1–19.

[3] J. L. Peterson, "Petri nets," ACM Comput. Surv., vol. 9, no. 3, Sep. 1977, pp. 223–252. [Online]. Available: http://doi.acm.org.pros.lib.unimi.it/10.1145/356698.356702

[4] E. Best and R. Devillers, "Sequential and concurrent behaviour in Petri net theory," Theoretical Computer Science, vol. 55, no. 1, 1987, pp. 87–136.

[5] A. Baratè, G. Haus, and L. A. Ludovico, "Music analysis and modeling through Petri nets," in Computer Music Modeling and Retrieval : 3rd International Symposium, CMMR 2005, Pisa, Italy, September 26-28, 2005 : Revised Papers, ser. Lecture Notes in Computer Science, R. Kronland-Martinet, T. Voinier, and S. Ystad, Eds., vol. 3902. Berlin Heidelberg, Germany: Springer-Verlag, 2006, pp. 201–218.

[6] ——, "Real-time music composition through P-timed Petri nets," in ICMC—SMC—2014 Proceedings, Athens 14-20 September 2014, A. Georgaki and G. Kouroupetroglou, Eds., Athens, Greece, 2014, pp. 408–415.

[7] "IEEE recommended practice for defining a commonly acceptable musical application using XML," IEEE Std 1599-2008, Sept 2008, pp. 1–110.

[8] D. L. Baggi and G. M. Haus, Music navigation with symbols and layers: Toward content browsing with IEEE 1599 XML encoding. John Wiley & Sons, 2013.

[9] A. Baratè and L. A. Ludovico, "IEEE 1599 applications for entertainment and education," in Music Navigation with Symbols and Layers: Toward Content Browsing with IEEE 1599 XML Encoding, D. Baggi and G. Haus, Eds. Wiley-IEEE Computer Society Press, 2013, pp. 115–132.

[10] M. Weber and E. Kindler, "The Petri net markup language," in Petri Net Technology for Communication-Based Systems. Springer, 2003, pp. 124–144.

Collaborative Music Composition Using Cloud Tools

Marco Morandi

Indire
Istituto Nazionale di Documentazione, Innovazione e Ricerca Educativa
Florence, Italy
Email: m.morandi@indire.it

***Abstract*—This paper illustrates an ongoing study to design and create a collaborative digital learning environment using new technologies, within the active-learning methodological approach. The aim of the research is to propose a new methodology for the development of composition and musical practice for upper secondary school students, based on Cloud computing, within a learning context characterized by the acquisition of skills in an informal manner.**

***Index Terms*—Music Composition; Cloud computing; Music practice; ICT Music education.**

I. Introduction

Digital technology has changed the world of music. Not only music that is "listened" but also, and especially, music that is played. The acoustic instrument has remained (almost) the same, but the approach towards every type of musical product has changed: the personal computer has become an almost complete "home studio" with costs considerably lower than a "real" professional recording studio. Digital technology has also made a big impact on the teaching of music at school, especially in recent years, with the widespread use of mobile devices (smartphones and tablets) that offer a variety of applications for music education, already used by many music teachers for their students [1].

By exploiting new technologies (software cross-devices, 2.0 applications), it is possible to offer students a digital environment that can bolster the informal type of school activities accompanying formal education subjects, to generate an "appetite" for musical practice, with the awareness that music "is essentially culture, knowledge that is reticular and interdisciplinary, that can shed light on other kinds of knowledge from which it continuously receives light in turn [2]".

The construction of an appropriate learning environment allows experiments with methodological solutions that give students the opportunity to enjoy musical experiences in contexts without external constraints, allowing them to temporarily abandon educational/formal practice and delight in the freedom of exploration during their music education.

Starting from a general outline of the educational basics that led to the writing of this paper, Section 2 will show the relationship between the construction of learning environments and 2.0 digital technologies. Section 3 will then show the technological context of music production and its development in the Cloud which, thanks to the constant increase in performance of web communication infrastructures, represents the main novelty for collaborative musical production activities not previously possible, when the characteristics of bandwidth and storage were insufficient to allow a quality/price ratio accessible to schools or individual students.

Section 4 looks at the details of constructing a learning environment: tools, facilities, objectives, technical feats, and examples of tasks. Section 5 identifies the expected results from the on-field study, both in general terms and from the standpoint of individual students learning. New developments and conclusions (Section 6) wrap up the paper.

II. Learning environments between Constructivism and didactics

The learning environment is the key element of the didactics of Constructivism, which bases its principles on the following conditions: "collaboration, personal autonomy, generativity, reflectivity, active involvement, personal relevance and pluralism. [3]"

Constructivism is an approach to teaching that puts the learner at the centre of the learning process as an alternative to an educational approach based on the centrality of the teacher.

In these environments, knowledge is the product of an active construction on the part of the learner, is connected to the concrete situation where the learning is taking place, and arises from social collaboration and interpersonal communication.

In these environments, so-called "significant learning" [4] is also born from social collaboration and interpersonal communication, integrating seven fundamental aspects: active, collaborative, conversational, reflexive, contextualized, intentional, and constructive. It follows that knowledge is a "making of meaning", a creative interpretation by learners in the process of understanding the reality that surrounds them [5], and as the product of an active construction by the learner, coupled with the concrete situation where the learning is taking place. The goal is not the learning of specific content, but the ability to internalize a methodology that makes learners independent within their own cognitive journeys: not knowledge that is already coded, but methods for personal growth, learning how to learn.

In 1990, Lavas and Wenfer [6] proposed the Situated Learning theory: that knowledge is not a set of learned theoretical concepts, but the result of a dynamic process, i.e., the active participation of a learner within a context, given by interaction with other members and the surrounding situation.

Constructivism has not developed a one-off teaching model. For Jonassen, "there are no predefined models for constructivist learning environments, and for many, they could never even exist, since the processes of constructing knowledge are always inserted into specific contexts. Thus, with every probability, the types of support for programmed learning in each context will never be transferred to another. [4]" Jonassen provides some basic suggestions for any learning environment and identifies the construction of knowledge as the main objective, while in the attention to the context and the use of internal communication tools, negotiation and problem-solving are the key aspects.

The teacher guides and supports the group, and a space is defined (physical or virtual) where the work tools are located. The current technological level inside the World Wide Web, especially with the deep shared use of social tools and Cloud services and the progressive growth in performance of web communication infrastructures, offers the possibility of preparing a digital learning environment in line with the assumptions of Constructivist teaching, abounding in stimuli for working groups and small communities. Teachers assume the role of facilitators of learning processes, and this represents a stimulus that creates conditions for positive collaboration, stimulating research and internal sharing, by focusing on the personalization of teaching strategies within the group/community.

III. The Technological Context of Music Production and the Innovation of Cloud Services

Since 1877, the year when Thomas Edison invented the phonograph, which made it possible to record and reproduce sound waves, the technology to record the human voice, singing, instrumental music, environmental effects, etc., has evolved through the recording and reproduction of sound using electrical and optical recording systems (photocells), vinyl, magnetic tape and cinema film.

In the beginning, all audio recording systems were based on the acquisition of analogue signals in the form of waves, which were physically recorded on supports (phonographic, vinyl or magnetic) with the aim of replicating the waveform, and then reversing the process and converting the tracks recorded on the various media into audio pulses and by using an amplifier, restoring the original waveform.

The large-scale introduction of digital recording has completely changed the technology of acquiring sounds, coupling the evolution of audio capture technology with the evolution of information technology.

Digital recording uses a tool that measures changes in sound pressure and converts and stores these on a support as a sequence of bits, thus creating an abstract model of the sound that varies in time.

The component that measures the sound pressure is the analogue-to-digital converter (ADC) which through an input device (e.g., a microphone) acquires a signal that is then converted by sampling, continuously measuring the level of the analogue sound wave and storing the binary number for each measurement on a support that can be: magnetic, a hard disk, an optical drive, or more recently, a solid state memory. The sampling frequency indicates the number of times per second that an analogue signal is measured and stored on the support in digital form, and thus measures the quality/accuracy of the digital signal obtained; for example, the standard for telephone communication is 8,000 per second, while for music it is 44,100 memorizations per second. For playback, the sequence of numbers is sent to a digital-to-analogue converter (DAC), which reconstructs the waveform, by interpolation, which is then amplified and sent to the speakers for listening. Despite an awareness of the physiological decrease in quality of the reproduced signal, digital recording presents numerous advantages, the main one being the versatility with which information can be stored/managed through computer media which are more efficient, compact, and inexpensive systems for analogue acquisition/copying.

The development of digital electronics and computers has without a doubt influenced the preference for digital sampling, leading to a vast public, something which, in the era of analogue acquisition, was the prerogative of a restricted reality: in fact, nowadays, ADC and DAC converters are to be found in every smartphone, computer, tablet, and digital music player, and allow the owners of such devices to record/playback their own voice, an instrument, the sounds of the environment, etc..

The gradual improvement in the performance of web communication infrastructures has allowed the transmission of large amounts of data in a very short space of time, and today operations are possible that were unthinkable until a few years ago, such as the digitization of musical performance and the ability to send it in real time to a remote server capable of processing the input data and structuring them inside multitrack music software.

IV. Construction of a Learning Environment for Collaborative Musical Composition

The learning environment that is the subject of this research (developed by the INDIRE project "Disciplinary Didactics and ICT"), is dedicated to the practice of music, music composition, and the planning and active participation of members in educational activities of an informal nature.

Participants can record their performances inside virtual spaces set up inside the environment, recording and over-dubbing music tracks, and adding their own recordings to those of other participants asynchronously, to realize/arrange a full track with all instruments as indicated/guided by the teacher.

The presence of a tool based on Cloud computing that can handle incoming data (i.e., the performance of a musician on his own instrument) solely by means of the browser, delegating the power of calculation to the "Cloud" server, is a technological aspect not previously available in the multimedia

landscape. This is a key factor for the potential access of all students with any device and an internet connection: the type of hardware/software owned is no longer relevant, but it is sufficient to have any device and a stable connection to the web to work fluidly.
The construction of such an environment requires two main methodological approaches: the active and collaborative learning, and its main point of reference is musical practice and composition plus the acquisition of skills in an informal way.
If on the one hand the active learning is a methodology that enhances the experimental approach to problem-solving by promoting its educational potential (fielding activities in which students are not mere executors of operations led by the teacher, but work reflecting on the ways the experiment can be carried out, and analysing the results [1]), cooperative learning is a method that involves students in group work to achieve a common goal, placing the emphasis on certain key features such as positive interdependence, individual responsibility, interaction, the appropriate use of skills in collaboration, and assessment of the work carried out [7].
In the process of creating a learning environment that fosters musical practice, the experiences and special features of the informal acquisition of skills have been considered, particularly within the framework of music.
John A. Sloboda [8] maintains that human beings can acquire implicit knowledge with regard to the structural characteristics of music in their own culture within the first ten years of life, by means of activities, rhythm games, songs, dance, etc..
Subsequently, this musical knowledge is fostered and maintained by means of exposure to the media (TV, radio, etc.); thus, all this happens informally. These skills are then possessed by many people without any explicit musical training or formal education.
Even earlier, James L. Collier conducted a study on Louis Armstrong, and on the informal acquisition of active musical skills without any allied formal education [9]. In the analysis of the contexts that led Armstrong to become such a brilliant musician in his musical genre and within the history of twentieth-century music (early exposure to a musical environment, freedom of exploration and expression, lack of distinction between practice and performance, etc.) Collier demonstrated that people can become experts even without specific formal education: "Musical involvement has the character of a visceral emotion, in total antithesis with situations of external constraint; i.e., that such experiences take place in almost all cases in the company of friends and family or alone, rarely with the presence of a teacher." [10]
Moreover, the construction of a digital learning environment for music cannot ignore the "electro-acoustic paradigm" [11], i.e., the effect that the introduction of digital equipment for the production and reproduction of music has had on individuals, and the change that the advent of digital technology has brought to everyday life, which can then become an all-out part of music education.
Prior to the introduction of recording/playback systems, there were two major means of creating and transmitting music: the oral tradition and writing. Electro-acoustic music has seen the appearance of music played through speakers and (subsequently) made in the studio by means of computers, samplers, and other digital systems.
Therefore, if "current musical pedagogy is linked to the musical attitude that preceded the advent of reproduction technologies, and within that attitude, more than a century old," [12] then what we need is a sort of "informalization" of music education, accepting that "formal education has been undermined and contaminated by the informal kind" [12].
The approach to teaching music in the environment that is the subject of this paper intends to use a workshop procedure, moving the centre of learning from information to training, promoting a more proactive attitude among students towards knowledge; in addition, it intends to rely on an equal interchange of work and collaboration between students and teachers, combining the skills of both, becoming a virtual lab to redefine teaching times by applying organizational and methodological innovation, facilitating hands-on teaching rather than lecture-style lessons. A space in which to enjoy experiences with others, using materials and methods that produce learning processes and "build" knowledge.
In this way, learning becomes the result of a continuous interaction of community members who, by interacting with each other, "build" knowledge through the elements typical of a workshop.
Within these learning communities, the teacher then becomes a "facilitator" whose task is to create the conditions for positive cooperation, to stimulate research and internal sharing, and to provide credible models for learning.

A. *Objectives and spaces*

The purpose of the learning environment is to allow the design, composition and production of music following instructions and guidance from the teacher.
The characteristics of the learning environment must allow students to tackle music using multimedia tools that can increase their awareness during their studies.
The a-synchronicity of the method facilitates the study of music: recording and listening back to what you have just produced is one of the main methods of acquiring musical awareness.
It is also possible to consider the digital recording approach as an "apprenticeship" towards the working world of music; a world in which musicians find themselves in the presence of very similar systems every time they offer their services in musical production situations.
The environment will be entirely online, and will use cross-device web interfaces, handling all incoming data through Cloud services.

B. *Tools and features.*

The tools that make up the learning environment are developed and/or integrated within a web platform, subject to login procedures, where the teachers can manage several groups of

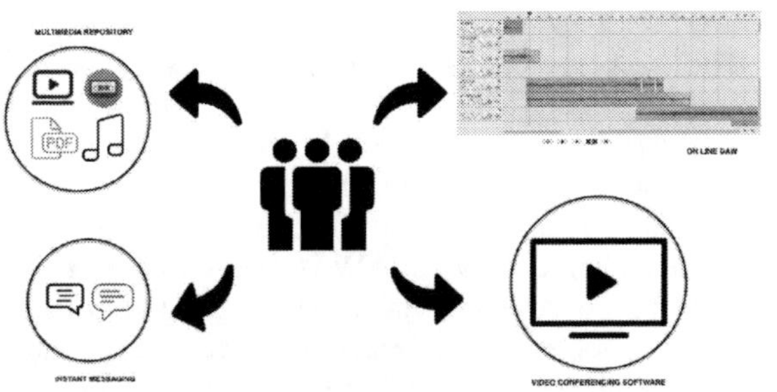

Fig. 1. Content type management: multimedia files, instant messaging, Video conferencing software, on line DAW

students (Fig. 1).
Each student can participate in the activities of several groups, and tools have been developed for peer evaluation of the results of each group, triggering a virtuous interaction between students who can also be in different classes/schools.

Online Digital Audio Workstation (DAW).

This is a software that allows the recording of analogue and digital music using computerised tools, by overdubbing multiple recordings/different instruments and allowing a final mix-down and export of an audio file readable by any device (Fig. 2).
The use of a Cloud-based online DAW, that allows access and recording directly from a browser window via a web interface, brings great benefits compared to desktop solutions, i.e., using a PC:

- Independence from the operating system and browser (Windows, Mac, Linux, Android, iOS). In fact, it is sufficient to have an internet connection and an access device;
- Independence from a device to access the Web (PC, Tablet, Smartphone, etc.);
- The software data and technical performance are managed server side, allowing access by almost any device user, regardless of the quality of the hardware owned;
- All participants can access the software at any time to record their performances, finding the work done by all the others previously;

Repository of multimedia materials. An area in which participants can share files of any type to plan a work, supporting the ideas with multimedia contributions (songs, audio-video bites, scores, etc.).

Instant Messaging. Instant messaging system present within all areas of the environment, to comment on the materials shared or as music design forums. The messages are saved and organized chronologically for correct navigation over time.

Video-conferencing software. Organized in circumscribed "rooms" accessible only to the working group in which the participants, moderated by the teacher, can organize the performance, editing and design of the work. Internal tools for

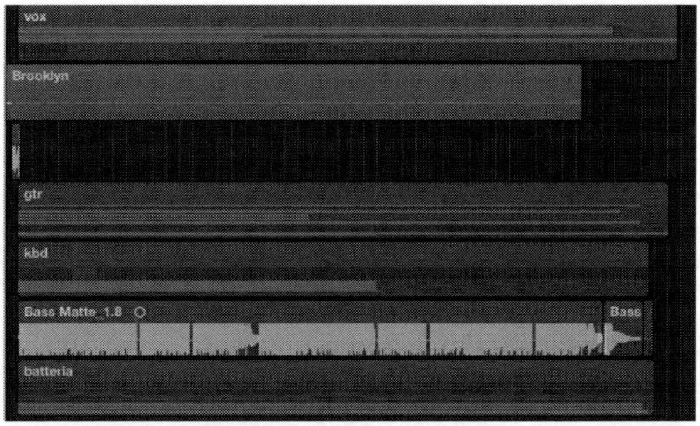

Fig. 2. Generic DAW session view

screen sharing and the upload of materials for instant sharing are the most efficient for the proposed use.

Devices to access the platform, manage the content, and record musical performances. The environment is accessible from all computing devices, to make it particularly suitable for the reference target: the use of cross-device programming languages (HTML5, JavaScript) makes the virtual space accessible and usable (as well as from any PC) also by common smartphones, widespread among the students of reference. These devices are accompanied by high quality microphones, suitable for converting the analogue signal of an instrument into a digital signal that can be saved and stored inside the online DAW.

C. Technical Realization.

A prototype of the environment has already been created by INDIRE as part of the projects to take a closer look at the relationship between disciplinary didactics and new technologies (Fig. 3).
An analysis was made of the technical aspects of the project, the communication aspects of the software produced, and the delicate issue of managing students privacy.

The following technical choices were then made:

- Programming languages: to maintain cross-device compatibility, the programming languages used for the areas to share materials, for instant messaging and bulletin boards, to create groups and manage teachers content and CMS, are HTML5, JavaScript (Angular), and CSS3, with Ionic Framework.
- Two third-party software packages have been used for the management of synchronous meetings and the DAW. Many commercial products are available on the market that can satisfy these needs, but instead those that provide Web-Services interfaces were chosen.
  These enable a transparent link to the user and a management of personal data that complies with the regulations in force on privacy. Using API and federated identity systems (OAuth) it is perfectly possible (if the third-party software supports and develops these services) to

Fig. 3. Prototype of the environment

authenticate a user by providing an alphanumeric code only, keeping the link to the actual personal data inside the source information systems.
In this way, users are authenticated directly and transparently using third-party products without any of their data being shared elsewhere.

D. *Description of an activity within the learning environment.*

To illustrate the features of the application in more detail, and how these can be integrated from the active-learning point of view, we can show one possible activity within the learning environment in which the teacher establishes the start-up mode and supervision with the intent of supporting/moderating the students' work.

1) The instructor divides the class into groups of 4-5 people and assigns each group a corresponding online environment, by fixing as an objective the composition of a pop song in a specific style (Italian / English pop, Hip Hop, Rock, etc.).
2) The teacher provides an essential discography that students must listen to (and expand to their liking) to evaluate the compositional aspects and the arrangements: the objective in this step will be to decide and establish the structure of the song (AABA, intro/verse/bridge/chorus/variation/finale/outro/etc.) and discuss the main aspects of the arrangement (instrumentation, melody lines, harmony, any modulations).
3) This activity will be carried out using instant-messaging tools and by sharing multimedia materials, and the teacher will moderate any discussions. Each student will be able to record and share audio files with their own compositional ideas or can share them synchronously using video-conferencing.
   This delicate and deeper phase ends with an indication by the group of the main parameters of the song:
   a) Metronomic tempo
   b) Bars
   c) Key
   d) Structure
   e) Electronic instrumentation needed (asking the teacher for help)
4) The teacher supports students in the realization of the structure of the piece inside the online DAW, building a template within which students can record their performances, and providing help with inserting electronic samples, rhythm loops or ambience effects.
5) Each student enters the DAW to record his or her performance, overdubbing their recordings until the desired result is achieved. No limits are placed on the number of overdubs nor the access times.
6) The teacher monitors the work and suggests changes to performances considered below par. When the recording work is finished, the teacher helps the groups in the mixing and mastering steps, to explain how a piece of music is produced.
7) Part of the sharing of materials is a specific evaluation of finished products among peers: tracks are shared in a particular form, and other groups of students are asked to evaluate them, anonymously, by responding to a preset questionnaire based on musical criteria, in order to offer their own opinion.
8) At the end, students write a report on the key points of the work carried out.

V. Expected Results

A. *Expected results in the learning of individual students*

Knowledge

- Learning of new languages and digital music codes using a Digital Audio Workstation (DAW) to record musical performances.
- Access to tools of collaborative learning online to exploit different points of view and approaches in a musical project.
- Knowing the importance of developing creative abilities
- Understanding interaction in the sharing of knowledge within social networking environments.

Skills

- Strengthening and valorization of musical practice.
- Mastering the use of the network by means of independent tools and collaborative environments, to search for useful material, and to share and discuss musical roads in the realization of a collaborative musical project.
- Ability to use tools for music creation through Cloud software and DAWs, in general. Developing a capacity to operate in technologically advanced environments and as part of a work team.

Competence

- Competently using dedicated software and technological applications and understanding the management mechanisms.
- Recording music using systems commonly employed in recording studios, precociously bridging the technological gap between a personal "acoustic" performance and the technological procedures to record this performance.

- Recording using a metronome, and overdubbing backing tracks/performance by other musicians, listening to the nuances and dynamics and trying out different approaches to better match the performances of their band mates.
- Musical performance skills aimed at recording.
- Working, studying and planning as a group, being responsible for the completion of a project and adapting personal behaviour to the circumstances in resolving problems.

B. Expected results in general terms

- Shared leadership. Making music "together" lets students grow, also and especially technically, and allows them to express a considered sensitive leadership and to develop skills of "mediation" in a group, sharing and making the most of the emotional elements of a musical experience in a working group (a band) to achieve an effective artistic product.
- Feedback and evaluation. Each student is an integral part of a group within an environment of communication-participation-collaboration, and is therefore placed in a direct relationship with all the other students, to realize a product in the most effective, fun and interesting way possible, using musical language. The interventions of revision and control of the activities carried out, and the assessment of the work of the group represent a constant within the environment, which manifests itself through synchronous and asynchronous tools of content sharing, to correct/improve the musical project.
- Simulation, through an educational and training project, of the concrete manner of operating in a musical production when it comes to organization, environment, compiling of reports and work tools.
- Assessment. It is not only the assessment of the "final" product that matters within a group of collaborative learning: elements such as the improvement of self-esteem, communication skills, and problem-solving abilities are of great efficacy in a workshop approach.
- Social skills. The quality of the work and the results are directly proportional to the communication and problem-solving ability of the participants, who are mutually supportive.
- Responsibility. The environment favours the self-realization and personal growth of each participant in the group, inside which is triggered a sense of mutual responsibility that promotes learning.

VI. CONCLUSIONS AND POTENTIAL NEW DEVELOPMENTS

This paper has illustrated a digital learning environment to develop musical practice and collaborative composition within small groups of students moderated by a teacher, and are considered the didactic outcome of the activities proposed therein.

The learning environment uses Cloud services for its operation and the necessary hardware for access is cross-device, allowing any web-connected device to exploit the potential offered and to deepen the students' knowledge, skills and abilities in connection with musical practice and composition.

As to future developments, the following guidelines have been considered:

- Testing of informal training in the composition, performance and remote sharing of musical tracks/projects with technological tools based on Cloud computing, within a virtual studio community, assembled under the supervision of teachers.
- Testing the efficacy of an informal learning model in a creative key as part of Italian school curricula, as indicated in the Italian "National Guidelines for Lower-Secondary-School Music Education' (p. 59).
- Testing ways of offering assistance and support to all students in the processes of learning within a virtual environment, not only in the planning of a project/song, but also in the management of teamwork communication.

REFERENCES

[1] A. Brown, *Music Technology and Education: Amplifying Musicality*. Routledge, 2015.

[2] G. L. F. Bianconi, "The musical journey of education: closed streets and highways. "music education and teaching," in *Music education and teaching*. Franco Angeli, 2008.

[3] D. Lebow, "Constructivist values for systems design: five principles toward a new mindset," *Educational Technology Research and Development*, no. 41, pp. 4–16, 1993.

[4] *Thinking Technology, Toward a Constructivistic Design Model*, vol. 34, 1994, number 4.

[5] J. Bruner, *After Dewey: The process of learning in the two cultures*. Armando, 1966.

[6] J. Lave and E. Wenger, *Situated Learning: Legitimate Peripheral Participation (Learning in Doing: Social, Cognitive and Computational Perspectives)*. Cambridge University Press, 1991.

[7] M. Comoglio and M. A. Cardoso, *Teaching and learning in groups*. LAS, 1996.

[8] J. A. Sloboda, "Music structure and emotional response: Some empirical findings," *Psychology of music*, pp. 110–120, 1991.

[9] C. J. Lincoln, *Louis Armstrong: an american genius*. Oxford University Press, 1983.

[10] G. L. F. Bianconi and F. Frabboni, *Music education and teaching*. FrancoAngeli, 2008, vol. Music education and teaching.

[11] D. François, *Le son des musiques*. Paris: Buchet-Castel, 2001.

[12] R. Maragliano, *New media and new sounds*. FrancoAngeli,, 2008, vol. Music education and teaching.

Method for Quick Identification of Computer Operations Performed by a Student

Kenta Morita
Graduate School of Information and Telecommunication Engineering
Tokai University
Tokyo, Japan
e-mail: morita.k@star.tokai-u.jp

Haruhiko Takase
Graduate School of Engineering
Mie University
Mie, Japan
e-mail: takase@elec.mie-u.ac.jp

Naoki Morita
Graduate School of Information and Telecommunication Engineering
Tokai University
Tokyo, Japan
e-mail: morita@tokai.ac.jp

Abstract **– In classes where personal computers (PCs) are actively used as a part of lesson plans, it is important for teachers to be able to quickly locate the operations that students have performed on their individual machines during exercises. To identify such operations, a method using a global hook has been utilized previously. However, when this method is used, numerous successive screen-captured images must be examined and it is difficult to find the changed portions that allow the operations to be identified. Herein, we propose a method that presents changed portions in an easily recognizable manner and reduces the number of captured images to be examined.**

Keywords- Compute-assisted instruction; Operation Process.

I. INTRODUCTION

Recently, classes in which students use personal computers (PCs) or tablet devices have become more commonplace [1]. In most such classes, students learn how to use applications, such as Microsoft Word or Excel, or practice programming techniques, by operating their PCs in accordance with instructions from a teacher.

When teachers present processes that students can manipulate on their PCs during class, lessons can proceed more smoothly and students can better understand the class contents. However, when a student is unable to operate his device in accordance with the teacher's instructions, the instructor must identify which parts of the student's operations are incorrect and correct the student's misunderstandings.

Unfortunately, when a student has made a mistake, the teacher may not be able to identify the errors in the student's process simply by viewing the student's screen. For example, as shown in Fig. 1, in which an exercise for calculating the sum of list of values using Excel is displayed, there is no visually identifiable difference between using the SUM function and directly inputting a value. More specifically, either 21 has been manually input into cell B6 or the "=SUM(B2:B5)" operation has been completed, but it is impossible to know which method has been used simply by looking at the screen.

Since it is difficult to identify where mistakes have been made in cases where screens look identical, determining the process the student used on his/her PC can help the teacher identify the incorrect operation. Additionally, in programming classes, it is important for teachers to know the processes that students use when editing source code because such processes contain information that the teacher needs to assess whether students followed instructions correctly. This allows the teacher to determine whether students have adequately grasped their lesson content.

Until now, while it has been possible for a teacher to observe all student operations if the student's PC screen is continuously captured in the form of video [2][3], this process includes all the screen time during which the student is not operating the PC, most of which is superfluous to the teacher's needs. Therefore, a method [4][5][6] that allows only (operational) changes made by the student to be collected is desirable.

Accordingly, in this paper, we propose a method by which all computer operations and the corresponding changes made by a student can be recorded and rapidly presented to the teacher, and by which unnecessary screen captures are eliminated. The use of this method can be

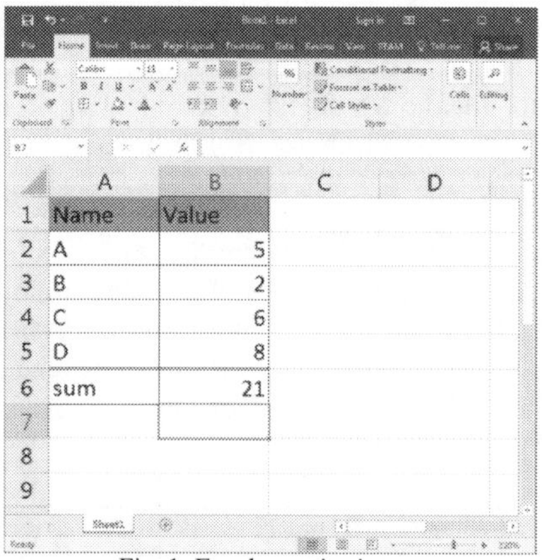

Fig. 1: Excel exercise image

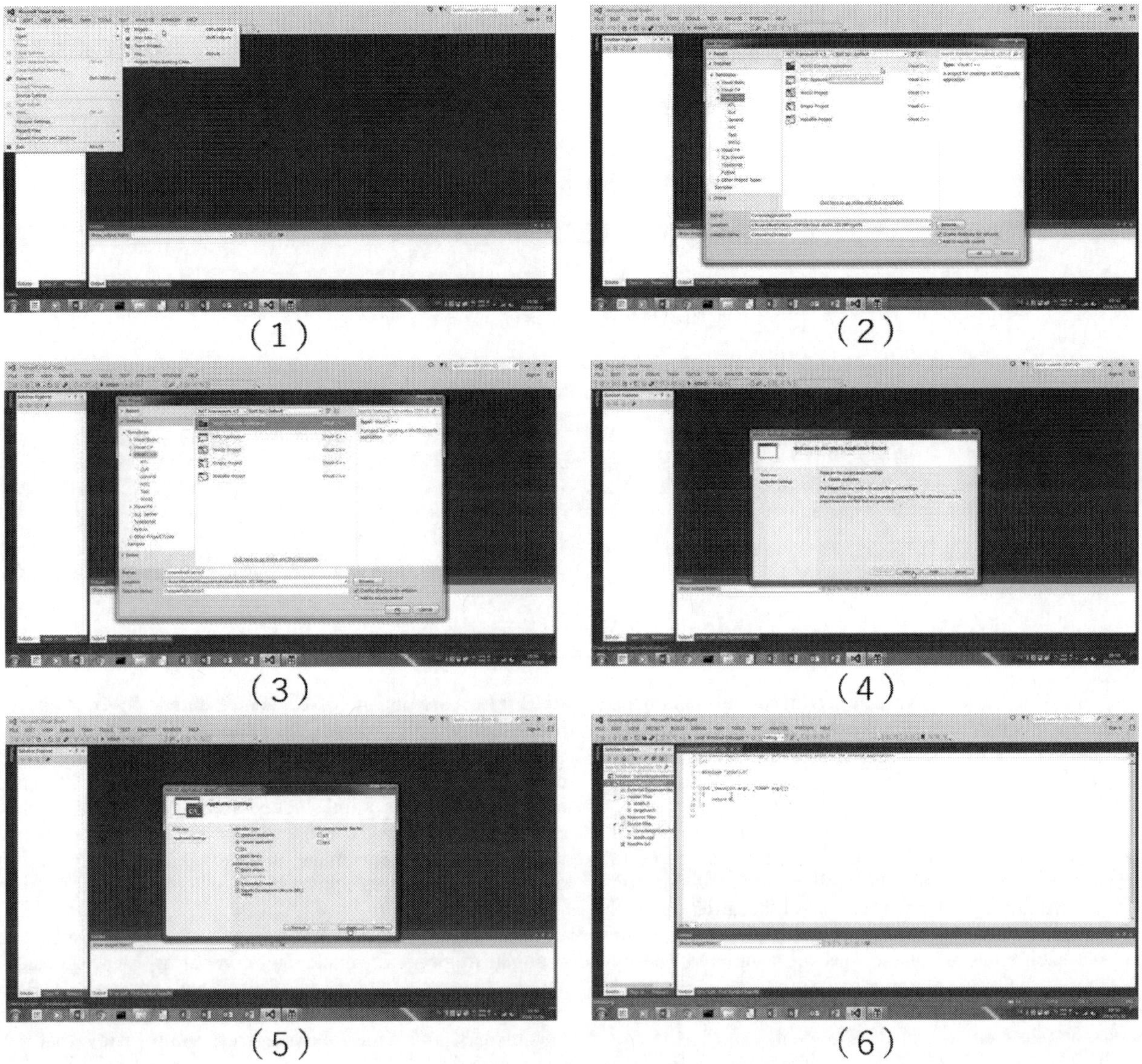

Fig. 2 Confirmation using global hook method.
(1)Select [New Project], (2) select [Win32 Console Application], (3) select [OK], (4) select [next], (5) select [Finish] (6) mouse click.

expected to help the teacher quickly ascertain the student's lesson comprehension.

This paper describes the previous methods and problems in Section II. In Section III, the method for quick identification is proposed. We discuss the effectiveness of our proposed method in Section IV. Section V presents the conclusion and future work.

II. PREVIOUS METHODS AND PROBLEMS

Currently, there are two methods that use dedicated applications [4] [5], and one global hook method [6] that can be used to restrict the information provided to the teacher to just changes in the student's process.

However, the dedicated applications only target programming operations and acquire the process taken in creating source code by using a dedicated text editor. Thus, while this method is capable of presenting information regarding the process used, it can only acquire changes that were entered via the dedicated text editor. This means it will not acquire operations, such as file openings on the desktop, nor can it acquire and recode the computer operations performed by students. As a result, this method cannot present all operations performed by the student.

There is also a global hook method that can be used to collect all of the operations carried out on a PC. This method monitors messages the operating system (OS) sends to an application, takes screen captures when it detects keyboard

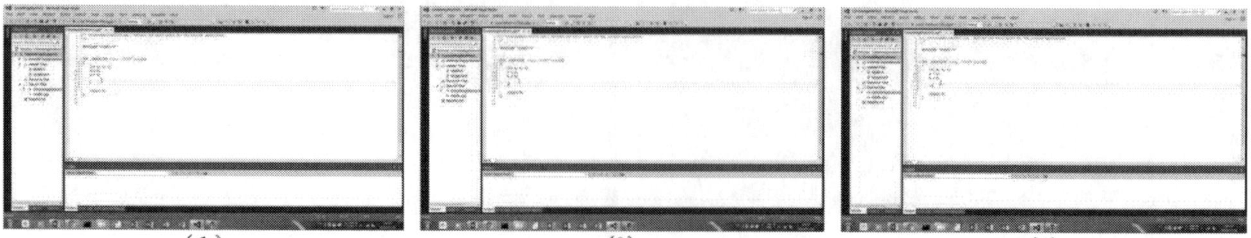

(1) (2) (3)

Fig. 3 Editing programming source code.
(1) Insert [Enter], (2) insert [c], (3) insert [=].

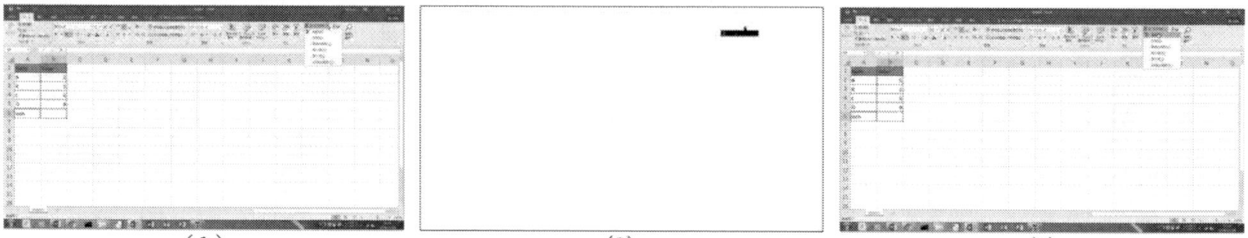

(1) (2) (3)

Fig. 4 Confirmation using proposed method.
(1) Previous image, (2) differential image, (3) next image.

input or mouse clicks, and saves the screen captures as image data. The process can then be determined by reviewing the captured images one by one, in order, as shown in Fig. 2, and noting the changes. By looking at the order in which they were captured, faulty operations can be determined.

However, while the global hook method acquires all of the operations that the student has performed and can present the information to the teacher, the problem with this method is that it is difficult to locate the path taken because a screen capture is made whenever student operates the keyboard or mouse, and each captured image must be examined one by one. Moreover, editing programming source code results in less visible changed portions of the screen because the input characters appear very small, as shown in Fig. 3, thereby making it necessary to scrutinize each image carefully. This makes reducing the number of screen capture images desirable.

Our goal was therefore to develop a technique that teachers can use to quickly identify operations performed by a student, while also reducing the number of images captured via the global hook method.

III. PROPOSED METHOD

In this section, we propose techniques that will permit teachers to identify computer operations performed by a student by identifying changes in successive screen captures while reducing the number of captured images required.

A. Finding changed portions

The basic idea behind our method of finding changed portions is to present only the portions that have been changed. For example, if there is an operation B that takes place after operation A, existing methods presents an image of B after the image of A is presented. In contrast, our proposed method presents the image of A next to an image that shows only the changed portions, which is the difference between images A and B. By examining the differences between previous and successive images, a teacher examining a student's process can predict where changes will occur in the next image, and more easily understand the operations performed, which is where his/her attention should be focused.

The image (difference image) used to display the changed regions is made by comparing two successive screen captures and consists of black and white pixels. Black pixels correspond to pixels that have changed between the two images, and white pixels correspond to pixels that have not changed.

To clarify the changed portion, the system shows the difference image between two successive images. For example, Figure 4 shows transition images of confirmation using the proposed method. Here, it can be seen that even if a teacher examines captured images one by one, he/she can easily understand the student's process simply by noting the black pixels in each successive image.

B. Reducing captured images

The basic idea for reducing the number of images to be captured is to refrain from creating screen captures if the changes in the screen are insignificant.

Existing methods generate a screen capture whenever the student operates the mouse or keyboard, which means that numerous captured images have very small changed portions, or no changes at all. However, it is still necessary for the teacher to examine each image to be sure no important changes are present. In contrast, our proposed method compares each new captured image with the one before it, calculates the number of changed pixels, and then creates a computer screen capture when the number of changed pixels exceeds a certain preset threshold value.

Using our proposed method, the number of screen captures is significantly reduced compared to existing methods. This method captures the screen if the number of black pixels exceeds the threshold, thus reducing the number of captures. For typing programs, the system captures occasionally, since black pixels appear only for characters that are being typed. For application menus or windows, the system captures frequently, since black pixels will appear over a wider area. Therefore, since only major operations are captured, it is possible to reduce the number of screen captures.

IV. EXPERIMENTS

In this section, we discuss the effectiveness of our proposed method based on the results of a simple experiment.

A. *Experimental setup*

In this experiment, in which the proposed method is compared to an existing method, we found it is easy to identify the changed portions, the number of captured images is low, and it is easy to determine the operations carried out by the student.

We selected a class of undergraduate students studying Java programming to test the method. This class involved a three-hour long practice session that mixed small operations with operations producing large changes to the screen. Students were required to manipulate text-editor-typed source code as well as run an application that converts the source code into an executable file. Three test subjects confirmed the operations.

Regarding the total number of changed pixels used as the threshold to reduce the number of captured images, 1/20 of the screen size of the PC seemed to be appropriate.

B. *Results*

We will begin by discussing whether it was easy to determine the portions of the screen changed by student operations using our method. One of the authors asked all test subjects whether it was possible to identify operations performed by the students when looking at their screen capture images one by one. The subjects stated that it was easy to find the changed portions because all they had to do was find the parts displayed as black pixels.

Next, we asked whether the number of captured images was low compared to existing methods. An existing method captured 1860 images, while the proposed method captured 584 images. Since the programming of the proposed method limited captures to large screen changes rather than capturing all changes, including relatively small screen changes caused by programming, there was a significant reduction in the number of images captured. Since the teacher wants to know all the operations of the student, we think that all these images are useful.

Finally, regarding whether it was easy to locate changes, we asked all test subjects to interact with the tool and to identify any operations performed by the students. Three test subjects responded with the name of the operation the student had actually performed, such as "press this button", or "type A". Teachers can find mistakes such as, student is not operating PC as instructed.

V. CONCLUSIONS

We discussed methods that teachers can use to determine the computer operations being performed by his/her students. We began by discussing an existing method that is difficult for teachers to use because it requires them to examine numerous sequential screen capture images in order to identify changed portions in the images.

We then introduced our proposed method in which new images are compared to the image captured immediately before it, and the portions that exhibit significant differences are output using different pixel colors. In our method, no screen capture is performed if the number of changed pixels is less than a preset threshold.

After examining the results of our experiment, we confirmed that our proposed method makes it easier for teachers to identify the changed portions and is capable of reducing the number of required captured images.

The proposed approach always captures the screen when the user switches from applications repeatedly. Such an image may not be useful for the teacher, so it is necessary to reduce it.

In the future, we want to confirm the effectiveness in more classes Since the number of subjects and students in the experiment of this paper is small.

ACKNOWLEDGMENT

This work was supported by JSPS KAKENHI Grant Number 16K16324.

REFERENCES

[1] G. Thavamalar, "Successful implementation of e-learning: Pedagogical considerations" The internet and higher education, Vol.4 No.3, pp.287-299.

[2] R. Stannard, "Screen capture software for feedback in language education" Second International Wireless Ready Symposium, MAR. 2008, pp. 16-20, ISSN 1995-4557.

[3] J. Nigel, P. Georghiades, and J. Gunson, "Student feedback via screen capture digital video: Stimulating student's modified action." Higher Education Vol.64 No.5, pp.593-607.

[4] Y. Katagiri, Y. Tateiwa, D. Yamamoto and N. Takahashi, "Implementation of a Context-Aware Programming Instructor Assistant Using an Analysis Function of Programming Activity" IEICE Technical ReportET2009-83, pp.181-186.

[5] H. Igaki, S. Saito, A. Inoue, R. Nakamura and S. Kusumoto, "Programming Process Visualization for Supporting Students in Programming Exercise" IPSJ Jornal, Vol.54 No.1, pp. 330-339.

[6] N. Morita, "A Programming Process Visualization System With Global Hooking" Society for Information Technology and Teacher Education(SITE2014), MAR. 2014, pp. 1945-1953, ISBN 978-1-939797-07-0.

CoWaBoo: A Descriptive Protocol of Learning Driven Applications

Athanasios Priftis
Information Systems Department
HES/HE G-GE,
Geneva, Switzerland
e-mail: athanasios.priftis@hesge.ch,

Jean Philippe Trabichet
Information Systems Department
HES/HE G-GE,
Geneva, Switzerland
e-mail: jean-philippe.trabichet@hesge.ch,

***Abstract*— Algorithms, data, services seem to create a net of semantic stability for users to consume information but come with concrete disadvantages regarding the way we understand, discuss and teach them. Social bookmarking applications are no exception to this, as they follow a similarly opaque way to organize and publish data. This article will examine the possibility to shift from predetermined results to open and descriptive protocols and applications that revisits fundamental web user activities such as search, classification, group formation and valorization of participation. This approach combines both a data handling protocol (CoWaBoo) and an application (collective observatories) that serve as wider concept and practice of application use and development. Our initial results from 2015 and 2016 university group course works, contributes to shifting our attention from how things end up, to how things *become*, an important competence in the field of ICT training and education.**

Keywords-ICT opacity; open protocols; learning driven applications

I. Introduction

Scholars agree that we need to look more deeply into the opacity of a growing algorithmic reality, where users perform prescribed tasks. The nature of the ‘opacity’ of these tasks is related to sociological interests in classification and discrimination, framed around ‘digital inequality’ that has frequently focused on the distribution of computational resources and skills [1]. How people may be subject to computational classification, privacy invasions, or other surveillance methods in ways that are unequal across the general population, could be in violation of existing regulatory protections [2]. This is crucial for several reasons but in this paper, we will focus on its possible effect on our training practices in education.

This “click on the most often” culture [3] is exemplified by Google’s searching normalization resulting from user habits that have “deeply ingrained habitual patterns” [4]. The result of this is a widely spread culture of opacity of web applications, data or machine learning algorithms assuming a certain normality: when a computer learns and consequently builds its own representation of a classification decision, it does so without regard for human comprehension. The examples of handwriting recognition and spam filtering illustrate how the workings of machine learning algorithms can escape full understanding and interpretation by humans, even for those with specialized training, even for computer scientists [5].

Algorithms, such as those underlying the Google search engine, are often multi-component systems built by teams producing an opacity that programmers who are ‘insiders’ to the algorithm must contend with as well [6]. The opacity concern arises in the middle of an input - black box - output approach. For the most part, we know how the data are fed into the algorithm: we produce it ourselves through our activities. We also typically know the outputs of the algorithm: we are either told, or we can reasonably infer how the algorithm has classified the data. What we do not know is what is going on in the middle, inside the ‘black box’, or which bits of data the algorithm selects and how it uses that data to generate the classifications.

To sum up, we cannot rely merely on the modern “disciplinary” methods and frameworks of knowledge in order to think and interpret the transformative effect new technology is having on our culture, since it is precisely these methods and frameworks that new technology requires us to rethink’ [7]. We need to propose and invent an analysis that intersects the current state of opacity and, at the same time, applicable in training and collaborative scenarios. Following sections of this paper will pursue this analysis, further. In Section 2, we, briefly, position protocols as an important, but not sufficient, parameter against an opaque, black-box culture of application use and development. This culture is exemplified by an analysis on social bookmarking applications and practices. Section 3 is devoted to CoWaBoo, a protocol assuming a socio-semantic logic, empowered by specific rules and architecture. In Section 4, we demonstrate how an application of collective observatories, built on the CoWaBoo protocol serves a double objective: validate the rules and functions of the protocol, while raising further research and learning questions in a context of collaboration and knowledge production. Finally, in Section 5 we highlight the initial training and experimentation results of using CoWaBoo and the collective observatories in university courses. Our conclusions include our future work and challenges.

II. On Protocols and Social Bookmarking Applications

Partnerships between legal scholars, social scientists, domain experts, along with computer scientists may chip away at these challenging questions of fairness in classification in light of the barrier of opacity. User populations can give voice to exclusions and forms of experienced discrimination (algorithmic or otherwise) that the 'domain experts' may lack insight into. Alleviating problems of black boxed classification will not be accomplished by a single tool or process, but some combination of regulations, audits, the use of alternatives that are more transparent, user education, as well as, the sensitization of those bestowed with the power to write such consequential code. Moreover, we need pedagogical concepts and tools that can form and carry a culture of educated openness. We would like to introduce protocols as an important parameter of future application analysis and design.

A protocol is founded on a contradiction between two opposing machines, one machine that radically distributes control into autonomous locales, and another that focuses control into rigidly defined hierarchies. In order for protocol to enable radically distributed communications between autonomous entities, it must employ a strategy of universalization, and of homogeneity. It must be implementing, at the same time distribution and anti-diversity. It must promote standardization in order to enable openness, while organizing peer groups into bureaucracies. A protocol, then, becomes an ambivalent space where both opacity and transparency are possible and certain short-term goals are necessary in order to realize one's longer-term goals [8]. Applications running on protocols can use or, sometimes, play down this contradiction but never break away from it.

Social bookmarking applications can be understood as social machines, a collective of humans and machines and computers (or algorithms) working collaboratively on some area. This assemblage involves large numbers of users, some level of interaction, responding to a certain task. Software or applications mediate between the user and other users or machines' in a way that obscures how searching, tagging, curating posts and bookmarks, or forming groups take place. Their users are involved in a "many to one to many" schema of directive search and classification where the intermediator the "one" is setting the agenda of how the documentation itself takes place. This combination of directive searching, leads to limited diversity for retrieving information and, results, to "one-click" driven documentation. We will use the terms atonal posts and reticular search to frame the results of this process, as a components of how prescription works in social bookmarking.

Atonal posts appear as flat bookmarks with standardized description that carry no actual engagement on behalf of the user. Atonal posts are produced with the minimum number of clicks, where decision and curation process are merely mentioned, and, thus, a post exists without any other event connected. They flood search engines and information aggregators, while creating impressive numbers of individual posts. They are prescribing information items as something distant but true, a set of data of something classified, thus becoming important, with a minimum effort of description or documentation.

The term *reticular search* carries the user expectation that searching of information, in the connected networks of our times, is a sufficient proof their own intentionality access knowledge. In this sense, searching and documenting information is imagined within fixed patterns: being efficient in information search implies knowing the "right tricks" as to cut down the time needed and the diversity of the possible results. This creates a kind of reticular search where a minimum set of keywords, thrown in a sea of algorithms, consist of a sufficient process. Both reticular search and atonal search help us frame how users interact with protocols and social bookmarking applications, nowadays. Producing atonal posts based on a culture of reticular search acts as an explicit normative context to a future self that is mediated as time-series structured data streams. Take the example of social media: we are often prescribing parts of ourselves, within few clicks, words and images, creating more and more (atonal) posts, or data for more (reticular) search.

III. The CoWaBoo protocol in a descriptive socio-semantique logic

CoWaBoo starts as a concept and an ambition to understand and change user actions and results in social bookmarking. It enters the field of information search by integrating, in a conscious manner, the reuse of results that are available in existing curating communities. Searching in CoWaBoo means identifying experts as mediators, or trusted entities in the research of information. This search is not to be inscribed in an immediate response but in a wider logic of information culture and curation of information. CoWaBoo attempts to move the boundaries of social bookmarking from an, opaque, click and post culture towards a storytelling event that involves serendipitous browsing and learning. The term "serendipitous browsing" is used to refer to information search that result in discovery of relevant information as by-product of the main task [9].

It is heavily connected with its possibility to stimulate competences including "sagacity" as penetrating intelligence, keen perception and sound judgment [10], "intellectual readiness" as the ability to recognize clues which may lead to meaningful discoveries, "openness" as the ability to seize an unexpected and unplanned event [11] as well as "preparation, training and knowledge" [9]. The CoWaBoo approach on social bookmarking is based on the identification of users who share common interests. The goal is to find information and websites and to identify experts in a field [12] not so much as a final, unmovable product but more as an unexpected travel. In this sense, information research process can be described as a travel with discoveries, information, websites and people. CoWaBoo opens this process to community-curated resources, while the users are gathering selected discoveries: they need to make choices and engage in some kind of a result that contributes back to the original sources.

In this sense, CoWaBoo opts to explore, not so much on "what is social bookmarking", but "how social bookmarking is". It is drawing on the previous work on user driven data search and management, social bookmarking applications and uses cases, online collaboration skills and user capacities, in order to reposition them in the proposed mediation interface. Positioning CoWaBoo "in between" current search and organization of information trends and algorithms, means reusing social bookmarking data, connecting with communities and users, producing results both locally and globally, decentralized and centralized.

Our next step in this direction is putting trust in the work of others by creating a circular understanding of searching and curating information. This comes in contrast with web 2.0, algorithmic based, ways of capturing data, seeking to extract value through an unintentional capacity of participation and opens a virtuous circle of social bookmarking. A different logic open to iterative transformations of the work of others, a possibility to produce knowledge through the act of redocumentation. CoWaBoo, then, is positioning itself, not as another collaborative application, but a protocol. We consider the addressee of these wider computational systems made up of arrays or networks as a future actor of it design. As the interaction needs to be open to further development, the code of CoWaBoo protocol needs to apply the following default rules:

- Assure the lucidity of past (as stored data), present (as current data collection, or processed archival data), and future (as both the ethical addressee of the system and potential provider of data and usage).
- Store objects that do not resemble to complex computational models but act as a section to existing social (bookmarking) practices, structuring assumptions, conditions generated from their use.
- Demonstrate in a transdisciplinary way that code's mediation can be rethought, researched for intervention, contestation and the un-building of code/software systems.

The overarching concept of the protocol is to formalize an always-editable space realized by the rules set above. This space stays vague if we do not experiment its utility. This is why we bring in the collective observatories application, as one, of the possible many applications, built upon the protocol. In this application, the protocol would store and allow us to recover a general index of a given subspace (observatory) and then be able to navigate through the different versions of the entries in this observatory. To achieve this within the application, we introduce two more layers of representing information reusing data from the protocol: a) the use cases, or the way we propose users to explore the possibilities of the protocol, through the creation of collective observatories and b) the graphic representation of classified information. The use cases need to be concrete with a measurable result. Users can search information that communities have already curated and form groups. The graphic interface attempts to address how users will experience the above.

In terms of communication, data and account handling the CoWaBoo protocol adopts the following approach. All data are stored on InterPlanetary File System (IPFS), a p2p storage protocol, with its current state available in the application. Community management is based on Stellar, an open source protocol, blockchain based, for value exchange. CoWaBoo is utilizing a NodeJs server with a Stellar Javascript SDK to provide the CoWaBoo API with a way to communicate directly with Stellar. Every time that a new member is subscribed, a new Stellar account is also created. This account receives the minimum amount of lumens (Stellar currency) to work properly as a CoWaBoo account Once the account is created, it automatically give its consent to carry out currency exchanges created by the "bank" of CoWaBoo in Stellar. Consequently, all transactions (votes in groups) are stored on Stellar blockchain infrastructure creating Stellar exchange community with a cryptographic Public Address and Secret Key. While Web 2.0 applications tend to prescribe our participation, in CoWaBoo we seek to re-open the discussion on the group rules and results as entries or definitions are editable and possible to change from everyone, as long as her/his entry is voted in a group. In the following sections, we will discuss in detail the utility of this function.

It is important, however, to demonstrate if and how the default rules are applied. Once an entry is added, modified or deleted, the observatory created a new version of itself that is registered to a different place of the old. To achieve this we have drawn from the blockchain paradigm. Blockchain as a distributed, cryptography boosted, database technology is a thing of the 80s, that computational capacity of our time brought to full implementation with the Bitcoin deployment. Blockchain, can also be understood as an implementation of distributed ledgers that comes with a unique set of possibilities in its design. It opens up the way to shared databases, where multiple entities can transact, with no or some trust between them, co-existing with no intermediation.

The CoWaBoo protocol reproduces the main blockchain synchronous properties, as described above in the following generic approach: a) accessible and affordable shared databases with resilience through replication and no single point of failure and control, b) where multiple entries are possible, c) based on the possibility of disintermediation. Blockchain implementation comes with two more interesting features: d) interaction "in and between" transactions (or more commonly framed as smart contracts). Going back to our collective blockchain application, we will try to point out the exact process and code that demonstrate the above

CoWaBoo can be understood as a re-documentation effort opening to possible, iterative transformations of the work of others, to produce knowledge, in three ways. Firstly, searching is based on existing "community curated" resources already available in existing socially curated results from Diigo, Zotero, two social bookmarking applications, and Wikipedia, inviting users to develop an intentional logic of collaborative indexing evaluation and curation of information. Secondly, groups are initiated with the possibility of voting in all group decisions using a currency that allows their users to valorize their effort and the results in the group. Thirdly, the rules of the protocol are themselves configurable and re-applicable in a variety of applications, with our collective observatories serving as an initial experimentation.

IV. IMPLEMENTING THE PROTOCOL THROUGH THE COLLECTIVE OBSERVATORIES APPLICATION

A protocol is never neutral in the sense that all decisions regarding its functions are already set to bring some kind of normality on users (agents) behaviors. Thus, it becomes crucial to describe in more detail the use cases of the collective observatories application and illustrate how the interaction with the protocol will take place. We present the use cases as a descriptive middleware, between the protocol and collective observatories application, appearing itself to its users:

- **Build your story:** A prompt to click on the start the button and move to an empty text area is the first step. The empty text area is destined to be the user's notebook, potentially filled up with search results discovered using the connected APIs for search on tag, bookmarks, articles and existing entries (linked to the Visualize tags and stories in observatories use case). Keywords for initial search lead to tags to visualize existing stories in bookmarking software or CoWaBoo observatories with the selected info are inserted in the text area, as part of the actual user story. This tentative story-result can stay local, private and unfinished, to-be-posted posted in an observatory, or become the first entry in a new possible observatory. Adding a post in an existing observatory is subject to a verification process depending on the rules of the observatory: self – validated means that the post is validated by the user, peer – validated are linked with a "vote" from someone of its existing members".
- **Edit a story:** A click on the full text search button of the application connects the user's keywords, then transformed to used tags, to visualize existing stories in observatories or observatories themselves (linked to the Visualize tags and stories in observatories use case) and select them as content for further editing into the text area (linked to the Build your story use case)
- **Start a community of transactions (group)**: The click on the community button initiate a community creation function with the possibility to add emails, each participation verified through the related email account and attributed both public and secret keys. The group creation launches the possibility to start, transparent, intra-group transactions where all group users being informed on energy limits to credit or store value of the group. Group participants use the secret key to perform transactions, while the results of the effectuated transactions as well as the user balance remain publicly linked to each user's public key. New members are proposing themselves through direct demands to join an observatory (group) or through accepted stories when observatory entries are accepted from someone of its existing member". The user in this instance can be a part of a multiple, group transactions possibility, his/her public key is added to the group users for further transactions.
- **Editing tags**: CoWaBoo treats tags as distributed objects, recasting the tag object as an autonomous transaction providing its user with an opportunity to redefine, rebuilt and redistribute through the work of others. Tags in CoWaBoo acquire a multiple meaning as they, simultaneously, represent: a) "Tags to be": user typed search keywords in the text area leading to tags used by other users, b) Keywords that are then selected as Tags (CoWaBoo step by step search), leading educated choices of stories description and proposed entries or definitions for observatories, c) Tags are treated as semantic elements pointing to entries in observatories (list of tags per observatory), d) names of observatories are also treated as tags (list of observatories) and proposed to users in order to contribute or consult before creating a new observatory
- **Propose or "vote" an entry or a member** (validation & valorization). Each story is accepted as entry (definition) when posted and voted by at least one group member as a verification (the fastest reply - user is considered for attributing the value of the transaction). Each accepted entry is tokenized with one (1) energy (limit +10 for every user), while a vote for an entry uses 1 energy, (- 10 for every user). The variation in personal energy is, initially, anonymous but transparent, connected to each user's public key.
- **Visualize tags and stories in observatories**: This use case is connected to user keywords (full text search) becoming tags and visualizing an index view with linked tags, entries and observatory names.

Here follow some important questions that will guide to the presentation of the initial results of the protocol and its collective observatories application: Firstly, do tags serve at the same time descriptive keywords, linked data (to stories) and ongoing collections (observatories names)? How do they connect entries and observatories? Do they provide some kind of navigation through the information initiated by the application and stored by the protocol? Secondly, the protocol does not promise, or highlights, a completed story or observatory but a possibility create stories and edit all products in future events. How is this appearing in the existing digital space? Can the CoWaBoo (protocol and application) unfinished social bookmarking space serve as an experimentation understood both in semantic, representational and process level in a context of collaboration and knowledge production? The following pages will present the initial answer to these questions.

V. Initial Results

Our efforts on introducing re-documentation and collaboration, as pivotal skills in students group works, starts during spring 2015, a full semester course, with twenty participants. All results of this initial effort entitled HEG Digital – Lectures on "Wikinomie are documented at the Diigo web social bookmarking application [13]. At that time, we used Diigo to document various group activities including: thematic awareness on selected areas, business and process analysis of Diigo and co-design of a collaborative social bookmarking application on the CoWaBoo protocol. Each of these activities would deserve a separate presentation and analysis. At this point, we will focus on the quality of social bookmarking posts produced from students during their curse activities. In both the examples used below, be it the "expert", from another existing Diigo group or the "student", from our own HEG initiative, we see the emergence of atonal posts, presented in Section 2: entries in a system produced with the minimum number of clicks, where decision and curation process are omitted.

In this context, posts exist with the minimum set of information and without any other rule or event connected (Figure 1 and 2).

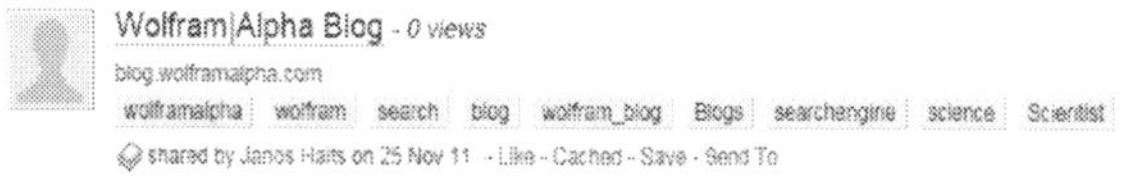

Figure 1 Atonal post – Typical example of an expert's bookmark in a Diigo group (Web 3.0) [14]

Figure 2 Atonal post – Typical example of a student's bookmark in a Diigo group [15]

These two posts are indicative of current social bookmarking trends: the "expert" will post a minimum set of information, using a rich set of tags but shows no further engagement in describing the bookmarked resource. The "student" provides the bookmark with a minimum set of tags and description. Both posts expect the potential user to have a specific interest on the topic in order to pursue further with their reading or reuse.

The results of the 2015 experiment led to the creation of the collaborative observatories application on CoWaBoo protocol. This application was introduced in our university courses the during spring semester of 2016. This new experimentation organized with twenty-four students of the University of Applied Sciences in Geneva during the HEG Digital – Lectures on "Wikinomie [16]. This group of, 3rd year, bachelor students were invited to work in groups of three, around a specific thematic area (i.e. Blockchain, Bitcoin, Wikipedia, Airbnb, Uber, Free and Open source software, Open licensing, Open innovation) using CoWaBoo as the main space of redocumentation, producing four concrete results for further evaluation: a) an introductory course presented in class, b) a collaborative documentation space in CoWaBoo, c) an infographic presentation and d) an accepted contribution to an existing Wikipedia article.

Once more, we are presenting selected results regarding the use of tags from students in their respective observatories. This is connected to our Editing tags use case and our understanding of tags as descriptive keywords, linked data and ongoing collections. *The first remark* on this work comes on the way the information of each observatory (eight in total) is presented with a certain tags selection. Let us use the "blockchain" observatory to see how its tags are visualized:

Blockchain (theme and name of the CoWaBoo observatory) with selected tags:

|| DAO || France || IDE || Parlement || analysis || badge || banques || bdd || bitcoin || blockchain || chain || concept || crypto-money || ethereum || finance || finance on blockchain || fonctionnement || governance || infographie || peer-to-peer || plate-forme || politique || presentation || questionnaire || reference || smart contract || technologie || wikinomie || wikipedia ||

The second remark is the way that each tag find is linked to other tags. This uses data coming from all other CoWaBoo observatories as linked tags with the word blockchain.

Linked Tags (in English and French) to other observatories for the "tag" blockchain:

Cowaboo, properties, avantage, bitcoin, monnaie, concept, fonctionnement, infographie, smart contract, reference, presentation, wikinomie, badge, questionnaire, Wikipedia, peer-to-peer, innovation ouverte, plateformes, copyleft, creativecommons, smartcontract

A third remark has to done on the entries (stories) that are being created and edited in the respective observatories, with the tag blockchain in each entry. **Entries using the tag blockchain:**

- CoWaBoo

|| CoWaBoo || blockchain || properties ||

- Bitcoin

|| avantage || bitcoin || blockchain || monnaie ||

- Blockchain

	blockchain		concept		fonctionnement		infographie	
	blockchain		smart contract	
	blockchain		reference	
	blockchain		presentation		wikinomie	
	badge		blockchain		questionnaire	
	blockchain		smart contract		wikipedia	
	bdd		blockchain		peer-to-peer	

- Innovation Ouverte

|| R&D || blockchain || innovation ouverte || plateformes ||

- Copyleft

|| blockchain ||copyleft || creativecommons || smartcontract ||

A fourth remark needs to be placed around the use of the word blockchain in all the observatories that CoWaBoo is hosting. **Observatories using the tag CoWaBoo:**

- CoWaBoo
- Bitcoin
- Blockchain
- Innovation Ouverte
- Copyleft

These four remarks summarize the possibility of an application, like our collective observatories, to use the CoWaBoo protocol's functions in order to reclassify user data. The protocol therefore formalizes all the necessary functions:

- Data storage, recording new data in an observatory: entry, member list, configuration
- Ensuring the current state of an observatory
- Possibility to add, change and delete data from an observatory
- Registration and acceptance of new members
- Vote counted and executed through blockchain intra-community transactions
- Configurability and re-applicability of the rules of the group in the protocol itself.

It is also important, to describe if and how the default rules are applied. Once an entry is added, modified or deleted, the observatory created a new version of itself that is registered to a different place of the old. This is important because whatever change on this code is reposted as a new block of information [17]. In the following figure (4), we can the current state of the blockchain observatory. This includes its id, entries, members, date, configuration (public or private) author and, most importantly, the path (hash) to its previously stored version. This process applies to all data stored from the CoWaBoo protocol and generated from the collaborative observatories application: observatories, entries and member list.

Figure 4. A CoWaBoo (blockchain) observatory stored on IPFS

As already mentioned the InterPlanetary File System (IPFS) is a content-addressable, peer-to-peer hypermedia distribution protocol. Nodes in the IPFS network form a distributed file system. IPFS plays a crucial role in CoWaBoo acting as a public ledger of all posted or edited data. The same goes for any rule, or post. All changes in membership, authorship and rules of this observatory are re-traceable in the blockchain logic of the protocol with the previous version always available. Content wise, things are also significantly different, compared to a standard social bookmarking application. Entries are taking more of wiki form with descriptive and links. The image below shows the text of the || France || Parlement || banques ||finance || politique || technologie || entry

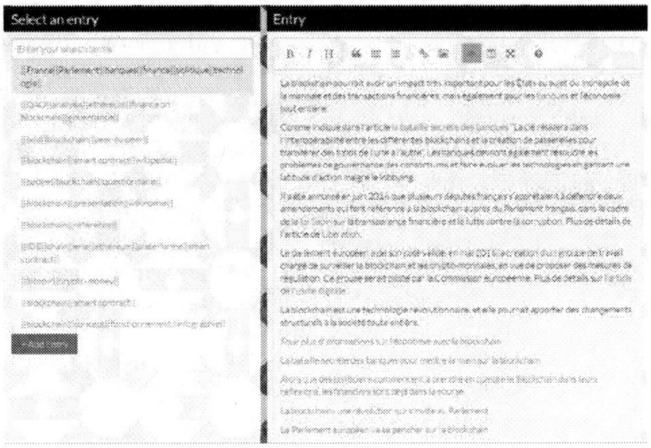

Figure 5. A CoWaBoo entry on the blockchain observatory

There is a clear shift, in all observatories, to adding text and sources in entries and forming them more as stories. This is due to the discussion related to CoWaBoo lecture on social bookmarking and the evaluation criteria but it goes hand in hand with our initial anti-click-culture approach. However, the creation of a tag dictionary based on group decisions and a diverse user participation including researchers, students, professors, experts and professionals from all project's entities is, now, emerging CoWaBoo's next step. In the table below, we summarize how CoWaBoo introduces the redocumentation process in steps:

TABLE 1. COWABOO REDOCUMENTATION PROCESS

Step title	Description	Process
Search and Post	Users are invited to search in existing communities, discern knowledgeable others, edit text and post result in existing groups	Search through tags on existing community curated resources Select resources and edit a story Publish on a group a shared "block of information" with tags ⇒ Create unique link (URI) that could be posted on selected web services
Reuse and Curate	Initiate a process of critical scrutiny and group content production for participants	Engage in a group - observatory, where an exchange between users, data and group rules is possible. Provide feedback on group's entries Contribute to the implementation of the group's collective observatory Provide history of group decisions and documentation

VI. CONCLUSIONS AND FURTHER WORK

This paper tried to demonstrate how the CoWaBoo protocol aims to reverse our habits to prescribe information and describe how various processes around this can take place. Although we can give not a binary answer as to whether (protocol and application) provide with a semantic and representational tool, in a context of collaboration and knowledge production, we have demonstrated how such a process could be initiated. Further work on the use of the protocol and its applications include the validation of the results of these use cases, during the spring semester 2017, within a targeted course in the Information Systems Department (HEG) of the University of Applied Sciences in Geneva. This pilot will continue the documentation of the work of 30 students in 15 sessions in 2017. This involves reusing the protocol through its use cases and functions, experimenting on:

- More complex group rules and valorization of transactions between participants in various groups. This should include testing of the default rules of the protocol and evaluation of the transactions functions in the application, while leading to group rules and results editable and possible to change from everyone, as long as her/his entry (definition) is voted in a group through the CoWaBoo currency.
- An alternative search experience based on an understanding of community resources as a reference to information search. Our goal is to stimulate competences as penetrating intelligence, keen perception and sound judgment.
- Creating new applications, scenarios and early implementations, based on the CoWaBoo protocol API (including both IPFS and Stellar protocols). These scenarios can be deployed using the protocol and its rules, or being inspired by it.

Finally, we believe that understanding web applications as potential open and descriptive protocols is a crucial step towards more transparency, less opacity, in our digital era. We intend to continue our research both as a way to unmask current opacity in digital technologies and experiment on new tools that could support collaborative and critical competences.

REFERENCES

[1] E. Hargittai and A. Hinnant, "Digital inequality" in Communication Research vol. 35 (5), pp. 602, 2008.

[2] S. Barocas, "Data mining and the discourse on discrimination" The Data Ethics Workshop, Conference on Knowledge Discovery and Data Mining (KDD 2014), 24—27 August, New York City.

[3] K. Zetter, "Junk food algorithms and the world they feed us" Retrieved February 10, 2017, from, URL: http://bit.ly/iaHTWq.

[4] E. Fisher and M. Naumer, "Information grounds: Theoretical basis and empirical findings on information flow in social settings", in New directions in human information behavior, A. Spink & C. Cole, Eds. Amsterdam: Kluwer, pp. 93-111, 2006.

[5] J. Burrell, "How the machine 'thinks': Understanding opacity in machine learning algorithms" SAGE Publications, 2016, DOI: 10.1177/2053951715622512.

[6] C. Sandvig, K. Hamilton, K. Karahalios and C. Langbort, "Re-Centering the Algorithm" Governing Algorithms, (NYU School of Law 2014), New York, NY, USA.

[7] F. Coffield, D. Moseley, E. Hall, and K. Ecclestone, "Should we be using learning styles? What research has to say to practice". London: Learning and Skills Research Centre, 2004.

[8] A. Galloway, "Protocol: How Control Exists After Decentralization", MIT Press, 2004.

[9] J. Gritton, "Of Serendipity, Free Association and Aimless Browsing: Do They Lead to Serendipitous Learning?", unpublished. Retrieved February 10, 2017, from, URL: http://www.education.ed.ac.uk/e-learning/gallery/gritton_serendipitous_learning/conclusion/assets/assignment_print_version.pdf

[10] M. Rosenmann, "Serendipity and scientific discover"in Creativity and Leadership in the 21st Century Firm", vol. 13, pp. 187-193, 2002

[11] E. Riley, "The Effects of a Cuban Musical Exchange Tripon the Musical Journeys of Students from a Sydney High School" Bachelor of music's thesis, University of Sydney, 2007, Retrieved February 10, 2017, from, URL: http://ses.library.usyd.edu.au/bitstream/2123/2177/1/Riley%202007.pdf,

[12] O. Le Deuff, Du tag au like, Paris: FYP Editions, 2012.

[13] The 2015 group work results on Diigo web social bookmarking application are available at https://groups.diigo.com/group/heg-digital

[14] The source of this expert group in Diigo is available at https://groups.diigo.com/group/web_3_0/search?what=wolfram+alpha

[15] This example comes from the HEG – Digital 2015 group work on Airbnb available at https://groups.diigo.com/group/heg-digital/content/tag/airbnb

[16] All HEG – Wikinomic 2016 results are available at http://project.cowaboo.net

[17] The link for the blockchain observatory is now available at: http://project.cowaboo.net/observatory/Blockchain, with all of its data stored on IPFS, a p2p storage protocol. Its current state (blockchain observatory) is available at https://gateway.ipfs.io/ipfs/QmaDv45G23aRmwveRgpqYEu5GKgqUu1bWqF2vST5SX7SmK

Learner Satisfaction in eTexbook Co-reading

A comparative study of internal and external forums

Sinini Paul Ncube, Hussein Suleman
Department of Computer Science
University of Cape Town
Rondebosch, Cape Town
e-mail: ncbsin004@uct.ac.za, husseins@uct.ac.za

***Abstract*—A textbook is a boundary object among students within given communities, in some instances, regions or the whole country. Students in such communities can engage collaboratively to study and gain better understanding of common content. While discussion forums have been an operative platform for social collaborations, learners are faced with the challenge of referencing their posts to linked informational resources. A system based on two chapters of a Python eTextbook was co-designed with students to evaluate its usefulness in supporting textbook based interactions. An experimental study compared the traditional external discussion forums to the developed internal forums which are embedded within eTextbooks. A systematic content analysis of learners' interactions demonstrates insights to their experiences, their needs and the potential benefits of combining discussion forums with eTextbooks to encourage more collaborations. Learners preferred internal forums.**

Keywords-collaborations; eTextbook; forums; interactions.

I. INTRODUCTION

A textbook is a common resource that is consistently used by teachers and their students from various communities. Usually, for every course, there is a standard textbook that students rely on to study. This makes the textbook a boundary object; a boundary object is an entity of interest across school communities. Students tend to meet after school to collaborate on course materials [12]. Students who do not have the opportunity to study with others may now partake in collaborations using their mobile devices on virtual environments that have no time, space or cultural barriers [12]. This creates an opportunity to structure and frame a platform that brings students from various communities together, in order to build a shared understanding of textbook content. Although research states that there should be a significant move away from textbook dependence to adopting a variety of sources for teaching, many teachers and students still depend highly on textbooks [4].

Students are increasingly choosing to purchase eTextbooks for their mobile devices as an alternative to traditional textbooks because of their low cost, light weight and ease of use [9]. Although they provide a cheaper source to information they, however, do not improve learning outcomes as students sometimes may not comprehend what they read [3]. The flexibility of eTextbooks allows for the exploration of interactive technologies to incorporate within digital textbooks to enable better understanding of content [11][18]. While individual digital reading has been the subject of much investigation [11], research into co-reading is scarce [9][14]. Co-reading normally occurs in classrooms, book-clubs, and in less coordinated ways through mass media yet it may also be explored for formal resources like eTextbooks [9][14].

Providing the student with an environment that cultivates a strong personal interest in constructing knowledge when given resources is the most effective way of learning [16]. Building effective mobile applications that encompass all aspects of collaborations instead of merely delivering resources to students is important [16]. In this paper, we ask the question: How should discussion forums be presented to promote the use of textbook based interactions? As a result, experiments in this paper explore the rationale for separating or combining resources like textbooks with their discussions for active collaborative learning.

The rest of this paper is organized as follows: Section II describes the background and related work. Section III describes the approach taken in the system design. Section IV presents and discusses results. Section V concludes the paper and gives future research guidelines.

II. BACKGROUND AND RELATED WORK

In this section we discuss how discussion forums have been utilized in learning environments and how they are linked to electronic resources which students discuss. The section is concluded by explaining the gap in the discussed literature.

A. Discussion Forums in Learning Environments

Several researchers agree that group learning as well as dialogue based instructional settings are key to learning. Students that are involved in group learning improve their problem solving and critical-thinking skills by deepening their understanding of concepts [13]. Problem solving is made easier when people work together because, within a group, everyone has something distinctive that they may contribute since people have their own unique ways of thinking. Exposure to multiple conceptual constructs helps create knowledge. Student engagement in networking platforms has been stated to be successfully measured by discussion forum posting [7].

Discussion forums are defined as threaded discussions that capture the exchange of asynchronous messages [7]. Forums are a primary means of interaction in most online distant learning platforms [13]. They are widely employed in e-learning setups to support social constructivism. Previous explorations of discussion forums have promoted active learning [10]. Traditionally, they are used within Course Management Systems (CMSs) like Moodle and Blackboard as a means for enabling dialog and collaboration among connected individuals [11]. Although forums facilitate better learning, in reference [13], they argue that forums are not good at managing a huge number of posts with fragmented topics over too many threads. They also state that forum usage is usually limited to a few participants. Also, peer answers to posts may be incorrect and counter-productive [15][18].

Although earlier studies indicated that discussion forums were not as effective for learning [17], a number of studies state that they are very essential to learning [1]. The effectiveness of threaded discussions has been discussed extensively in literature and results note their affordances in enhancing individual thinking capabilities, promoting participation, enabling reflection of peer contributions and allowing the sharing of diverse ideas [1][13]. Learners are also able to analyse their own ideas before sharing them, thereby improving the quality of discussions.

The popularity of MOOCS for larger student populations as well as CMSs for smaller student populations especially at University levels is indicative of the latest trends toward interactive online course related learning [11]. The discussion forums have become the knowledge source to the course work [10][18]. Reference [10] describes discussion forums as an integral part of online learning, however states that they are presented as an afterthought for students to use as they wish, which may make them dysfunctional. Reference [2] states that forums tend to attract many student complaints or topics focused on course administrative issues instead of focusing on course challenges. A more directed discussion forum may filter such posts. In reference [2], they conducted a study that identified if discussion forum posts were content related. Their study revealed that, of all the posts, only 28% were related to content even though the course offered other dedicated areas for asking on non-content related matters.

Reference [10] investigated the idea of producing high quality interactions through seeding the forum with content and varying the sections of comments revealed to students. Results from their study indicated that seeding, which is selecting prior-semester comments from stimulating topics and incorporating them into the new semester, inspired an above average amount of discussions. They found that the quality of annotations increased when sections were seeded.

Reference [19] attempted to improve the quality of posts by removing confusing posts that tend to lead to student drop outs or lack of participation. Other research focuses on encouraging more interactions. Reference [19] also states that making many posts improved learning while contradictory research argues that a high number of posts does not necessarily improve learning outcomes [13]. Reference [19] explores increased interactions through instructor's presence and the value of their input in directing the forum discussions.

B. The use of Interactive eTextbooks for Learning

Discussion forums are usually linked to various resources like course eTextbooks. eTextbook related studies have incorporated dictionaries within textbooks so that students do not have to exit the textbooks in order to seek word definitions in trying to understand the content. Various eTextbooks also incorporate automatic assessment through interactive exercises in order to help students test themselves as they read [11]. Content interactions through iPads and kindles exist, most research tends to focus on creating a great individual experience through the incorporation of videos, annotative features, etc. [11][14].

Electronic content with instructor annotations can also provide guidance to students beyond the classroom as they read a textbook [3][6]. This may improve the way that students interpret and understand content. Underlining and highlighting also contributes to recall [8]. Asking questions contributes to meta-cognitive monitoring, thereby improving learners' self-regulation, recall and comprehension [8]. Exercises are the most important pedagogical feature of interactivity since they provide a better experience on a topic, especially since students try exercises as they read [5]. In reference [5], they did a study which showed that a high number of completed exercises results in high performance on written tests.

Reference [3] states that other research projects have focused on redesigning the eTextbook because of its flexibility; the kindle and iPad provide new formats of presenting these books, with lots of multimedia. However, high costs of producing multimedia books makes them harder to scale for every textbook [3]. As a result, they suggest that it would make more sense to tailor existing eTextbooks to the needs of students at low cost. This means focusing on how students and their instructors interact with the content and each other and doing minimal redesigns.

C. The Gap in Literature

The literature above has demonstrated the importance of interactions, however the gap in the literature is in that the studies are not attempting to explore the way in which discussion forums are presented in trying to improve collaborations. A majority of research seeks to identify strategies for improving the quality and quantity of traditional forum posts. Discussion forums already provide a platform for interactions, however they are presented separately to resources as a choice for students to use [10]. In this paper, we attempt to create a discussion forum around the intellectual content of textbooks by limiting the distance between the forum and the resources to be discussed. In references [3] and [6], the researchers describe an idea of sharing annotations which may enable students to communicate with each other through their personal notes. In reference [6], they conducted an experiment that investigated on how to improve the quality of annotations for learning. However, little systematic research has been conducted to explore the practicability of conversing instead of just sharing readable annotations within common content by integrating social interactive activities through discussion forums within eTextbooks in the hope that this promotes more collaborations. The design and presentation of discussion forums may have an effect on the way that students interact.

III. RESEARCH DESIGN

An experimental study was conducted with students. The aim of the experiment was to determine the feasibility of an internal discussion forum within an eTextbook. To achieve this, we created an internal forum as well as the traditional discussion forum, which we will refer to as the external forum in this paper.

A. System Design

An experimental system was designed by 15 university students in Computer Science who underwent a participatory design session in order to define the needs of a collaborative eTextbook system that could be relevant to them. The system was specifically designed to explore the possibility of including interactive discussions within eTextbooks. The design experiment helped outline how discussion forums can be presented inside eTextbooks to support interactions within books. The design session resulted in inline editing eTextbook paper sketches whereby various readers work together in group work sessions on mobile phones so as to understand the textbooks. In order to test the feasibility of this system, we developed two systems using a Python Web framework called Web2py. The first platform is the traditional external forum that has links to an eTextbook resource. The second platform is an internal forum, that is, an eTextbook with embedded interactions within it.

The two platforms were designed in a similar manner using similar eTextbook content, see Fig 1. The eTextbook used was a relevant support textbook found on the CMS for the Python course at the time. Two chapters (Loops and Strings) of the Python eTextbook that were being taught in parallel to the experiments were chosen for the system.

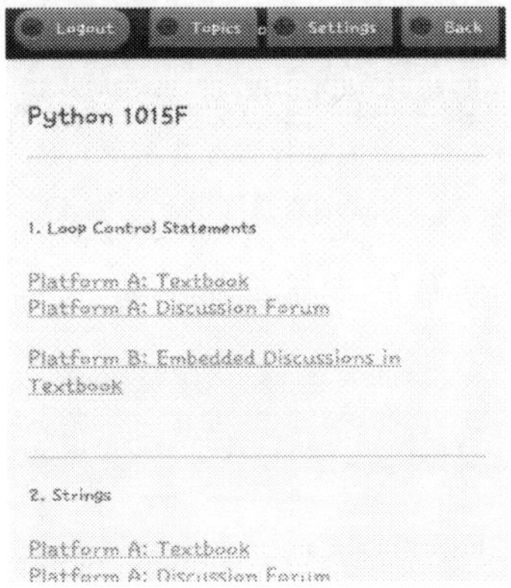

Figure 1. Initial page showing the two platforms.

From Fig. 1, one can see the topic of Loop Control Statements. Below that, there are three links. When a user clicks on the "Platform A: Textbook" link, it opens the book chapter. Otherwise, when a user clicks on the "Platform A: Discussion Forum" link, it opens a page where users can initiate and respond to discussions, see Fig. 2a for a clip of the discussion page. When a user clicks on the "Platform B: Embedded discussions in textbook" link, it opens the book chapter whereby the user can read as well as initiate or participate in discussions that are found within the book chapter, see Fig. 2b for a clip of the book chapter with discussions within it.

The only differentiating variable between the two platforms is the location of the forums for conducting discussions. The external forum separates the eTextbook from the discussion forum while the internal forum integrates the eTextbook content together with discussion forums. The internal forum represents the controlled setup of the experiment. The purpose of having the two systems was to test whether including discussions in textbooks promotes better interactions for students thereby suggesting that the location of forums for discussions is important to the design of collaborative systems.

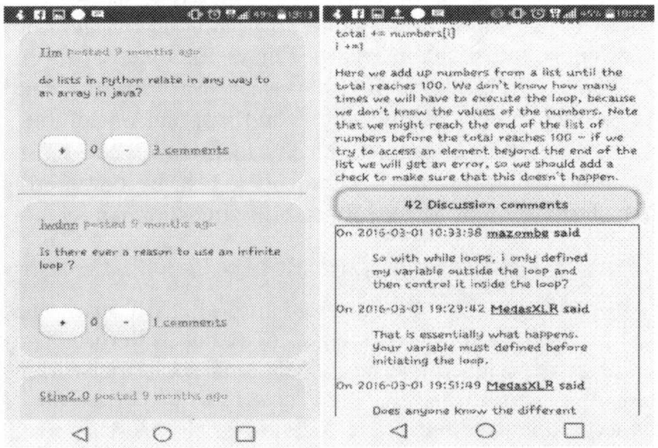

(a) (b)

Figure 2. Snippets of (a) the external forum discussion page and (b) the internal forum of textbook with discussions within the text

B. Research Participants

Research participants were randomly recruited from approximately 200 first year Computer Science students enrolled in a Python programming course at the University of Cape Town. A call for participation was emailed to all the students in the Python class and the first 30 respondents were selected for the experiment. Only 24 participants completed the experiments.

C. Experimental Procedure

The experiment occurred over a period of two weeks. Two tasks were presented to the participants. Before the experiments commenced, a pre-questionnaire was given to all participants to assess their prior experiences about eTextbooks, discussion forums and Internet usage on mobile devices. Each participant was given a token payment of approximately $15 after participation. The amount of $15 was considered a standard token of appreciation for students which is not too small for participants to lose interest in doing the experiment and yet not too large an amount for participants to only be interested in doing the experiment for monetary purposes. Following are the tasks performed by the participants:

1) Task 1

The first task was meant to give students the opportunity to have a feel of both platforms that were being compared. They therefore used both the external forum and the internal forum. The chapter topic of discussion was Loop control Statements. Students were asked to post at least two questions and respond or comment to any two other questions on each of the two platforms of the system per day for one full week. At the end of the week, the task was concluded by completing a survey that evaluated participants' experiences in using the two platforms.

2) Task 2

In the second week, participants were each asked to choose one of the two platforms they preferred using after experiencing both platforms in task 1. This means that they either chose to use the internal forum or the external forum. The topic of discussion for that week was Strings. They were asked to post two questions and respond or comment on any two other questions per day for a full week on the platform they selected. They ended the task by completing the task survey plus an overall usability questionnaire.

IV. RESULTS

According to the pre-questionnaire, all participants had used discussion forums as well as eTextbooks before. They had prior experience in using CMSs and social networking platforms. This means that they could easily participate in this experiment as they were technologically savvy enough to rate and compare the two platforms. Following are results of the experiment.

A. Using Alias names vs. real names on academic forums

Although on social media networks, people usually sign in using their real names for easy identification, in an academic platform this might not be preferred. Participants had the option of logging onto the system using their Facebook names which is usually the name that one is known to by friends or using an alias so as to be anonymous. Facebook was used as an easier way to centralise users without registrations. According to the results, 69% of the participants opted to use an alias name as opposed to their real name when using the system.

The findings showed that 31% of the participants used their real names and found it unnecessary to be anonymous on an academic platform, claiming that everyone was on the site to learn hence there was no need to hide identities. They also explained that being identifiable increased chances of possible meetups for face to face interactions. Although they were comfortable to share their identity online, they emphasized that this experimental application should not post anything on their behalf on the Facebook platform. However, of the 69% that used alias names, the participants highlighted the need to be anonymous and to owning anonymous posts. Students like to protect their identity and have a sense of security and privacy as they tend to feel uncomfortable to share their identity with strangers. Also, they chose alias names to avoid feeling stupid, especially if they ask obvious questions or answer other posts wrongly. Some mentioned that using alias names for online activities had become a habit.

When the participants who opted for alias names were asked what their challenge would be in using their Facebook names on the platform, they stated that they feared being classed academically or being judged negatively by peers. Other participants stated that some students may become biased when answering their posts because they know them in person. Even people who would never help them in person had the opportunity to do so if they kept their identity anonymous. Others insisted on being anonymous because they were shy to express themselves freely, hence using a real name would result in fewer posts and comments from them. Students felt that using alias names improved their participation levels and gave them liberty in asking any types of questions. Students also felt much safer when hiding behind alias names.

1) Discussion

It is evident from the results above that the use of alias names should not be overlooked when creating academic online platforms. University students also have confidence challenges on online platforms. Not everyone prefers hidden identity, however for discussion forums to cater for everyone they should be presented such that students have the choice to be anonymous or not. CMSs tend to have discussion forums but, because the students have to be registered for the course, they can only use their real names. Often this is to protect against inappropriate posts. Although this is very important, 69% of the participants indicate their need to freely express themselves without being judged for better participation.

B. External Forum (Discussion forum plus a separate link to an etextbook)

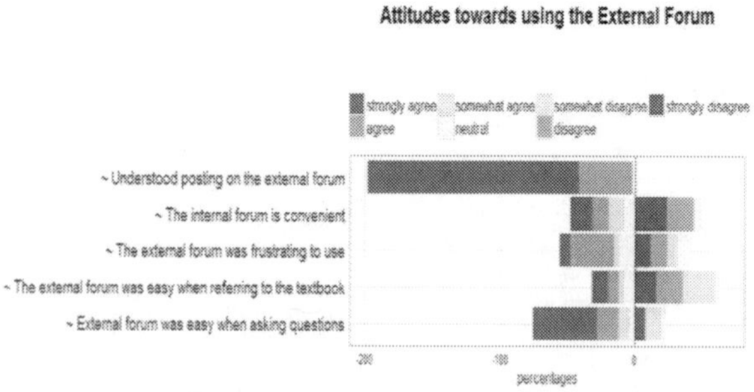

Figure 3. Experiences of participants when using the external forum

Fig. 3 above shows that participants had no challenges in using and understanding the external forum. Participants found the platform easy to use. Some participants found the external forum frustrating to use and this was attributed to the fact that one had to switch back and forth from the forum to refer to the textbook and also the external forum presented different ungrouped topic posts. Not all the participants found it convenient to separate the textbook from the forum. Reasons were that sometimes one wanted to focus on the textbook without any distractions, hence separation encouraged focus to those participants. Some participants stated that they only used the discussion forum when they had finished reading, hence it was easy to refer to the textbook if they had written sections and challenges down.

Results highlight favourable qualities of the external forum to be the convenience of focusing on questions and answers without the interruption of the textbook. Participants highlighted that it is easier and faster to view all posts in separate dialogues and, since posts were easily identifiable, they could be answered much faster. Participants also liked that one has the freedom to identify and select questions of interest to them among many questions. This also enabled participants to respond to posts as they browsed questions they needed answers to. Another positive quality of the external forum is the promotion of general enquiries. Each question had its comments, which made it easier to scroll and identify answers to a post.

The not so favourable points of the external forum included the difficulty of switching from the forum to the eTextbook for referencing. They found the process of continuously exiting the forum to open the linked eTextbook cumbersome. The participants also stated that the forum ended up with many posts such that it was harder to navigate and easily identify relevant or particular posts as the forum posts were general and covered numerous topics. Participants also noted that if a response is delayed the post may never be answered as participants said they were usually biased to earlier posts and were reluctant to search for older posts. Participants also stated that they would have liked a notification system as it was sometimes hard to find particular questions to check if they had been answered.

Participants suggested incorporating Web links on comment boxes so as to share useful links that explained their answers. Other media, like videos, pictures and audios, were noted to aid users in providing explanations for their posts, although these options where provided on the system, learners did not utilize them. Participants also suggested

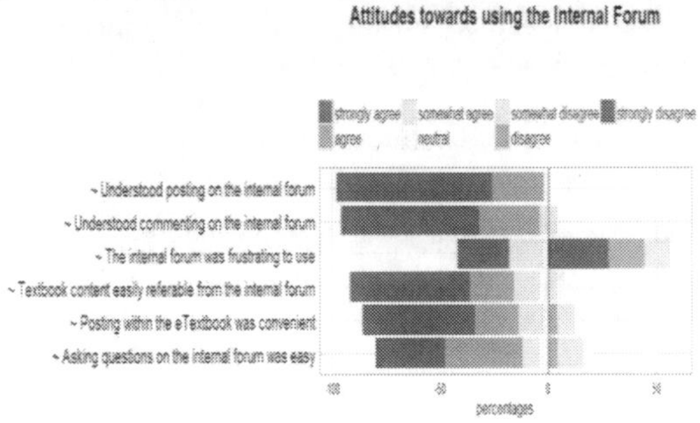

Figure 4. Experiences of participants in using the internal forum

inserting a sidebar linked to the textbook for easy referral by tagging relevant sections of the textbook. Questions listed on the forum should also be categorized and grouped to avoid repeats.

C. Internal forum (eTextbook with embedded discussion forum

Participants understood how the system worked without much training. A short demo was given when participants filled the pre-questionnaire. Fig. 4 above shows that some students found the internal platform frustrating to use and this is attributed to students who liked the external forum better. The frustration was because they could only ask questions related to the textbook and that the textbook had been altered. A large number of participants, however, found the internal forum easy to use when asking and answering posts. They also found the system to be highly convenient and referencing the textbook when making posts to be much easier.

Participants were asked what they liked most about their experience in using the internal forum. Results showed that dividing the textbook so that questioning and relevant content was sectioned made reading the book desirable and convenient. They highlighted the convenience of having the textbook and posts being combined. Each section of a textbook was directly above a discussion forum section, making it simpler to make references to the relevant textbook content for clarifications. According to the participants, viewing the internal forum comments based on textbook sections made it easy to verify and argue answers in response to other participant posts. The eTextbook was more flexible since examples were right next to exercises, making it easy to switch between the text and discussions when attempting to answer the exercises.

The internal forum system offered a platform to ask specific questions related to the topics at hand. Participants stated that the internal forum allowed for a more focused in-depth analysis of a given topic of the textbook as many had their own views to share per section. The direct approach of topic based discussions made it easier to find answers to similar problems. It was also easy to identify which section one had to read to attempt the questions before asking. Participants stated that having one area that centered on a particular topic promoted a wide range of posts, leading one to view the topic in many dimensions. The hub of questions related to a particular topic enabled participants to find answers to common challenges while also making students aware of hidden challenges. The highlight of the internal forum to many participants was the access to help from other users of the system being readily available as they read. Because one could easily verify answers from others or the textbook if in doubt, participants stated that most answers or opinions made sense. Participants also agreed that the discussions around a single topic flowed and were easy to understand. On this platform, they stated that it was easy to see what other people were saying about a given topic.

The internal forum was convenient in that there was no need to exit the eTextbook while reading so as to ask a question on another page. The organization of comments below each section, aligned by topics, was easy to follow. Each section had few posts enabling one to first check if their question had been asked before asking the same question. One could also easily test if they understood a section by attempting to answer questions from others within that section of comment posts.

Some participants even stated that this platform enabled them to obtain help on some challenges that they were facing in class since the topics used in this experiment ran concurrently to the topics they were learning in class at the time. Some already made a comparison of this platform to an external forum and chose the internal forum, with embedded discussions, as their preference. Others also committed to using such a system as it provided a platform to easily collaborate while reading.

The internal forum system was designed such that people could comment below a section since one of the suggestions was to break down the book for easy reading on mobile devices. However, one was not able to comment on a comment. Most of the negatives about the internal forum centered on not being able to respond to a specific person below their post. The reason for this not being favourable was that a thread may deviate to other questions; as a result that thread may remain unanswered. Also, when a section has many comments where one cannot tell if a comment is a question or answer, the many comments may become cluttered and difficult to follow.

Suggestions for improving this platform included the ability to switch off the forum should one need to focus on the textbook. Participants also desired that the system would load faster despite the compressed images and comments on the pages.

D. *External Forum vs. Internal Forum*

The participants had the opportunity to compare the two platforms and select a platform that appealed to them. In Fig. 5, participants were in favour of the internal forum when compared to the external forum.

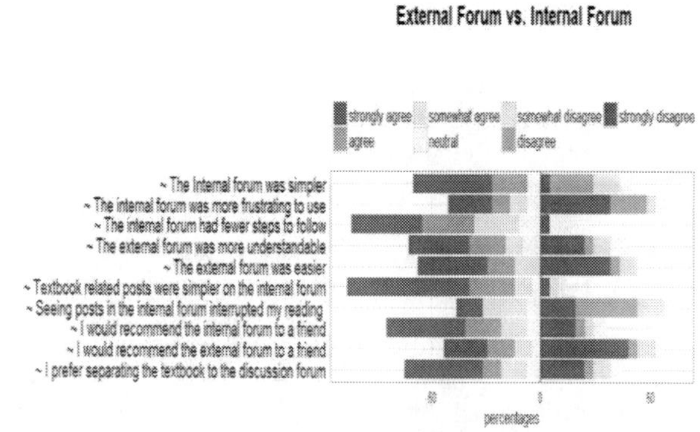

Figure 5. User comparison of experiences in using internal forums vs. external forums

They found it simpler and less frustrating to use, faster, with fewer steps to follow and easier to use than the external forum. The referral to the textbook was much easier. Some participants found combining the textbook with the forum to be interruptive while a majority did not think it interrupted their reading. Many participants preferred not to separate the textbook from the discussion forum and stated that they would recommend the internal forum more than they would recommend the external forum.

In Task 2, 63% of the users preferred the internal forum to the external forum. Of the 37% who selected the external forum, they found their platform more user friendly with much freedom for editing posts. They found that it was easier to ask questions and answer questions. Some of the users found that the internal forum was unfavourable because having discussions got in the way of the textbook content. They stated that there were too many writings on the internal forum platform. Their main negativity of the internal forum was the lack of posting within a post so as to better organize comments within each section.

The majority of the users who selected internal forum for task 2 identified the platform as more focused, specific to textbook sections, much faster to use, simple, more user friendly and convenient in overall. Incorporating everything onto one platform is what made the system convenient for participants. They described the platform as easier to read since the readily visible questions and answers helped one to learn easily from peers. They found the conversations easy to understand and follow. The reasons that led them to not choose the external forum included that the platform was more challenging to follow since posts were very independent and sometimes one may be clueless as to what others are discussing. Referencing specific sections of the textbook was difficult and time consuming on the external forum. One had to direct their peers to browse through pages of the textbook in order to find the relevant section to the questions. Separating the textbook meant that a user had to switch to the separate discussion forum every time they had a question. They insisted that the external forum actually stopped the flow of reading as one could easily get distracted reading questions instead of reading the textbook or even in following new topics instead of reading. Since the questions on the external forum were unordered except by date and number of replies, one had to go through a lot of unrelated material, which could be distracting for people who wanted to focus on particular topics.

In order to improve both platforms, participants suggested emoticons as a mechanism of grading answers. Emoticons are exciting and require little effort from the user. A high number of clicks on the academic emoticon would show a consensus among readers about their thoughts on the post. Other suggestions stated that notifications would be important in reminding people to follow up on their posts, as well as keep users motivated to read.

E. *Discussion of Internal vs. External Forums*

In many CMS platforms, the forum is seen as one of the major support mechanisms for learning offered to students. Discussion forums are often confined to a minority hence many tools are being established to increase the number of interactions. The use of the eTextbook with embedded discussions in it was perceived to be the best at meeting the student learning needs and increasing interactions with an average of 30 responses per thread. It is evident that perhaps we should investigate more about designing systems that allow co-reading within eTextbooks.

Since students had two weeks to use the platforms, they had ample time to learn and be able to choose what they figured was the most effective platform for their learning needs. There is an obvious difference between an internal forum and a traditional external forum. Despite the widespread use of traditional forums, there is still room for improving interactions and embedding discussions within textbooks as one of the strategies for improving engagement and locking students into a zone of relevant content to encourage participation. Perhaps more experiments should be conducted in figuring ways of presenting discussion forums. In this experiment, the addition of forums to the textbooks appealed to more learners. It is therefore evident from the results that students find it convenient to perform easier and faster tasks on collaborative platforms.

Even though preference was for the internal forum, those who preferred the external forum had valid arguments for separating the discussions with content. The structure of the independent external discussion forum encourages a question and answer kind of interaction, whereby people focus on receiving a response or asking a question. This was seen in the length of discussion forum threads, which tend to have an average of two or three responses only. Also, allowing the user to focus on the textbook without interruption is an important consideration. We therefore suggest a system that encompasses the best of both platforms evaluated in this experiment. Learners may toggle between having interactions within their textbooks and switching them off when they need to focus more on reading.

V. Conclusion and Future Work

Increasing student interactions is of great importance to the future of active learning. In this study, we investigated the effectiveness of social interactions embedded within eTextbooks. We built an application to enable students to collaborate on a Python eTextbook chapter, which was in line with course content. Our results demonstrate that: (1) allowing hidden identity is key to socialised learning platforms as it gives students the liberty to respond to posts; (2) incorporating interactions within eTextbooks encourages content related discussions; (3) sectioning the textbook with a discussion forum below each section promotes easy revision, understanding and referencing of textbook content; and (4) although students may find embedding discussion forums on eTextbooks to be convenient, combining the different aspects of the two platforms may result in a more usable system that encourages discussions while also promoting individual studying. We therefore conclude that interactions may be increased by reducing the gap between what is being discussed to its content. Internal forums may propel students to focus on their studies. The results in this experiment suggests that we reconsider how we present discussion forums to students, not as an afterthought as part of CMSs but within eTextbooks to encourage student engagement. We anticipate that our study will contribute to the exploration of forums within textbooks for more effective learning. Designers and operators of socialized learning platforms must therefore consider the possibility of presenting discussion forums in new ways that involves resources being discussed.

This work was conducted with Computer Science students at university level. Another experiment already evaluated high school students in the subject of mathematics. More experiments may test for other subjects. The experiment also does not test if internal forums promote better learning. Subsequent experiments could be conducted with a larger sample over a longer period of time like a full semester to promote the findings on this paper.

Acknowledgment

We acknowledge Hasso Plattner Institute and UCT for funding this project.

References

[1] C. K. Cheng, D. E. Paré, L. M. Collimore, and S. Joordens, "Assessing the effectiveness of a voluntary online discussion forum on improving students' course performance," Computers & Education, vol. 56, no. 1, pp. 253–261, 2011.

[2] Y. Cui and A. F. Wise, "Identifying Content-related threads in MOOC discussion forums," In Proceedings of the second (2015) ACM Conference on Learning @ Scale, pp. 299-303, 2015.

[3] A. R. Dennis, K. O. McNamara, A. S. Morrone, and J. Plaskoff, "Improving learning with eTextbooks, "In System Sciences (HICSS) 2015 48th Hawaii international Conference on Systems Sciences, IEEE, pp. 5253-5259, 2015.

[4] R. Duschl, "Science education in three part- harmony: Balancing conceptual, epistemic, and social learning goals," Review of research in education, vol 32, no. 1, pp. 268-291, 2008.

[5] E. Fouh, D. A. Breakiron, S. Hamouda, M. F. Farghally, and C. A. Shaffer, "Exploring students learning behaviour with an interactive eTextbook in computer science courses," Computers in human behaviour, vol. 41, pp. 478-485, 2014.

[6] J. Jan, C. M. Chen, and P. H. Huang, "Enhancement of digital reading performance by using a novel web-based collaborate reading annotation filtering mechanisms," International Journal of Human Computer Studies, vol. 86, pp. 81-93, 2016.

[7] R. F. Kizilcec, C. Piech, and E. Schneider, "Deconstructing disengagement: analysing learner subpopulations in massive open online courses," In Proceedings of the 3rd International Conference on Learning Analytics and Knowledge, ACM, pp.170-179, 2013.

[8] H. W. Lee, K. Y. Lim, and B. L. Grabowski, "Improving Self-Regulation, Learning Strategy Use, and Achievement with Metacognitive Feedback," Educational Technology Research and Development, vol. 58, no. 6, pp. 629-648, 2010.

[9] D. D. Matthew, "A call to embrace social reading in higher education," Innovations in Education and Teaching International, 2014, DOI:10.1080/14703297.2014.991934.

[10] K. Miller, S. Zyto, D. Karger, and E. Mazur, "Improving online class forums by seeding discussions and managing section size," In Proceedings of the first ACM conference on learning @ scale conference, ACM, pp. 173-174, 2014.

[11] T. Nakahara, T. Soga, Y. Nakamura, M. Mitani, and N. Kawana, "Development of an e-Textbook Connected with a Learning Management System and a Study of its Effective Use," In EdMedia: World Conference on Educational Media and Technology, vol 2014, no. 1, pp. 979-984, 2014.

[12] S. P. Ncube and H. Suleman, "Complementing formal learning with mobile technology outside the classroom," In Interactive Mobile Communication Technologies and Learning (IMCL) 2014 International Conference, IEEE, pp. 51-56, 2014.

[13] D. F. O. Daniel, J. Sinclair, and R. Boyatt, "Exploring the use of MOOC discussion forums," In proceedings of London International Conference on Education (LICE-2014), pp. 1-4, 2014.

[14] J. Pearson, T. Owen, H. Thimbleby, and G. R. Buchanan, "Co-reading: investigating collaborative group reading," In proceedings of the 12th ACM/IEEE-CS joint conference on Digital Libraries, ACM, pp. 325-334, 2012.

[15] B. Schweizer, "Confessions of an Unreconstructed MOOC(h)er," Thought & Action, vol 61, pp. 61-68, 2013.

[16] P. Thinley, S. Geva, and J. Reye, "Tablets (iPad) for m-learning in the context of social constructivism to institute an effective learning environment," International Journal of Interactive Mobile Technologies (iJIM), vol. 8, pp. 16-20, 2014.

[17] M. J. Thomas, "Learning within incoherent structures: The space of online discussion forums," Journal of Computer Assisted Learning, vol. 18. no. 3, pp. 351-366, 2002.

[18] J. J. Williams et al., "Connecting collaborative & crowd work with online education," In proceedings of the 18th ACM Conference Companion on Computer Supported Cooperative Work & Social Computing, ACM, pp. 313-318, 2015.

[19] D. Yang, M. Wen, I. Howley, R. Kraut, and C. Rose, "Exploring the effect of confusion in discussion forums of massive open online courses," In proceedings of the Second ACM Conference on Learning @ Scale, ACM, pp. 121-130. 2015.

Proposed Model for Using Open Educational Resources in Massive Open Online Courses (MOOCs)

Ahmed Hosny Saleh Metwally
School of Computer Science and Information Technology
Northeast Normal University
Changchun, China
E-mail: ahmed_hosny@nenu.edu.cn

Wang Yining
School of Media Science
Northeast Normal University
Changchun, China
E-mail: Wangyn814@nenu.edu.cn

***Abstract*— One of the most important events of the last few years was the propagation of Massive Open Online Courses (MOOCs). Indeed, MOOCs have managed to help huge numbers of online users, especially in higher education sector, to attend free courses and get certificates. Open Educational Resources (OERs) can be used in different ways in the learning practices because the concept of openness and reusability of these resources encourages many stakeholders to use these resources in online and massive courses. The main challenge faced by many experiments in using OERs in MOOCs is how to enhance interaction between students and educational content. Thus, there is an urgent need to address this challenge by building and maintaining links between these kinds of courses and the provided OERs by other universities. The specific objective of this paper was to propose a model for using OERs through the current MOOCs. Data for this study were collected by reviewing previous related work and models to present this model in three main Phases: Pre-using OERs, Using OERs, and sustaining of OERs. Every Phase includes attributes and components. This proposed model can be implemented when designers and developers of MOOCs intend to invest different open educational resources in engaging participants and exchange best learning practices.**

Keywords-Massive Open Online Courses; MOOCs; Open Educational Resources; OERs; Model.

I. Introduction

Recently, there has been renewed interest in the development and use of Open Education Resources (OER) and their potential in expanding access to higher education and improving the quality of course contents, particularly in the education domain, where there is a wide range of quality materials [1]. From official education materials such as the ones available in Massive Open Online Courses (MOOC), Higher Education domain is becoming critical to recognize that relationship between OERs and MOOCs [1].

In the light of elevating the meaning of educational resources, "OERs can be described as the five Rs of openness [2]:

• Retain—the right to make, own, and control copies of the content.

• Reuse—the right to use the content in a wide range of ways (e.g., in a class, in a study group, on a website, and in a video).

• Revise—the right to adapt, adjust, modify, or alter the content (e.g., translate the content into another language)

• Remix—the right to combine the original or revised content with other open content to create something new (e.g., incorporate the content into a "mashup").

• Redistribute—the right to share copies of the original content, revisions, or remixes with others (e.g., give a copy of the content to a friend)."

OERs "typically refer to electronic resources, and such materials are generally released under a Creative Commons or similar license that, can originate from colleges and universities, libraries, archival organizations, government agencies, commercial organizations or other individuals who develop educational resources they are willing to share" [3].

Despite the long history of OERs and its occupation high agenda of social and inclusion policies and supported by many stakeholders in education, their use has not yet reached a critical threshold, basically, the current concern on OER is on building more access to digital content [4].

MOOCs are free of charge courses for a massive number of learners on the web; it must be considered that course design and the way of presenting course materials, and interactivity trough social networks and study groups [5]. Learners must be self-organizer to participate in mutual interest subjects with other learners; massive courses have weekly timetable, no special prerequisites should be provided, no formal certification will be awarded [6].

In the context of OERs and MOOCs, for example, the course about Open Educational Resources (COER13) has been completely downloaded and re-uploaded to iMooX, The course was republished with some new videos and interviews for more than 500 users, so reusing and remixing allows for the reoffering of courses without additional costs [7]. Moreover, extensive research has shown that a cost efficient way and introduced OER at the Medical University of Graz which can be applied also to other institutions so the following steps are performed: (1) Identify the need, (2)

Identification of content which may be suitable also for general public, (3) Rights clearance, (4) Set-up of distribution channels [8].

MOOCs that implement OER practices implement the ethical dimension of e-learning much more successfully than MOOCs that might just offer free access to a MOOC at a given time or use proprietary resources that cannot be reused [9]; for example, in xMOOCs the course materials are provided during the course time, in some cases cannot be reused [9].

Ghislandi sees that "the main problem is how to implement Openness for achieving best learning results, provided that the OER and MOOC evaluation is still a fluid topic" [10]. The course materials in the majority of MOOCs are not designed to fit the concept of the OER movement, and protected under copyright regulations which do not allow adaptation or translation; therefore, the content con not be reused; since they are nonmodifiable, nonremixable, nonshareable [11][12].

Atenas recommended that "the fairest way to allow and encourage the use of resources from MOOCs is by removing copyright barriers, adding creative commons licenses to course materials and by using the General Public License (GNU) in the case of open codes used for modeling the contents or courses" [12]. This way may enforce sharing and reusing resources but it needs more awareness with related issues like ethical issues and quality assurance.

This research attempts to make explicit a systematic relationship between MOOCs and Open Educational Resources through proposing a model for using and implementing OERs in MOOCs. The rest of this research is organized as follows: Section II. OER vs. MOOC; Section III. Quality Approach; Section IV. Provide details of the proposed model for using OERs in MOOCs. Section V. Presents the findings of the research, focusing on the three key themes that connect using OERs in MOOCs; Section VI Taken together, these findings and highlighted new research tracks.

II. OER vs. MOOC

This section reviews and compares the main themes between OER and MOOCs [10]:

- "OER is a resource, and sometimes a course. MOOCs are courses including assessment, credits system, students support, curriculum, etc.
- OER is typically delivered on demand while MOOCs have a defined beginning and end.
- OER can be used by a single person while MOOCs are addressed to a massive cohort, during a given period.
- OER is for every school level while MOOCs are mainly dedicated to Higher Education and the Life Long Learning postgraduate or nonformal".

The term of "open" in MOOC refers to "open admissions" or the removal of any academic barriers to participation in a course or program[13]. While the term of "open" in OER entails, "it seems, at a minimum, no cost to the consumer or user of the resource" [14].

Although differences between OER and MOOCs are mentioned, it can be noted that approaches consider MOOCs as open resources. OER used for teaching, assessment, research purpose so it is supposed using and implementing these resources to formulate and construct massive courses.

III. Quality Approach

Developing and using OERs makes improvement in the quality of education when the teachers and students use the educational resources without barriers like copyright and paying barriers [15]. Moreover, OERs and MOOCs provide different opportunities for achieving quality in higher education through implementing strategic management approach [16].

The quality of instructional design of a massive course is a critical indicator and prerequisite of the potential of the course for effective learning.

There are quality standards and rubrics have focused significantly on the quality of OERs and MOOCs. Camilleri, Ehlers, Pawlowski figured out that "quality assurance requires pedagogical enhancement, pedagogical stakeholders, and pedagogical resources" [4]. Furthermore, open standards for quality assurance of OER and MOOC would assist in measuring quality in more globally accepted terms [11].

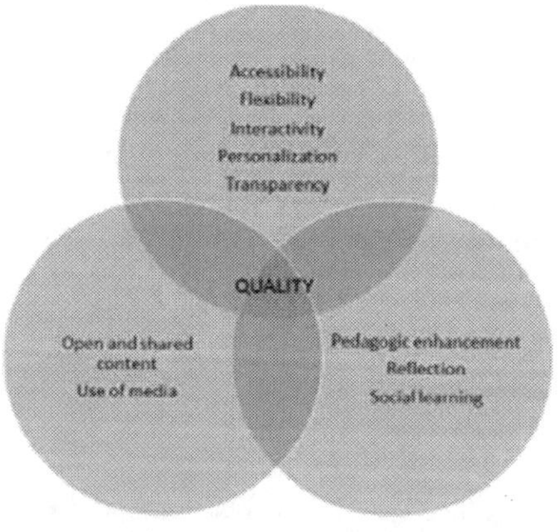

Figure 1. Quality indicators for OERs and MOOCs.

As shown in Figure 1. "accessibility, flexibility, interactivity, personalization, transparency, open and shared content, use of media, pedagogical enhancement, reflection, and social learning are the key indicators of high quality in the use of OERs and MOOCs" [16].

IV. Proposed Model for Using OERs in MOOCs

This section presents the proposed model for using OERs in MOOCs. This model has formed through reviewing previous works and models in this domain like:

potential model to guide the development of OER in public health and help an academic for producing and publishing OER through a matrix of questions and answers, according to various risks and benefits to them and their institution [17]. Another framework based on semantic web technologies to improve discovery, accessibility, visibility, and to promote reuse of open educational content in the massive course [18]. Moreover, Atenas' study proposed model for democratisation of the contents hosted in MOOCs through three strategies to open up MOOC contents includes: "deposit the materials in repositories of OER (ROER) as individual objects, to archive them in ROER in data packages as learning units or to convert them into Open Courseware (OCW) as self-taught courses" [12]. Furthermore, Shu-Hsiang, Jaitip, and Ana developed "a strategic planning process (SPP) model based on the concept of open educational resources, university social responsibility (USR), social entrepreneurship (SE), and strategic planning (SP), so the proposed SPP model will serve as a guide for mapping out a strategic plan and activities for aligning and implementing OER, which can tie strategic planning to a university's effectiveness and success in sustainability for the long term" [19].

It can be noted that the proposed model in this research has included three Phases as the following:

A. Phase 1: Pre-Using OERs

B. Phase 2: Using OERs

C. Phase 3: Sustaining of OERs

As shown in Figure 2. Proposed model contains three main phases for using OER in MOOCs.

A. Phase 1: Pre-Using OERs:

This Phase includes finding OERs through searching on the web by search engines to collect and download these resources in different formats. Also, MOOCs provider can provide other resources from previous educational softwares that produced before, repositories, open coursewares, and online courses. After collecting resources they can archive its.

B. Phase 2: Using OERs:

MOOCs platforms may provide a course in different subjects so MOOCs providers have to produce OERs if they found that the resources in phase (1) need to modify for serving the educational objectives or even producing OERs by authoring tools. Web 2.0 has provided effective tools for creating OERs so it will encourage authoring and producing many resources as well. In all cases, Creative Common License can be used to keep intellectual property rights and empower the concept of openness and reuse.

Repository in MOOC platform has great importance in this proposed model. It receives all of the resources either which are collected in the previous phase or produce in this phase. On the other hand, repository connects producing process with using process and encourages users' contributions by uploading their own resources and downloading other ones or even embed them through using embed codes. These activities for users could translate to points so it can be shown in their profile to reinforce sharing OERs.

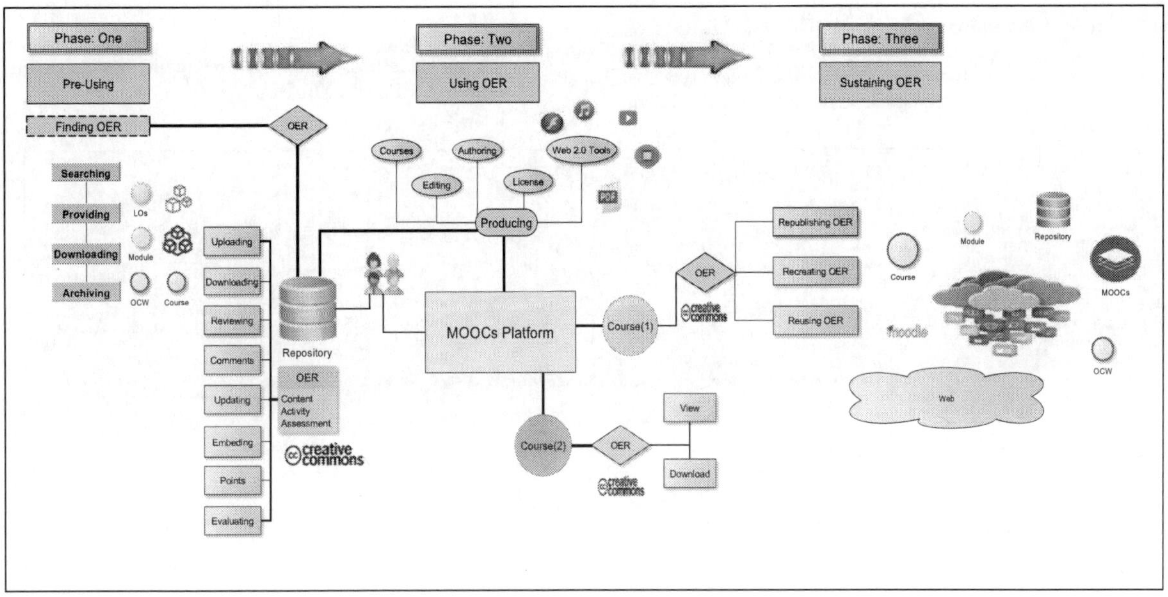

Figure 2. Proposed model for using OERs in MOOCs.

MOOCs providers and Users can evaluate OERs in repository in the light of quality standards. Repository supervisors can review new resources, update some of them, add comments. Registered users in MOOCs preview courses and resources for free.

C. Phase 3: Sustaining OERs:

In this phase, MOOCs providers have to come up with in the ways of supporting OERs, reusing, and sustaining. This may happen by creative commons license that helps users of MOOCs to reuse and share OERs which have been used in MOOCs. Furthermore, OERs will be available after studying courses on the web for reusing in other courses, republishing in another contexts through Learning management systems, Open course wares, learning objects repository, educational Softwares.

V. RELATED ISSUES FOR CONNECTING AND USING OERS IN MOOCS

The following part presents the findings of the research, focusing on the related issues that connect using OERs in MOOCs as it shows in Figure 3.

- Learning communities: support developing OERs that mainly used in MOOCs. being OERs in a social context that leads to developing and update content over time [20].
- Sustainability: it relates to financial issues and paying for getting certificates may be a good solution to keep sustaining OERs besides thinking of emerging business models.
- Quality Assurance: it must be taken into consideration for quality of MOOCs and OERs if we need to raise learning quality and learning outcomes.
- Legal Issues: and raising awareness about types of Licenses and consequences of using illegal resources.
- Trust and Reputation: if MOOCs providers need to gain a high reputation for courses, they have to give more concerns with the trust of OERs and search for good methods to keep the trust of users.
- Interoperability: that means designing OERs to be compatible with different MOOCs platforms, learning environments and standards.
- Instructional Design: It is a basic component of the overall quality and pedagogic effectiveness of learning practices [21]. Instructional Designer must implement models for developing massive courses and create educational resources in a systematic way upon educational approach.
- OER Distribution: after studying massive course and a possibility of reusing OERs in another course.
- Creative OER: crating educational resources is very important but not enough to keep using. Achieving a high level of learning objectives requires creative resources in their content, activity, assessment of these resources. The more producing creative OERs, the more using OERs.
- Ethical Issues: have a relationship with legal issues and the degree of awareness about authors copyrights; either OERs used for educational purpose or research purpose.
- MOOC and OER Models: designing and developing models in the field of MOOCs and OERs contributes in an effective way to discuss the main attributes which have main importance for encouraging implementing OERs in MOOÇs.
- Learning Analytics: will help in recognizing to which extent stakeholders used OERs in massive courses. It leads to design and renews strategies for efficient use.
- Technical Issues: in the light of quality standards of both of OERs and MOOCs.

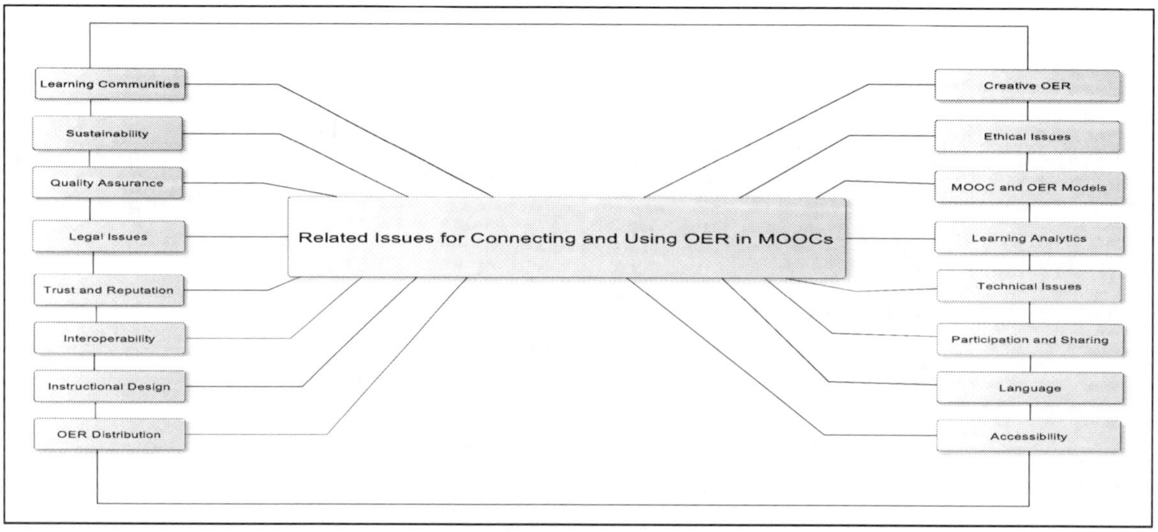

Figure 3. Related Issues for connecting and using OERs in MOOCs.

- Participation and Sharing: for maximizing benefits from OERs and providing tools in MOOCs platform to share, publish, and upload resources by users.
- Language: it may cause troubles especially to non-English speaker countries, so there is a need to find the best ways to use OERs in other languages.
- Accessibility: and providing resources for disabilities users and special needs, and developing accessibility standards to be compatible to fit their needs.

VI. Conclusion and Future Work

In general, therefore, it seems that MOOCs and OERs concepts include common features such as openness and serving educational purposes. Although the expansion of creating and sharing OERs on the web, there are researches study strategies and recommendations in the context of implementing OERs and MOOCs for achieving best educational practices. This research has addressed connecting between OERs and MOOCs through proposing a model for using OERs in MOOCs which included three phases: Pre-Using OERs, Using OERs, and Sustaining OERs. Every phase contained attributions started from finding OERs passing to preparing, and conserving these resources through the repository and distributing its. There are important factors to encourage users to share educational resources like providing repository in MOOCs platform with a point system, and allow them to evaluate resources with repository's evaluator. Sustaining OERs could be done by paying for getting a certificate to support costs of producing OERs. Last but not least, research has presented the finding focusing on the related issues for connecting open educational resources and massive open online courses: Learning communities, Sustainability, Quality Assurance, Legal Issues, Trust and Reputation, Interoperability, Instructional Design, OER Distribution, Creative OER, Ethical Issues, MOOC and OER Models, Learning Analytics, Technical Issues, Participation and Sharing, Language, Accessibility. Considering the findings of this research may direct future research, it would be desirable to develop a prototype of the proposed model. Further into the future, Studying related factors of using OERs when applying the proposed model will encourage using OERs in the massive courses. Furthermore, studying the criteria of using OERs in MOOCs, and applying qualitative research for studying the rates of using OERs in MOOCs could be important research directions in the future.

Acknowledgment

This research is supported by Northeast Normal University. Special thanks to the research team in educational technology seminar, and school of computer science and information technology at Northeast Normal University.

References

[1] A. M. F. Yousef, M. A. Chatti, M. Wosnitza, and U. Schroeder, "A Review of the State-of-the-Art," in *Proceedings of CSEDU2014, 6th International Conference on Computer Supported Education*, 2014, pp. 9–20.

[2] D. wiley, "The Access Compromise and the 5th R," 2014. [Online]. Available: http://opencontent.org/blog/archives/3221. [retrieved: January, 2017].

[3] EDUCAUSE, "7 things you should know about Open Educational Resources," *EDUCAUSE Learning Initiative*, pp. 1–2, 2010. [Online]. Available: http://net.educause.edu/ir/library/pdf/ELi7061.pdf. [retrieved: February, 2017].

[4] A. F. Camilleri, U. D. Ehlers, and J. Pawlowski, "State of the Art Review of Quality Issues related to Open Educational Resources (OER)," JRC Scientific and Policy Reports, Publications Office of the European Union, Luxembourg, Rep. EUR 26624 EN, 2014.

[5] L. Pappano, "The Year of the MOOC," *The New York Times*, 2012.[Online].Available: http://www.nytimes.com/2012/11/04/education/edlife/massive-open-online-courses-are-multiplying-at-a-rapid-pace.html. [retrieved: January, 2017].

[6] A. Mcauley, B. Stewart, G. Siemens, and D. Cormier, "The MOOC Model for Digital Practice," 2010. [Online]. Available: http://www.elearnspace.org/Articles/MOOC_Final.pdf. [retrieved: February, 2017].

[7] M. Ebner et al., "How OER Enhances MOOCs—A Perspective from German-Speaking Europe," in *Open Education: from OERs to MOOCs*, no. August, J. M, Kinshuk, and M. K. Khribi, Eds. Berlin, Heidelberg: Springer Berlin Heidelberg 2017, pp. 205–220.

[8] H. Rehatschek, U. Leopold, and S. Kerschbaumer, "Introduction of OER at the Medical University of Graz: Practical tips to introduce OER with a minimum of additional budget and efforts," in. *International Conference on Interactive Collaborative Learning (ICL)*, Dubai, 2014, pp. 121-126.

[9] P. Arnold, S. Kumar, S. Schön, M, Ebner, and A. Thillosen, "A MOOC on Open Educational Resources as an Open Educational Resource : COER13," in *The MOOC Case Book: Case Studies in MOOC Design, Development and Implementation*, J.R, Corbeil, M.E, Corbeil, and B.H, Khan, Eds. NY: Linus Learning, pp. 247-258.

[10] P. Ghislandi, "A tale about Zen philosophy and a motorcycle. (that is: OER & MOOC quality)," *Research on Education and Media*, vol. 7, no. 1, P.P.-, 2015.

[11] I. F. Silveira, "OER and MOOC: The need for openness," *Issues Informing Sci. Inf. Technol.*, vol. 13, pp. 209–223, 2016..

[12] J. Atenas, "Model for democratisation of the contents hosted in MOOCs," *RUSC. Universities and Knowledge Society Journal*, vol. 12, no. 1. pp. 3–14.

[13] S. Downes, "The quality of massive open online courses," in *International Handbook of E-Learning, Volume 1: Theoretical perspectives and research*, B. H. Khan and M. Ally, Eds. 2015, pp. 65–77.

[14] S. Downes, "Models for Sustainable Open Educational Resources," *Interdisciplinary journal of knowledge and learning objects*, vol. 3, no. 1, pp. 29–44, 2007.

[15] C. R. Wright and S. A. Reju, "Developing and Deploying OERs in sub-Saharan Africa: Building on the present," *Int. Rev. Res. Open Distance Learn.*, vol. 13, no. 2, pp. 181–220, 2012.

[16] E. Ossiannilsson, Z. Altinay, and F. Altinay, "Towards Fostering Quality in Open Online Education Through OER and MOOC Practices," in *Open Education: from OERs to MOOCs*, M. Jemni, Kinshuk, and M. K. Khribi, Eds. Berlin, Heidelberg: Springer Berlin Heidelberg, 2017, pp. 189–204.

[17] A. Hemingway, C. Angell, H. Hartwell, and R. F. Heller, "An emerging model for publishing and using open educational resources in public health," *Perspect. Public Health*, vol. 131, no. 1, pp. 38–43, 2011.

[18] N. Piedra, J. Chicaiza, J. López, and E. Tovar Caro, "Supporting openness of MOOCs contents through of an OER and OCW framework based on Linked Data technologies," in *2014 IEEE Global Engineering Education Conference (EDUCON)*. April 2014, pp. 1112–1117.

[19] C. Shu-Hsiang, N. Jaitip, and D. J. Ana, "From Vision to Action – A Strategic Planning Process Model for Open Educational Resources," *Procedia-Social and Behavioral Sciences*, vol. 174, pp. 3707–3714, 2015.

[20] N. Sclater, "MOOCs, Open educational resources and social networking: bridging the gap between informal and formal learning," *Revista Mediterránea de Comunicación*, vol. 7, no. 2, pp. 9–19, 2016.

[21] A. Margaryan, M. Bianco, and A. Littlejohn, "Instructional Quality of Massive Open Online Courses (MOOCs)," *Computer & Education.*, vol. 80, pp. 77–83, Aug. 2015.

Personalized Links Recommendation Based on Learning Analytics in MOOCs

Ahmed Mohamed Fahmy Yousef
Fayoum University

Fayoum, Egypt
Email: amf00@fayoum.edu.eg

Abstract— **Increasingly, Massive Open Online Courses (MOOCs) are widely used and have become a key instrument in Technology Enhanced Learning (TEL) models in the last few years. However, the key challenge with this kind of larger scales platforms is how to provide course participants with a quality learning materials that promote effective learning based on their needs. Indeed, this requires careful planning, monitoring and evaluation of all learning activities. Recently, learning analytics and Recommender systems are widely used in MOOCs to overcome this challenge in providing personalization and accessibility learning materials for course participants. The purpose of the current study was to determine the usability and effectiveness of a personalized links recommendation tool based on learning analytics in MOOCs. This personalized links recommendation tool was undertaken the power of crowd sourcing to provide course participants with an high quality learning material from externals recourses, e.g., Open Education Resources (OER). The present study makes several noteworthy contributions such as researching the mapping of learning data, an open personalized - links recommendation architecture, and a user-friendly and dynamic interface to deliver the recommendations.**

Keywords-Massive Open Online Courses; MOOCs; Viedo-Based Learning; Learning analytics; Recommendation Systems.

I. INTRODUCTION

Since then new technologies such as Smartphone's and tablets in combination with social media such as YouTube have contributed to increasing social interaction and have made it easier as ever to integrate video applications in education [1]. More recently, Massive Open Online Courses (MOOCs) have offered a whole new perspective for Video-Based Learning (VBL) in education sector. MOOCs incorporate video-based lectures and new ways of assessment in courses that are offered on the Web and have potentially thousands of participants [2]. In MOOCs teachers, create and share videos related to the learning topic. The learners can then study the topic by themselves and discuss it back by solving problems and doing practical work [3]. In video-based collaborative learning learners, are able to share responsibilities for their learning. Much of the literature since the mid-2000s validates the efficacy of collaborative learning especially in VBL environments. They report on some educational benefits of learners working cooperatively in groups such as shared goals, ideas, resources, activities, and supporting each other [4]. Less than 28% of the studies applied the individual learning style that was consistent with the theory of multiple intelligences [5]. According to this theory VBL should focus on the particular intelligences of each student [1].

The questions that arise here are: what are advantages and disadvantages of current MOOCs? How can the current MOOC environments be improved? To answer these questions a state-of-the art study was conducted in 2015 [6]. The most interesting aspects of this study are:

- MOOCs platform consist of several units comprising video lectures with support of many learning materials such as PDF files, PPT and lecture notes. At the same time the participants can discuss the content in various groups.
- MOOCs are used by several thousand learners per course; the teaching assistance offered to support the learning activities becomes a critical issue.
- Closer inspection of the study results shows the lack of human connection as a big challenge, especially in MOOCs. The learners in these open courses come from all over the world. They speak English in different levels and have different cultural believes.
- The current versions of MOOCs use traditional assessment methods. These include e-tests, quizzes, multiple-choice and short answer questions. These methods are limited in evaluating course participants in open and distributed environment effectively.
- Providing life-long learning for more and more participants for free, facing a big challenge how to deal with information overload caused by massive activities.

Based on these analyses, it can thus be suggested that educational recommender system is a powerful tool enable learners to share their opinions and benefit from each other's experience. Indeed, recommender systems are an emerging field that has the potential to analysis learners' interaction data with MOOC environments to better understand their learning process [7]. One important opportunity to develop MOOCs is to leverage personalized links recommendation based on learning analytics techniques to collect, evaluate, analyse, and report data about learners and their learning activities in the MOOC environments, in order to achieve better learning outcomes. This paper analyzes how personalized links recommendation based on learning analytics techniques can be applied to current MOOCs to guide course participants in personalized inclusive open learning scenarios. The remainder of this paper presents the research methodology, the theoretical dimensions and design criteria of recommendation systems in educational scenarios e.g., MOOCs, the design, implementation, and evaluation results of the use of recommendation systems tool in the MOOC in more detail.

II. RESEARCH METHODOLOGY

This work employed case study research methodology, seeking for exploring new processes or behaviors based on the learning experiences surrounding the class of "*Producing Educational Programs*" offered by Fayoum University, Egypt using a blended MOOC platform includes a creative video tool allows learners to upload and collaboratively annotate videos online as shown in Figure 1.

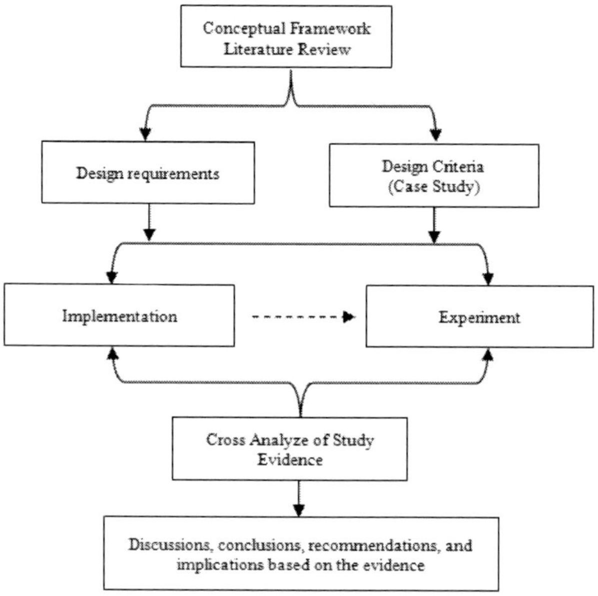

Figure 1. Case study methodology [8]

In addition, the analytical process is collected and combined data from different learners' activities when they interact with learning elements. The approach of the study is depicted below and is based on the work of Yin 2003 [8].

III. CONCEPTUAL FRAMEWORK

Recently, a considerable literature has grown up around the theme of recommender systems and their potential in the educational sector e.g., eLearning and MOOCs. In fact, recommender systems are widely used to handle the current challenges of MOOC environments in providing standards-based solutions for learners as well as, for providers (Professors) [9]. One of the greatest challenges, professors who taught MOOCs have troublesome in recommending learners to select suitable learning materials due to the wide range of educational material and knowledge shared in MOOCs platforms. On the other hand, MOOCs participants feel lost and dispersing to select the educational resources and the learning style that meet their characteristics the best [10],[11],[12]. Thus, research is needed to investigate different approaches of user recommendation in MOOCs. This work proposes a novel approach which applies recommender system techniques for video lectures and discussions forum in MOOCs. The contributions of this work are these design requirements:

- Capture and store large data sets from learners' activities when they watched video lecture.
- Observing the items that a user views the video lectures.
- Keeping a record of the items that a user discusses in the forum and newsgroup articles.
- Analyzing the user's social network and discovering similar likes and dislikes "Only for MOOC lectures".
- Provide a recommendation mechanism that enables learners to discover external video lecture and learning resources based on their interests and activities on the learning environment.

This end has led to a renewed interest for developing video heatmap tracking feature in an educational recommender systems, which are able to visualize exactly where each course participant navigated, second by second, by retracing individual viewing sessions. In this regard learners acquire knowledge and educators support the learning process in order to provide them with external learning material in MOOC environments.

IV. RECOMMENDER SYSTEM IMPLEMENTATION

In their interesting analysis of MOOC design criteria, Yousef et al (2014) collected design criteria regarding the interface, organization, and collaboration in video lectures and discussion [13].Based on the design criteria in this study and the recommender system requirement collected above in Section III, the study at hand aimed to collect more user requirements.

A. *User Requirements*

To gain as full an understanding as possible, an Interactive Process Interviews (IPI) with target learners was conducted to determine which functionalities they are expecting from personalized links recommendation tool. These interviews involved 12 students who were between the ages of 19 and 15 years and all of them had prior experience with MOOCs and recommender systems. Almost two-thirds of the participants (70%) are set out the following additional requirements and functionalities:

- Collect as much data as reasonably possible form the video timeline.
- Support for a wide variety of current and future mobile devices.
- The system must deal with privacy police of the university. The user must be aware about the fact that the application is running, that it is collecting data, or what data it is collecting.

B. System Architecture

The architecture of the recommender system follows from the design requirements explained above. Figure 2 shows the learners actions are events explicitly generated by them, for example by tapping on the forum, entering text and similar.

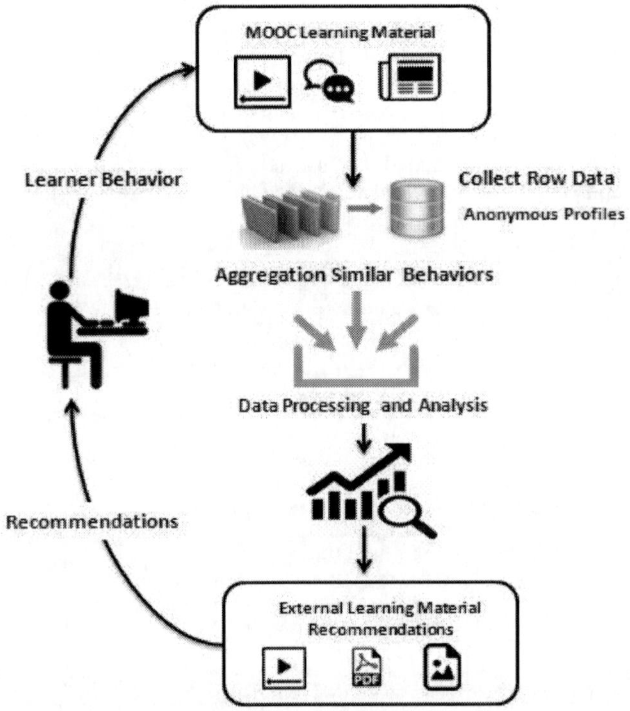

Figure 2. Recommender System Architecture

It would be possible to collect more data by analyzing video time line data or generating a graphical representation of data where the individual values contained in a matrix are represented as a video heatmap. All recommender learning materials presented in this study are based on observed learner's behavior.

V. CASE STUDY

The case study of this experiment took place during the summer semester 2016 with duration of four weeks. It was offered both formally to students from Fayoum University and informally with open enrollment to anybody who is interested in *Producing Educational Programs*. A total of 478 participants completed this course. 89 are formal participants who took the course to earn credits from Fayoum University. These participants were required to complete the course and obtain positive grading of assignments. The rest were informal participants undertaking the learning activities at their own pace without receiving any credits. The teaching staff provided 8 main video lectures and personalized links recommendation tool has suggested 38 related videos, 12 PDF articles and 7 images. This course was taught in both languages Arabic and English and participants were encouraged to self-organize their learning environments, present their own ideas, collaboratively discuss the video lectures, and share knowledge through forum and newsgroup articles.

The case reported here illustrates the an example (video heatmap analysis) of how a timeline of a video was marked-up at various points of analysis with total number of views as seen in Figure 3.

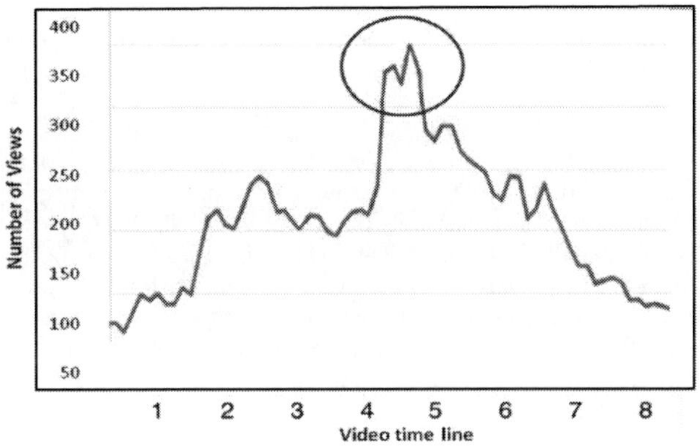

Figure 3. Video Heatmap Analysis

In fact, this case confirms the importance of the personalized links recommendation to predict the learning difficulties and misunderstanding concepts. From the data in Figure 3, it is apparent that minutes between 4:00 and 5:10 are the highest views traffic. By tracking the discussion forum associated with the video time line as presented in Figure 4. It's clear that course participants are comments and asked many questions regarding the minutes between 4:00 and 5:10.

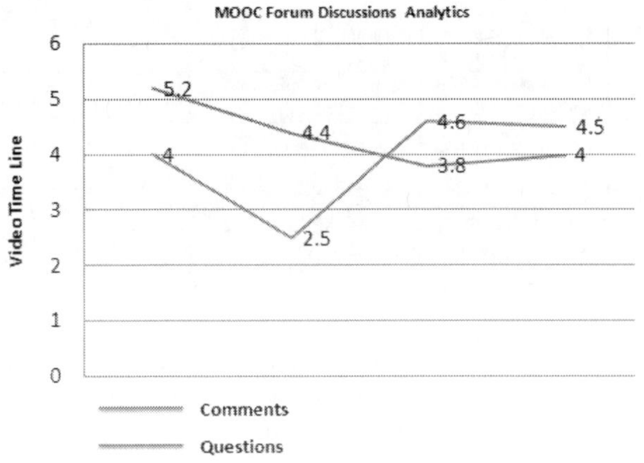

Figure 4. MOOC Discussion Forum Analysis

The personalized links recommendation tool then suggested some related videos and articles for particular participants they are watched this video part as well as for those who are comments or asked questions for the same video part.

VI. EVALUATION

The next sections are providing the evaluation details of the personalized links recommendation tool. We employed a mixed-method evaluation approach based on the System Usability Scale (SUS) which is a simple, ten-item attitude Likert scale giving a global view of subjective assessments of usability as a general usability evaluation [14] and a custom effectiveness questionnaire reflecting the personalized links recommendation tool.

A. *Usability Evaluation*

The System Usability Scale (SUS) was invented by John Brooke who, in 1986 and provides a "quick and dirty", reliable tool for measuring the usability [14].The System Usability Scale is a Likert Scale which includes 10 questions which users of your website will answer. Participants are asked to score 10 items with one of five responses that range from Strongly Agree to Strongly disagree. Of the study population, 213 subjects completed and returned the questionnaire.

TABLE I. SYSTEM USABILITY SCALE (N= 213)

No	System Usability Scale (SUS)		
	Item	***User Rating***	***SUS Score***
1	I think that I would like to use this website frequently	4.3	3.3
2	I found the website unnecessarily complex	2.3	2.7
3	I thought the website was easy to use	3.9	2.9
4	I think that I would need the support of a technical person to be able to use this website	2.1	2.9
5	I found the various functions in this website were well integrated	4.6	3.6
6	I thought there was too much inconsistency in this website	1.9	3.1
7	I would imagine that most people would learn to use this website very quickly	4.6	3.6
8	I found the website very cumbersome to use	1.1	3.9
9	I felt very confident using the website	4.8	3.8
10	I needed to learn a lot of things before I could get going with this website	1.2	3.8
SUS Total Score			84

The majority of respondents were in the 18-25 age range. Male respondents formed the majority (56%). Participants have a high level of educational attainment: 70% of participants are studying Bachelor's degree at Fayoum University and 30% have a Bachelor's degree or higher. They also have an experience with TEL courses, nearly, 75% reported that they attended more than two TEL courses.

The overall System Usability Scale (SUS) score from the questionnaires was 84, which translates to "Users like your site and will recommend it to their friends".

B. *Effectivness Evaluation*

The second part of this evaluation aimed to examine the effectiveness of using personalized links recommendation tool in MOOCs. Effective evaluation questionnaire was designed to collect feedback from the course participants' reflection the most applied objectives reported in Section III, as shown in Table 2. A 5-point Likert scale was used from (1) strongly disagree to (5) strongly agree. In addition to ensure the relevance of these questions, we sent this questionnaire to a small panel of 5 learners as well as 5 learning technologies experts. They were asked for their opinions and suggestions for revising the questionnaire. Their feedback included a refinement of some questions and replacing some others. The revised questionnaire was then given to the course participants.

TABLE II. EFFECTIVENESS EVALUATION (N= 213)

No	Effectiveness Evaluation		
	Item	***Mean***	***SD***
1	I think that I the system is able to provide specific recommendation for me	4.3	0.45
2	I thought the system is able to recommend me (four to five) relevant learning material.	4.3	0.73
3	The remmended learning material help me to better understand the course content.	4.1	0.91
4	I think that items recommended to me are diverse (Videos, PDF, Images).	3.45	1.20
5	I found the rating system (Likes) helps me to assess the quality of the learning material	4.6	0.62
6	I found it is too easy to obtain the recommened learning resources for me form OER.	3.9	1.13
7	The personalized links recommendation helps me to reflect on my own performance.	4.6	0.61
8	I found the system is very respect of my praivacy.	4.6	0.34
9	I think the discciions formu helps me to improve collaboration with peers.	4.8	3.8
10	I can get help at any point that is tailored to where is me.	4.2	0.82
Effectiveness Evaluation Average Score		4.28	1.06

The aim of this research was to explore and explain the personalized links recommendation tool in MOOCs. According to Table 2, responses regarding recommendation provided through this tool were largely positive. However, some learners received only recommended videos. One possible reason for this is that, those participants didn't participate in the discussion forum or students news group [15]. It would be interesting to compare experiences of individuals within the same group activities.

VII. CONCLUSION

The concept of Massive Open Online Courses (MOOCs) is currently accredited with high relevance for prospective developments in eLearning technologies in higher education. MOOC providers worldwide are hard pressed in meeting the challenges of teaching an increasing number of course participants and dealing with growing student heterogeneity. Recommendations can be applied to overcome current limitations of MOOCs in providing personalization and accessibility features such as recommending resources (e.g., papers, books, images. Video lectures). In this investigation, the aim was to assess the personalized links recommendation tool in MOOCs. One of the more significant findings to emerge from this study is the use of information aggregation capabilities of a recommender system to improve the teaching assistance and consulting course participants in an automated way and thus scale tutoring and consulting in a personalized way for a large scale of learners worldwide. To validate this approach, a mixed-method evaluation approach was employed based on the System Usability Scale (SUS) as a general usability evaluation and a custom effectiveness questionnaire reflecting the personalized links recommendation tool. The findings from this study make several contributions to the current literature. First, experimental results show that the proposed personalized links recommendation tool can enhance learners' performance. Second, create dynamic system architecture and finally, a user-friendly and accessible interface to deliver the recommendations.

REFERENCES

[1] A. M. F. Yousef, M. A. Chatti, and U. Schroeder, "Video-based learning: A critical analysis of the research published in 2003-2013 and future visions," In eLmL 2014, The Sixth International Conference on Mobile, Hybrid and On-line Learning, pp. 112–119, 2014.

[2] A. M. F. Yousef, M. A. Chatti, U. Schroeder, H. Jakobs, and M. Wosnitza. "A Review of the State-of-the-Art" In Proceedings of CSEDU2014, 6th International Conference on Computer Supported Education, pp. 9-20, 2014.

[3] J. Daniel, J. "Making sense of MOOCs: Musings in a maze of myth, paradox and possibility", Journal of interactive Media in education, vol. 3, 2012.

[4] A. M. F. Yousef, M. A. Chatti, and U. Schroeder, "The state of video-based learning: A review and future perspectives", Int. J. Adv. Life Sci, vol. 6, no.(3/4), pp. 122-135, 2014.

[5] R. A. Berk, "Multimedia teaching with video clips: TV, movies, YouTube, and mtvU in the college classroom" International Journal of Technology in Teaching and Learning, vol. 5, no.1, pp. 1-21, 2009.

[6] A. M. F. Yousef, M. A. Chatti, U. Schroeder, H. Jakobs, and M. Wosnitza. "The state of MOOCs from 2008 to 2014: A critical analysis and future visions" In International Conference on Computer Supported Education, pp. 305-327, Springer International Publishing, 2014.

[7] O. C. Santos, and J. G. Boticario, "Requirements for semantic educational recommender systems in formal e-learning scenarios", Algorithms, vol. 4 no. 2, pp. 131-154, 2011.

[8] Yin, R. K. (2003). Case study research: Design and methods (3rd ed.). Thousand Oaks, CA: Sage.

[9] N. Thai-Nghe, L. Drumond, A. Krohn-Grimberghe, and L. Schmidt-Thieme, "Recommender system for predicting student performance" Procedia Computer Science, vol. 1 no.2, pp. 2811-2819, 2010.

[10] C. E. McLoughlin, and E. Catherine, E. "The pedagogy of personalised learning: exemplars, MOOCS and related learning theories" In Proc. EdMedia, 2013.

[11] J. Knox, J. Ross, C. Sinclair, H. Macleod, and S. Bayne, "MOOC Feedback: Pleasing All the People? " In Krause, S. Lowe, C. Invasion of the MOOCs: The Promise and Perils of Massive Open Online Courses, pp. 98, 2014.

[12] J. Wilkowski, A. Deutsch, and D. M. Russell, "Student skill and goal achievement in the mapping with google MOOC" In Proceedings of the first ACM conference on Learning@ scale conference, pp. 3-10,. ACM., 2014.

[13] A. M. F. Yousef, M. A. Chatti, U. Schroeder, and M. Wosnitza, "What drives a successful MOOC? An empirical examination of criteria to assure design quality of MOOCs" In *Advanced Learning Technologies (ICALT), 2014 IEEE 14th International Conference on*, pp. 44-48, IEEE, 2014.

[14] J. Brooke, "SUS-A quick and dirty usability scale" *Usability evaluation in industry*, vol. *189, no.,* (194),pp. 4-7, 1996.

[15] A. M. F. Yousef, M. A. Chatti, I. Ahmad, and M. Wosnitza, "An evaluation of learning analytics in a blended MOOC environment" In Proceedings of the Third European MOOCs Stakeholders Summit EMOOCs, pp. 122-130., 2015.